LOST
ON THE
MAP

A memoir of colonial illusions

ISBN: 978-1-77995-000-0
e-ISBN: 978-1-77995-001-7

First edition, first impression 2022

Published by Bookstorm (Pty) Ltd
PO Box 4532
Northcliff 2115
Johannesburg
South Africa
www.bookstorm.co.za

Edited by Janet Bartlet
Cover design by Dogstar Design
Book design and typesetting by Dogstar Design
Printed in the USA

LOST ON THE MAP

A memoir of colonial illusions

BRYAN ROSTRON

BOOK**STORM**

For my wife Sunny, as always
&
My Italo-Aussie grandson, Nicolò

CONTENTS

William Wallis + Susannah Moncur
(1812–1885)   (1813–1871)

William Moncur Wallis + Frances Weale
(1837–1905)   (1836–1914)

Isabel Weale + Charles Lenox Simpson
(1853–1926)   (Customs official, China, d. 1909)

Beatrice Wallis + Lewis Rose Macleod
(1876–1968)   (1875–1941)
'Granny Trixie'

Bertram Lenox Simpson
(1877–1930)
'Putnam Weale'

Rodolfo Savelli + Esmé Simpson + Saul Almagià
1st husband   (1887–1972)   2nd husband

Alix Simpson + Maj. Gen.
(1895–1982)   Wulff Grey
'Auntie Alix'   (1876–1961)

Luigi Savelli
(1913–1979)
'Gigi'

George Grey
(1918–1944)

René Dyker + Beatrice Macleod
'Uncle René'   'Auntie Betty'

Barbara Macleod + Frank Rostron
(1912–2004)   (1907–1989)

Bryan Rostron
(1948–)

I
·╬·
BRIEF INTRODUCTIONS, TALL TALES

A family treasure trove

WHEN I WAS eight years old, my fearsome Auntie Alix informed me solemnly that I was distantly related to faraway royalty. An illustrious seafaring ancestor, Captain Samuel Wallis, she announced, had been the first European to discover the island of Tahiti. Then, following a charged pause to allow this news to sink in, she added that shortly after his discovery – most unfortunately for Captain Wallis – he had been eaten by the queen of that idyllic isle. Alix was sombre as she delivered these strange tidings and I realised she had judged me old enough to be inducted into this vital family lore. She explained that if a member of the Tahitian royal clan had selected someone for the honour of consumption, well … according to local custom, this gastronomic privilege made all the victim's descendants, for ever after, honorary members of the Tahitian royal lineage.

'And that, Bryan,' beamed Alix, 'includes you!'

For over 250 years my family went forth and colonised. Yet, until recently, I had little idea of this imperial epic of adventurers, rogues, swashbucklers and subversives, as most of it had been either forgotten or kept secret. My ancestors, I have now learned, abandoned the mother country to crisscross the globe, helping to paint the map red. Some made good; others went bust. What united them was that they all felt entitled, however humble, to settle in distant lands

I

as though it was their divine right.

They also created self-glorifying myths. My mother, Barbara, occasionally retold that venerable Tahitian saga, though altogether more amusingly, and later I found references to it in letters from relatives I'd never met. It wasn't true, of course. Even so, like other tales passed down the generations, this had been an article of faith: our invisible family legacy, illuminating how we were supposed to see ourselves. Yet when I finally did discover the truth about our 'royal' Tahitian heritage, the actual story, faithfully recorded in Captain Wallis' own log of his voyage on *HMS Dolphin*, proved to be altogether far more bizarre, if less socially exalted; almost, in fact, unbelievable.

Painting the map red

As an only child, my family tree appeared sadly stunted, ending abruptly with my only living grandparent: beyond Granny Trixie in Johannesburg, it was blank. Now that I have explored our ancestral map, it is filled with a ghostly legion of relatives.

Britain eventually staked a claim to control one quarter of the globe. That much I knew. But the more that I filled in the blanks on our family tree, exhuming our role in this astounding imperial enterprise, the more I began to wonder: what did they believe and what were they thinking – all those Rostrons, Macleods and the Wallis dynasty – when they scattered so confidently across the face of the earth? Naturally, they carried in their heads, as we all do, a subjective mental map. And on that global chart, it seems, absolutely nowhere was out of bounds for us to either claim or occupy, irrespective of who already lived there and had to be dispossessed.

Our zigzagging family saga is a tantalising mix of adventure and misadventure: personal, familial, and occasionally apocryphal. Yet what also propelled that astonishing expansion of empire were at times parallel beliefs in outlandish myths. Captain Wallis' instructions from the British Admiralty were to discover the fabled 'unknown southern land', reputed to contain fabulous riches – and where higher beings were so advanced that they could communicate telepathically. As this was merely a figment of European desires, Wallis bumped into Tahiti instead. Similarly, in Africa, feverish legends about the Empire of Monomotapa swelled to such ludicrous proportions that they inspired European expeditions to locate its imaginary treasures of gold and precious stones.

So, this is not a sober history. I am more intrigued as to how we finally got to South Africa, with many a detour, and to understand what three generations of us, myself included, imagined that we were doing here. Myths, I have found, can often prove as powerful as facts in revealing what our forebearers truly thought they were doing in helping to paint the map red. Testing those myths might also shape how we, the orphaned grandchildren of empire, now think of that lingering legacy.

A personal odyssey

In one of the cheap exercise books, where I recorded my initial researches, there's a pencilled note that I was present in the majestic British Library Reading Room the very Saturday that it finally closed its doors at the British Museum. On that day, beneath the sky-blue dome and surrounded by 25 miles of stacked shelving, there were only four months left before I returned to South Africa, the land of my birth, after a 28-year absence. I was reading the original accounts of early explorers who long ago set forth from the southern tip of Africa into territory hitherto unknown to Europeans. Late on that final day, waiting for another hefty eighteenth century volume to be delivered, it finally occurred to me to look up Captain Samuel Wallis. That was the first of a great many surprises, delightful and shocking, unearthed during this quest, compelling me to reassess almost everything; in particular, why do we cling to cherished family stories and historical assumptions, often despite all the evidence or common sense?

As our family map filled out, illuminating a receding hinterland of identifiable names and startling landmarks, it was as though the long dead had begun to whisper to me over the centuries: an ancestral chorus of forgotten witnesses. There were no dukes on safari in Africa or Viceroys of India. Most of my predecessors were ordinary folk, many of them tradesmen. With no qualifications or the need for passports, they set off with high hopes, and nowhere in the entire world, it seems, was out of bounds.

This freedom of movement is reflected in my own life. Starting out under the straightjacket of apartheid, I subsequently lived in England, France, Italy and the United States, experiencing the reverberation of over 2,000 years of different empires.

After delving into our family's past, and the empire which allowed them to flourish, some common threads emerge: one is the prevalence of secrets. Another is an obsession with colour. Over a century ago a distant cousin of mine, a notorious adventurer, wrote a popular book about race, sounding a panicked alarm that the white race was about to be swamped by the yellow and brown races. However, my relative reserved his most histrionic vituperation for Africa, under the heading, 'The Black Problem'. Insidiously, the furies of ethnic insecurity are bubbling up again in the former imperial powers of Europe and in the United States. It's as though some of the racial terrors that I've been excavating are hissing in our ear again, ready to reawaken the sullen beast of white supremacist rage: a reminder that the past still haunts us.

Debates about colonialism rage on, as do its aftereffects.

In February 2018, the British Treasury tweeted: 'Did you know? In 1833, Britain used 20 million pounds, 40% of its national budget, to buy freedom for all slaves in the Empire. The amount of money borrowed for the Slavery Abolition Act was so large that it wasn't paid off till 2015.'

This tweet didn't mention that the cash (approx. 17 billion pounds today) only went to compensate slave owners for the loss of their human chattels. Nevertheless, the Treasury crowed, 'Which means that living British citizens helped pay to end the slave trade.' Not everyone was thrilled to learn this, myself included. Eighteen years of working on UK newspapers, and paying taxes, meant that I too had helped to settle that massive debt. Taken aback by the public response, the tweet was rapidly deleted. Nevertheless, that Treasury 'Friday Fact', having hopelessly mangled the facts, had briefly exposed the self-justifying amnesia that afflicts current apologists for colonialism.

If we owe any debt to the past, it is to face it squarely. The recompense paid to Cape Colony slave owners, for example, trickles down to the present, part of the rich patrimony of their white descendants. For their estimated 38,742 slaves, the 1833 legislation stipulated that they had to continue as unpaid 'apprentices' for a further several years.

Above all, what has been laid bare by my search for lost family and empire are the invisible influences which have helped shape me: the sum of where I have come from and who I am. For good or ill, this should be faced. The account has largely been assessed, but the bill not yet paid. It's time for an honest reckoning. And where better to examine all this than from South Africa, long the mad laboratory of racial prejudice?

Today, my wife and I live at the back of Table Mountain, overlooking a bay that may have been visited by the first European to round the Cape of Good Hope. The exact location of the bay named by Bartolomeu Dias, the representative of yet another vanished empire, is hard to pin down on a sketchy early sixteenth century map. It probably identifies this bay upon which I gaze as I write. Then again, it may not.

Like much of my chronicle, the 'facts' remain stubbornly provisional, even ambiguous. Nevertheless, *Porto Fragoso*, a description bestowed by Dias, suggests that this is the perfect perch from which to mull over the finds of my long search: *Porto Fragoso*, or Rocky Port.

Posing the vital question

On first returning to South Africa after an absence of nearly three decades, there came an inescapable moment with nearly all our foreign visitors. They would lean forward, narrow their eyes, and you knew that they had at last judged the moment suitable to pose a question which had been preying on their minds ever since landing in Cape Town. As though they feared that you were perhaps temporarily emotionally unstable or had contracted some appalling disease, they would lower their voice and, with funereal delicacy, ask 'But ... are you optimistic?'

Of course, they weren't concerned about the roasting summer droughts or violent winters we can get here on the southern tip of Africa. As none had experienced the emissions from the local fish factory, nor were they worried about the effects on our health of that oily reek which occasionally perfumes the valley so pungently. Oh no. Those tactful probes about our mental state were really a coded question, implying that now there was a democratic (black) government in South Africa, were we quite sure that we had done the right thing in leaving London?

There is a peculiarly European ambivalence to Africa. This combines a sense that Africa must somehow be 'saved' along with an atavistic terror of what they might actually find here. Charles Dickens astutely caught this contradictory attitude in *Bleak House* (1853) with the meddlesome Mrs Jellyby; a plump, pretty woman whose eyes seem to gaze a long way off as though 'they could see nothing nearer than Africa!' A martyr of 'telescopic philanthropy', she works remorselessly on her latest cause, 'the Borrioboola-Gha venture', to the neglect of her own large brood of underfed children.

'You find me, my dears,' Mrs Jellyby informs visitors, 'as usual, very busy; but that you will excuse. The African project at present employs my whole time.' Though as a result, 'I am happy to say it is advancing. We hope by this time next year to have from a hundred and fifty to two hundred healthy families cultivating coffee and educating the natives of Borrioboola-Gha, on the left bank of the Niger.'

Mrs Jellyby sits 'in quite a nest of waste paper' and elaborates on 'the brotherhood of humanity', though later she fails to notice when her demoralised husband goes bankrupt and tries to throw himself out of the window. Despite her unstinting labour, towards the end of *Bleak House* we discover that 'She has been disappointed in Borrioboola-Gha, which turned out a failure in consequence of the king of Borrioboola-Gha wanting to sell everybody – who survived the climate – for rum …'.

After all that: am I optimistic?

The most truthful reply might be that of the diligent Mrs Jellyby when visited at her dishevelled central London home in the busy district of Holborn; where in fact I'd worked for a while on a national newspaper. Asked about the climate of Borrioboola-Gha, the single-minded philanthropist declares it to be the finest in the world. Met with some incredulity, the self-important busybody has a surprisingly sensible reply.

'Certainly. With precaution,' retorts Mrs Jellyby. 'You may go into Holborn, without precaution, and be run over. You may go into Holborn, with precaution, and never be run over. Just so with Africa.'

My imperial inheritance

Peering back through a narrow familial telescope, the picture shrinks drastically and reflects back a peculiarly white world. For this is also the tale of two grandfathers. Both migrated to South

Africa shortly after the turn of the twentieth century. My maternal grandfather, Lewis Rose Macleod, sailed from Australia, where the skinny young man had been an enterprising journalist and author of flippant verse and droll amateur plays. He docked in Durban, but quickly made his way to the gold frenzy of Johannesburg. Though he had left school in Sydney at 13, Lewis Rose soon developed into a benignly rotund and thoroughly establishment fellow, and by the 1920s he was editor of the *Rand Daily Mail*, at that time the voice of the plutocratic 'Randlords'.

On the other hand, my paternal grandfather, William Rostron, was a working-class printer from Lancashire. Tough, irascible and a boxing aficionado, according to my father he also squandered most of their meagre housekeeping money at the racetrack. In 1903 William had landed in South Africa as a penniless emigrant, and his orphaned, tubercular wife, Annie Maguire, recalled being lowered onto the dock in a wicker basket. A dedicated trade unionist, by the 1920s William was printing the small weekly newspaper for the recently founded Communist Party of South Africa. He also printed pamphlets for the violent 1922 Rand Insurrection, during which a prominent slogan was 'Workers of the World Unite and Fight for a White South Africa!'

The magnetism of the 'mother country', however, remained formidable – even for those colonial subjects who had never been there. Lewis Rose didn't travel to Europe until he was 41, when he wished to volunteer (unsuccessfully) to serve 'his country' in the First World War. Later, in the 1930s when editing South Africa's leading newspaper, he was apparently astonished when my mother told him that she planned to visit Victoria Falls.

'But my dear,' he chided, 'when one goes on vacation one goes to Paris.'

Europe and its rituals remain a significant focus for many white people. Even here where we live, half an hour from Cape Town, many imperial influences persist into the twenty-first century. In this amphitheatre of mountains enfolding our alluring bay, we are left with the echo, and even some ruins, of three great European empires. The Dutch, the first European settlers at the Cape, christened this valley Hout Bay after its magnificent forests. Leading to our home high above the rock-fringed bay is Pondicherry Avenue, named for the French regiment dispatched from India to support their Dutch allies as a European war threatened. On either side of the bay, cannons still stand guard, aiming at fishing boats as they chug into the Atlantic. Residues of the British Empire lurk round every corner. From Victoria Road, we turn left toward the sea along Empire Avenue, passing Manchester, Liverpool, Oxford and Brighton, till we arrive at Princess Street opposite the beach and its constantly shifting dunes.

View of Hout Bay with cannons

Both my father, Frank, and maternal grandfather chose to identify themselves explicitly as 'Empire men'. As late as 1948, the year I was born, my father flew over the entire continent of Africa on a marathon four-day flight in a BOAC flying boat, from Johannesburg to Southampton – and at no point soaring over the entire continent were they not above territory either governed or indirectly controlled by the British. Looking back, it even seems to me that as I grew up, I was largely educated, in fact, to be a dutiful and upright district officer in an empire which no longer existed.

Dreams of elsewhere

As sometimes only a stuffed shirt colonial can be, my splendidly pompous Uncle René was comically snobbish. Somehow Uncle René got himself made the honorary consul for Monaco in Cape Town. He utterly adored the tubby Prince Rainier and his glamorous consort, the former Hollywood star Princess Grace. Uncle René's voice would lower reverently whenever he referred to their Royal Highnesses, even though they reigned over a seedy Riviera statelet mostly renowned for the casino in Monte Carlo. Quite late in life, Uncle René had married my mother's older sister Betty, and they rented a cottage on a battery chicken farm in the suburb of Tokai outside Cape Town.

By day Uncle René was an undistinguished office manager. But by night he was transformed in his imagination into a debonair Edwardian *bon vivant* who dressed formally for dinner, even though at the table there was usually only himself and his wife.

When I was 16, with my mother and I as the sole guests, Uncle René appeared for dinner with a bulky chain of office round his neck that proclaimed him as president of his local wine tasting society. At dawn the following morning, peering out of a window at the back of their modest cottage, I was astonished to observe him in his garden raising the flag of Monaco. To mark the birthday of Prince Rainier, Uncle René wore a dinner jacket and white gloves, and when the flag finally reached the top of the pole he saluted stiffly – witnessed only by Auntie Betty and the battery chickens.

Today, many years after Uncle René paid his anonymous homage to little Rainier III, I live on the opposite side of the mountain chain that bisects the Cape Peninsula. And while South Africa has changed so dramatically, not all attitudes have kept pace.

Europe still exerts an almost magnetic pull, even for families who have lived in southern Africa for many generations. As a result, that startling doubt which first surfaced over half a century ago – on witnessing Uncle René's comic tribute to a European princeling six thousand miles away – now comes back to haunt me with unsettling insistence: *what on earth do we white people think we are doing here in Africa?*

2

✝

DISCOVERING NOBLE SAVAGES

The ballad of Captain Wallis

THE REASON I DIDN'T pay much attention when Auntie Alix told me we were related to Tahitian royalty was that she possessed something far more fascinating to a comic-reading lad. Her claim that our ancestor Samuel Wallis had been eaten by a queen had a certain creepy novelty, but obviously it happened an unimaginably long time ago; ages before photography, for instance. And Alix had a pair of fading photographs that I was always itching to see again. So, after what seemed like a diplomatic interval for an eight-year-old, I would pipe up, 'Auntie, may I see your Chinese photos, please?'

Alix had been brought up in China, and was a small girl when in 1900 the Boxer Rebellion erupted. Her father, Charles Lenox Simpson, was an official in the Chinese Imperial Maritime Customs Service. During the final decades of the sclerotic Qing Dynasty, acquisitive foreign powers were aggressively asserting their commercial muscle, and the nationalistic 'Boxers' attempted to drive them out violently.

There were two sepia snapshots in Alix's photo album that captured the drama of the insurgence. One was captioned 'Before' and the other 'After'. The first showed a Chinese man in a long robe kneeling down with his neck close to the ground; over him loomed another Chinese man with a huge sword raised above his head. In the second photo the kneeling man lay on the ground with his severed head a few paces away. This was inordinately interest-ing, especially as the executioner was encircled by onlookers who appeared curious, yet unmoved by the spectacle.

Only decades later did it occur to me, in the British Library, to investigate that other strange tale, first divulged to me by Alix: about our kinship with Tahitian royalty. *The Dictionary of National Biography* clarified that Captain Wallis, who had been born in Cornwall, enjoyed a long and distinguished career, dying peacefully at his home in London in 1795, aged 67.

Captain Samuel Wallis

Captain Wallis had indeed 'discovered' Tahiti in 1767; but he had not been eaten, not even by a queen. In fact, Wallis continued on his voyage, departing Tahiti undevoured, and successfully circum-navigated the globe.

A couple of years previously, Captain John Byron, grandfather of the poet, and known as 'Foul-Weather Jack', had been dispatched by the Admiralty in *HMS Dolphin* with instructions 'to make Discoveries of Countries hitherto unknown', and had claimed the Falkland Islands for Britain. Byron returned with a 'positive opin-ion' that the (imagined) Great Southern Land must exist somewhere in the South Pacific. So, the First Lord of the Admiralty, the Earl of Egmont, appointed Samuel Wallis as captain of *HMS Dolphin*. His mission was to search for this supposedly fabulous, unknown continent. Initially, Lord Egmont also wished Wallis to secure the Falkland Islands. But the cabinet split over this, fearing that such an act could provoke war with Spain and undermine their main objective. Egmont resigned, and Captain Wallis' new instructions made his objective clear: to explore the Pacific and locate 'Land or Islands of great extent, hitherto unvisited by any European power …'.

HMS Dolphin, commanded by my forebearer Captain Wallis, set sail in August 1766 and on its return nearly two years later, the ship's barber published a lengthy dirge, *The Dolphin's Journal Epitomised In A Poetical Essay*, which eulogised his captain, still very much alive, in heroic fashion:

> 'WALLIS I sing, the hero brave,
> Who to his country, like a slave
> Undaunted plow'd the southern wave,
> In search of land unfound.'

Alix had been entirely mistaken, as had my mother and other relatives. The family myth had gathered currency by fanciful repetition. After all, Auntie Alix wasn't actually my auntie either. She was my mother's great-aunt, consequently to me a cousin (at some remove). But 'Cousin Alix' sounded far too precocious. Instead, I was encouraged to adopt her as my 'auntie', although to a small boy, Alix appeared chillingly austere. According to my mother, when the topic of sex once arose, Alix pursed her lips and lapsed into French to distance herself from that distasteful subject.

'Ma chérie,' she admonished Barbara severely with strangulated, well-bred vowels, *'je n'aime pas absolument cette chose-là!'*

This may reveal the clue to our fiction of Captain Wallis being gobbled by the Queen of Tahiti. Were the facts simply consumed by imperial prudery? For it seems very likely that what Alix had confused for 'being eaten' was – squeamishly, Freudianly – sex.

Terra Australis Incognita

When *HMS Dolphin* hove into sight of Tahiti, Wallis' deputy recalled: 'We now supposed we saw the long wished southern continent, which has been often talked of, but never before seen by any Europeans.' Wallis had opened his secret instructions after having set sail. His orders stated that the Admiralty had 'reason to believe that Land or Islands of great extent hitherto unvisited by any European power may be found in the southern hemisphere between Cape Horn and New Zealand, in latitudes convenient for navigation and in climates adapted to the produce of commodities useful in commerce.'

The notion of a great southern landmass had been introduced by Aristotle in the tidy conviction that there had to be a counterweight to the known lands of the northern hemisphere. The world would tip over, others surmised, without such a balance. This belief steadily solidified, and by the eighteenth century settled into certitude, even depicted as a 'fact' on maps. As European explorers ventured into the Pacific without discovering that expected land, the elusive *Terra Australis Incognita* merely changed shape and size, becoming *Terra Australis Nondum Cognita* (the southern land not yet known), while simultaneously swelling in reputation.

Initially it was believed that the counterbalancing southern land would be an uninhabitable torrid zone; at best inhabited by monstrous beings or antipodeans who lived upside down. Theologians argued that as the torrid zone appeared unreachable, it could not be peopled by descendants of Adam and Eve. Nevertheless, what if beyond the torrid zone there existed a temperate region?

In the Middle Ages there was intense scholastic debate as to whether any inhabitants of a southern temperate zone would be mortal or even immortal. Some speculated that if man lived in a fallen state in the north, perhaps the Garden of Eden might be located to the south. Maps increasingly depicted 'the southern land not yet known' as a wonderland of marvels, including unicorns, inhabited by peaceful folk living in a garden of earthly delights. By the time Wallis embarked on his Pacific mission, the most influential British geographer of the day was fully convinced of the existence of this dreamland.

In 1767, the year of Captain Wallis' 'discovery' of Tahiti, Alexander Dalrymple stated flatly that a gigantic continent 'was wanting on the south of the Equator to counterpoise the land to the north, and to maintain the equilibrium necessary for the Earth's motion.'

As Examiner of Sea Journals for the English East India Company, Dalrymple promoted an alluring vision of that hypothetical land not yet known: 'The number of inhabitants in the southern continent is probably more than 50 millions, considering the extent.' A notoriously crabby Scot, Dalrymple's opinions were so valued that he was appointed as the first hydrographer of the British Admiralty – though his temper was always liable to get the better of him, and eventually he was dismissed after yet another quarrel. His death shortly afterward was diagnosed by his doctors to have been caused by 'vexation'. Nevertheless, his fervently held views doubtless helped to inspire the orders that sent Wallis on his chimerical quest.

Dalrymple even calculated the latitude and longitude of this phantasmagorical realm, booming: 'This is a greater extent than the whole civilised part of Asia, from Turkey to the eastern extremity of China. There is at present no trade from Europe thither, though the scraps from this table would be sufficient to maintain the power, dominion, and sovereignty of Britain, by employing all its manufacturers and ships.'

Wallis and the wanton women

HMS Dolphin was a 24-gun frigate with 150 men. Having sailed for nearly eight months, the ship passed from the Atlantic to the Pacific, after a rough passage through the Straits of Magellan – where the *Dolphin* became separated from the slower, less seaworthy *HMS Swallow*. Wallis, however, sailed on. Ill-winds and scurvy forced him to vary his instructions. 'I began now to keep the ship to the northward', he recorded in his meticulous, cursive script, the brown ink now fading after 250 years.

Wallis' original logbooks are today held in the Mitchell Library in Sydney, and the two volumes still carry their marbled wrappers inside velum covers. However, while a librarian, wearing white surgical gloves, turned the brittle pages, reading my ancestor's words across the centuries felt profoundly disconcerting. Wallis' factual log entries presented a disdainful rebuttal of that wild cannibal myth that my family had once taken as gospel.

Weather, latitude and daily progress were noted as *HMS Dolphin* sailed into warmer waters. By June Captain Wallis recorded that they were sighting a series of islands for which he chose prominent British names, including Queen Charlotte.

Sketch of HMS Dolphin *by Captain Samuel Wallis*

At daybreak, on 18 June 1767, land was again sighted. Wallis noted that 'The fog obliged us again to lie to, and when it cleared away, we were much surprised to find ourselves surrounded by some hundreds of canoes.' Rapidly raising sail, *HMS Dolphin* proceeded along the coast, eliciting the observation, 'The country has the most delightful and romantic appearance that can be imagined.' This was Otaheite, later Tahiti, which Wallis chose to name King George the Third Island.

There were several violent skirmishes. In one bay, a musket was fired, killing an 'Indian'. In another, wrote the *Dolphin's* second-in-command, George Robertson, the ship's nine pounders fired grapeshot and ball at a large canoe which they imagined carried the island's king, killing most of the canoe's paddlers. *HMS Dolphin* anchored in Matavai Bay, fringed with fine-grained, black volcanic sand and steep hills dense with tropical vegetation. On Wallis' successful return to Britain, the Admiralty commissioned an account to be compiled for publication from his logbook.

This log reported that after gestures of peace on both sides, Wallis dispatched a cutter to reconnoitre close to the beach while islanders swam out through 'very great surf' to offer them fruit and fresh water: 'They said that they were very importunate with them to come on shore, particularly the women, who came down to the beach, and stripping themselves naked, endeavoured to allure them by many wanton gestures, the meaning of which could not possibly be mistaken. At this time, however, our people resisted the temptation.' They didn't resist for long.

HMS Dolphin *fires on Tahitians, sketch by Captain Wallis*

The following day Wallis sent boats ashore with nails, hatchets and other trinkets to exchange for water and food, and 'the young women repeated the allurements ... with still more wanton, and, if possible, less equivocal gestures.'

George Robertson felt uncomfortable going ashore, 'espetially as I hade now killd two of them.' He was also startled that the young women stripped naked before them, adding 'this new sight attract our mens fance a good dale, and the natives observed it, and made the young girls play a great many droll wanting tricks.'

Soon enough, of course, such enticements had the desired effect on the sailors. Trade was quickly established, allowing the crew to 'fare sumptuously every day'. It was Robertson, the ship's Master, who discovered quite how lavishly the crew now fared.

Ashore one day Robertson was accosted by three smiling girls, who managed to communicate that they wished for nails, so Robertson handed over three. It was only later, *HMS Dolphin's* naïve Master confessed, that the ship's gunner succinctly clarified the racy goings-on: 'He like-way told me that the price of the old trade is now fixt at a thirty penny nail each time.'

For want of a nail

Iron was unknown on Tahiti, so the sailors discovered that they could readily buy sex with nails from their ship. Owing to their rarity, nails rapidly became a status symbol and valued item of exchange. The Tahitian girls rejected gold and silver. They wanted only nails, and – a stark indication of rampant inflation – started to demand more and bigger nails. This trade rapidly escalated to crisis proportions. On board it began to be noticed that nails were vanishing from the ship at an alarming rate, but it took longer for the *Dolphin's* captain to discover the cause.

'The commerce was carried on for some considerable time before the officers discovered it, for while some straggled a little way to receive the lady, the others kept a look out,' Wallis admitted later. 'When I was acquainted with it I no longer wondered that the ship was in danger of being pulled to pieces for the nails and iron that held her together.'

A 'most diligent enquiry was set on foot', but even the offer of a large reward failed to flush out any culprits. 'I was mortified at the disappointment,' the published account of Wallis' journal continues, 'but I was still more mortified at a fraud which I found some of our people had practised upon the natives. When no nails were to be produced, they had stolen lead, and cut it up in the shape of nails.'

Wallis, till then extremely ill, had been slow to react. 'It was now thought necessary,' he declared, 'to look more diligently about the ship, to discover what nails had been drawn; and it was soon found that all the belaying cleats had been ripped off, and that there was scarcely one of the hammock nails left. All hands were now ordered up, and I practised every artifice I could think of to discover the thieves, but without success. I then told them that till the thieves were discovered, not a single man should go ashore: this however produced no effect, except that Proctor, the corporal, behaved in a mutinous manner, for which he was instantly punished.'

Robertson, ordered by Wallis to identify the culprits, overheard the crew saying that they would rather face a thrashing than have their shore leave cancelled. Wallis was alarmed to discover that this 'old trade' affected not just the sound structure of his ship, but discipline too. The entire mission was at risk. 'I found it necessary therefore,' he stated, 'to read the articles of war.'

Food-gathering parties, though, continued to be sent ashore. And the 'old trade' carried on. Days later, after more provisions had been bartered, one of the sailors, Pinckney, was caught stealing iron hooks and spikes.

'Having secured the offender,' wrote Wallis, 'I called all the people together upon the deck, and after taking some pains to explain his crime, with all its aggravations, I ordered that he should be whipped with nettles while he ran the gauntlet thrice round the deck: my rhetoric, however, had very little effect, for most of the crew being equally criminal with himself, he was handled so tenderly, that others were rather encouraged to repeat the offence by the hope of impunity, than deterred by the fear of punishment.'

The situation was dire. Wallis concluded despairingly: 'To preserve the ship, therefore, from being pulled to pieces, and the price of refreshments from being raised so high as soon to exhaust our articles of trade, I ordered that no man, except the wooders and waterers, with their guard, should be permitted to go on shore.'

Saucy tales of endless love

After five weeks in what Wallis described as 'one of the most healthy as well as delightful spots in the world', *HMS Dolphin* sailed away on 27 July 1767, with her captain on deck, a great deal healthier than when he had arrived. So, along with the departure of Wallis, any claims of our kinship with Tahitian royalty also vanish.

Nevertheless, his farewell witnessed an affecting scene. There were tears, wailing and gestures imploring him to return. Wallis had established a firm affinity with what the British crew took to be the island's queen. According to Wallis she was 'about five and forty years of age, of a pleasing countenance and majestic deportment'.

This was Purea, or Oberea as the sailors called her. The *Dolphin's* captain refers to her variously as 'my princess', 'fair friend', even 'my Queen'. Oberea, though a powerful woman and a leader, was not a queen. Nevertheless, Oberea treated Captain Wallis regally.

At first Wallis had been bedridden with what he called 'bilious cholic', so ill he could barely crawl. Eventually he had to be carried ashore. Oberea herself helped lift the captain over streams and commanded her female 'attendants' to massage this Englishman, dress him in soft cloth and feed him. Oberea became a regular visitor to the ship, always bringing gifts of food, as well as continually displaying generous signs of friendship. On the day of departure, 'The queen came on board, but not being able to speak, she sat down and gave vent to her passion by weeping.' Wallis, in turn, was deeply moved, 'as filled both my heart and my eyes'.

On such a slender and poignant thread, mixed with the escapades of his men, an amatory legend was born. After Wallis' return to England, spiced-up accounts spawned a series of dramas, satirical poems and limericks portraying Tahiti as a licentious Eden.

The somewhat innocent, perhaps even prudish Samuel Wallis was clearly taken with his fair friend. Yet he was not 'taken by' her, nor consumed in any sense. They shared feasts of fruit, hogs and fowl, but my ancestor was not eaten by this powerful Tahitian

'Queen'. Even so, nearly three centuries later, straitlaced Alix had evidently, primly, mistaken that prolific published innuendo about sex for cannibalism.

The 'discovery' of Tahiti and subsequent depictions of Oberea launched in the European imagination an enduring romantic notion of the Pacific islands as a fecund utopia, uncorrupted by the vices of civilisation. This fed into new philosophical ideas in the late eighteenth century about the virtues of the loosely-termed 'noble savage'. Most immediately, however, it fuelled that persistent and apparently almost universal suspicion that someone, somewhere – but not here – was enjoying unfettered fun.

The injured islanders

The bawdy literature generated by reports of Captain Wallis' adventures, and the ensuing Pacific voyage of Captain James Cook, is known today in scholarly argot as 'The Oberea Cycle'. *An Epistle (moral and philosophical) from an officer at Otaheite* (1774) is characteristic of this lascivious genre, boasting such poetical nuggets as 'Oh spread thy empire, Love, from shore to shore, / Till wedlock cease, and cukoldom's no more' – followed by the more prosaic but tartly pointed couplet, 'With nails we traffic for the blooming maid, / And the ship's planks supply the dangerous trade.' Tahiti became a byword for easy living and easier sex ('Each Oberea feels the lawless flame, / Nor checks desires she does not blush to name').

This libidinous reputation is substantially due to the Admiralty's desire to publicise the expansion of British sea power. A disciple of Dr Samuel Johnson, the lexicographer, was hired to write up the journals of Captains 'Foul-Weather Jack' Byron, Samuel Wallis and James Cook.

In 1773, John Hawkesworth produced a three-volume work which gained instant notoriety thanks to titillating passages highlighting the charms of Tahitian women and haphazard sexual encounters with crew members. The wealthy and patrician naturalist Joseph Banks, who accompanied Captain Cook on *HMS Endeavour*, had supplied the author with racy accounts of Tahiti's erotic delights. Though criticised for corrupting British morals, the effect of Hawkesworth's literary efforts was to launch a cult of Tahitian sensuality.

London theatres, in addition to saucy comedies and revues, offered 'wanton dances' in the Tahitian style. A few verses (almost always by 'Anon') were obscene, while most merely groaned with innuendo. Banks invited crude botanical puns. *An Epistle from Mr Banks, voyager; Monster Hunter and Amoroso to Oberea*, has the fictional Banks boasting 'but what a plant I did produce to thee!'

After versifying upon the imagined offspring that the vigorously *amoroso* Banks had left behind, the poem cautions that reading about such profligate exploits could have a detrimental effect on the virtue of British womanhood:

> 'One page of Hawkesworth, in the cool retreat,
> Fires the bright maid with more than mortal heat:
> She sinks at once into the lover's arms,
> Nor deems it vice to prostate her charms;
> 'I'll do', cries she, 'What Queens have done before';
> And sinks, from principle, to common whore.'

There was soon, however, a genuinely dissenting voice. *The injured islanders; or the influence of art upon the happiness of nature* (1779) was fuelled by indignation. The long poem attacks the pretentions of colonial acquisition and subjugation. At one point the British Library oddly attributed it to Captain Wallis. In fact, the author was a Doctor of Divinity at Dublin University. Gerald Fitzgerald was appalled at the crude mockery of 'hospitable and happy islanders' in what, with Irish partiality, he termed O'Taheite. The Rev. Fitzgerald's intention was to turn 'ridicule' to 'Panegyrik'.

He takes it for granted that Wallis and 'Obera' were lovers. Poetically, Oberea yearns for his return ('And Love still whispers, lo! Thy Wallis near; / Oh joyful hope! – to greet Thee I prepare.') But now the focus of competing colonial powers ('Pride at the Prow, Presumption at the Helm'), an unhappy fate is foreseen for the islanders:

'Mark'd out for Plunder, Servitude, Despair …'.

Infected dreams of paradise

Nine months after Samuel Wallis 'discovered' Tahiti, the aristocratic Frenchman Louis-Antoine de Bougainville arrived in the *Boudeuse* with orders to explore the Pacific and establish colonies. Though unaware of Wallis' prior visit, his sojourn followed a similar pattern. The French also first killed some islanders, then established friendly relations. Bougainville named the island *La Nouvelle Cythère* and took possession of it in the name of Louis XV. The two volumes describing his global circumnavigation, *Voyage autour du Monde*, caused a sensation, especially his lyrical depiction of Tahiti which nourished burgeoning ideas of the 'noble savage'.

The cultivated Bougainville rhapsodised, 'I thought I was transported into the garden of paradise.' The French philosopher and writer Denis Diderot, in his fictional *Supplément au voyage de Bougainville*, employed this utopian image of innocent islanders to satirise eighteenth century European society. Diderot has an old Tahitian warn his fellow islanders that Europeans will approach bearing a crucifix in one hand and a dagger in the other.

Almost a year after the Comte de Bougainville, Captain Cook arrived in Tahiti by following the navigational coordinates of Wallis. Having observed the celestial transit of Venus as instructed, Cook set sail complaining that half his men had contracted venereal disease. There followed a furious dispute as to which nation was responsible. ('Ah, yes,' sighed a friend, 'the imperial transit of penis.')

Bougainville blamed Wallis. But Captain Wallis swore that none of his crew had the pox – save one who contracted the clap in Cape Town on their way home. This was confirmed, insisted Wallis, by the surgeon's register. Outraged, the Englishman pointed his finger back at Bougainville, huffing patriotically that 'The reproach of having contaminated with that dreadful pest, a race of happy people, to whom its miseries had till then been unknown, must be due either to him or to me, to England or to France; and I think myself happy to be able to exculpate myself and my country beyond the possibility of doubt.'

The sensual image of Tahiti, coined from those visits by Wallis and Bougainville, has persisted. The projection of European desire for a simpler life has been subsumed into a generic Polynesian idyll: a palm-fringed beach with swaying maidens in grass skirts and garlands of gardenias covering voluptuous breasts. Their doe-eyed look is by turns pliant and inviting. It also stares out from the paintings of Paul Gauguin, who did much to propagate the erotic Tahitian myth, whilst carrying syphilis with him from Paris.

Oberea, who treated Captain Wallis so regally although she wasn't a queen, remained celebrated in Europe for another hundred years, increasingly depicted as a strumpet. In the nineteenth century her name was displayed in advertisements for London brothels. This is not what Alix had in mind when she promoted us to royal kinship by spectacularly mistaking Oberea's intense curiosity about Wallis.

Perhaps the truth about my ancestor and Oberea is to be found concealed in one of the wash drawings that he made during his voyage. Wallis mostly drew scenes of islands and bays with *HMS Dolphin* hove to close by. But the largest, most detailed and decidedly intriguing is a sketch of the 'Queen's House' in Tahiti. Wallis depicts a long, open-sided thatched hut. Looming behind are jagged mountains and tall palm trees. It is what occupies the foreground that arrests the attention. A massive Tahitian woman, out of all proportion to the rest of the sketch, stands before a small group of British soldiers. This toga-clad woman, undoubtedly Oberea, dwarfs the Europeans.

Three pasty white solders with muskets line up behind an officer, almost certainly Wallis himself in full dress uniform, sword at his side, wearing a wig and hat. He grips some kind of staff of office. Invitingly the imposing woman holds out a palm frond. Facing her, however, the officer's staff, held stiffly erect, appears reedy and feeble in comparison. It is as if the puny Englishmen have shrivelled in her presence.

It could be that this image reflects Wallis' well-attested sense of wonder at this superb 'Queen'. Or does his sketch reveal a deeper, lurking fear of inadequacy in the face of such overwhelming femininity: a dread, reflected later in Alix's bizarre myth, that he will somehow be devoured by an unaccustomed sensuality?

Face-to-face with Oberea, sketch by Captain Wallis

On leaving Tahiti, *HMS Dolphin* sailed past other islands which, as the ship's barber and atrocious poet later rhymed, 'Respecting every son of fame, / Great Wallis gives to each a Name' (Duke of York, Lord Howe's, etc.). But after three weeks they espied a smaller island and this time, Wallis recorded, his men wished to honour their captain by christening it after him; thus permitting Mr Richardson, the barber/bard, to trumpet 'This Isle, which Time shall ne'er outlive / But ever crown your Fame.'

Not quite. Nevertheless, unlike King George the Third Island, which became Tahiti, 'Wallis Island' quietly retains its name today. Meanwhile his rival, the Comte de Bougainville, is memorialised by

Bougainville Island, an autonomous region of Papua New Guinea, as well as being altogether more widely and flamboyantly invoked for donating his aristocratic name to the gloriously colourful creeper, bougainvillea.

Samuel Wallis seems in retrospect to have been a relatively benevolent imperial pioneer. But Diderot was right to warn the Tahitians about foreigners bearing a crucifix in one hand, dagger in the other. By 1914 every Pacific island was occupied by Americans or Europeans.

This sea-girt empire

Although Wallis had not been eaten, his health was gravely impaired. With *HMS Dolphin* leaky, he turned for home. On 31 January 1768 they sighted the east coast of Africa, and Wallis noted in his logbook 'We saw the Land of Monopotapia.' A week later they anchored in Table Bay and arrived back in England on 19 May 1768, having – after two years – circumnavigated the globe. Captain Wallis sped straight to London to report to the Admiralty: definitively, his 'discovery' of Tahiti; more tantalisingly, that they had come across enticing but elusive hints of that fabled *Terra Australis Incognita*.

This instantly altered the instructions for James Cook, who only the day before had been appointed to command the first of his great voyages. It was now resolved that Tahiti would make an ideal location to observe the transit of Venus, designed to determine the size of the solar system and aid navigators with the perennial problem of calculating longitude. Cook was also handed new sealed orders, signed by the King, with a directive that they were not to be opened until after his departure from Tahiti.

The *Dolphin*'s crew had made several imagined sightings of the elusive unknown continent, but the traces always evaporated when approached. The Master, George Robertson, swore on one occasion that he had seen a high promontory to the south, yet 'the weather being so thick and hazy' others doubted it was land. Two days later they spotted what Robertson called 'the long wished for southern continent'. Once again, this proved intangible. His distant mountains were probably banks of dark cloud.

Robertson remained convinced that the object of their search was close by, hovering seductively over the horizon. This was partly because as they sailed out of the bay in Tahiti, he had glimpsed what he took to be pale-faced men in large canoes. They wore 'canopies' over their heads, he said, bearing 'great resemblance to the Jews'. Robertson also thought that they might have been speaking Hebrew.

In fact, these dignitaries probably belonged to a high-ranking Tahitian priestly caste. But Robertson's misconception fed into a stubborn European conviction that in addition to copious deposits of precious stones, diamonds and gold, the impressively abundant *terra incognita* sustained an extraordinarily advanced civilisation. The Royal Society suggested to Cook that the inhabitants would probably be skilled in arts and science and might possess 'a method of communicating their thoughts at a distance'.

Cook's secret orders were precise: he must not be 'diverted from the object which you have always to have in view, the Discovery of the Great Southern Continent so often mentioned'. On leaving Tahiti he was to sail south, locate the *terra incognita* and display

'every kind of Civility and Regard' to its eerily sophisticated inhabitants, while claiming any part of their land that he considered
valuable for King George III.

Cook, with three massive sweeps across the Pacific, finally dissolved that alluring mirage. On his second voyage, 1772–1775, *HMS
Resolution* was the first ship to cross the Antarctic Circle. Instead of
a sunlit land of fantastic wealth, all they glimpsed were ghostly sil-
houettes of icebergs. Thus, Cook finally proved that the longed for
bounteous Southern Continent *nondum cognita* (not yet known)
was a chimera that could never be known.

In contrast to Captain Cook, Wallis has faded into obscurity,
save for the unappetising role assigned to him in our family lore.
Greater anonymity, however, shrouds my great-great-great-great-
grandfather, even though at the age of 29 he sailed with Captain
Cook on that marathon second voyage.

James Wallis, of Portsea in Hampshire, is listed as the carpenter on *HMS Resolution*. Exactly 241 years after Cook's *Resolution*
penetrated the Antarctic circle, I flew over the fringes of Antarctica
on a flight from Sydney to Johannesburg that had been driven far
south by high winds. From the comfort of 30,000 feet above, peering down at the otherworldly monochrome sight, I thought of my
ancestor on a wooden sailing vessel in that numbing nether region
of glacial blues, translucent greens and blinding white. What could
it have been like for a working-class Kentish man in frozen latitudes
never plumbed by man before? Where icebergs 'as high as the dome
of St Paul's' made an explosion like cannon shot every time a chunk
broke off and crashed into the glacial sea? Aside from the names
of later ships that he served on, nothing at all is known about this

modest artisan.

When he died in 1833, a brief obituary in *The Nautical Magazine* noted 'At Deptford, aged 90, Mr James Wallis, Carpenter in the Navy, who accompanied Captain Cook on his second voyage of discovery around the world.'

Our accidental naval hero

Wallis men were traditionally shipwrights at the naval dockyard of Deptford in Kent. James Wallis' brother, Provo, having served as a shipbuilder during the American War of Independence, transferred to the British naval base in Halifax, Nova Scotia. His son became clerk at the Halifax dockyard, and that extensive Wallis naval legacy enabled them (as was a corrupt practice then) to register Provo's grandson, also named Provo, as an able seaman at the age of four. This was my distant relative who, after gaining national fame for gallant feats during a naval battle in 1813, eventually rose to become Admiral of the Fleet. Sir Provo William Parry Wallis GCB remained on the 'active list' till he died aged 100, the longest-serving naval officer in British history.

One reason for the British thrust into the Pacific, following the exploratory voyages of Samuel Wallis and James Cook, was a desire to establish a counterweight to the loss in the north of the 13 colonies after the American War of Independence. But that revolution against British authority left many matters unresolved, and they flared up again in the inconclusive 'War of 1812', when the United States, irked chiefly by trading restrictions imposed during the Napoleonic campaigns, declared war on Britain. The moment

Lieutenant Provo Wallis

of glory for Provo Wallis, then a 22-year-old lieutenant, is regarded as the decisive moment for control of the seas and perhaps the war.

It was a tale far more dramatic and gorier than any swashbuckling yarn from the imperial-minded adventure books that I consumed as a lad. The British fleet operating from Halifax had sustained a series of humiliating disasters. In the summer of 1813 a Royal Navy frigate, *HMS Shannon*, was blockading Boston when, with chivalric swagger, the British captain sent a note to his counterpart on an American frigate trapped in Boston harbour: 'As the *Chesapeake* appears now ready for sea, I request you will do me the favour to meet the *Shannon* with her, ship to ship, to try the fortune of our respective flags.' The captain of the *Chesapeake* never received this challenge, but had already resolved to put to sea. The ensuing battle is said to be the bloodiest ship-to-ship engagement in the age of sail.

The two frigates closed fast and waited till they were only 35 metres apart to open murderous cannon fire on each other. The *Chesapeake*, disabled, swung wildly, unable to aim directly, while *HMS Shannon* continued to pour lethal broadsides onto her enemy's decks. The ships collided and the British swiftly boarded the *Chesapeake*.

This battle, according to young Provo Wallis' timepiece, was over in a mere 11 minutes. The carnage was colossal: 71 men killed and

155 wounded. In those homicidal minutes there was a higher casualty rate than aboard *HMS Victory* during the entire four hours of hostilities at the Battle of Trafalgar.

The American captain, who had sallied forth with such bravado, lay mortally wounded. The British captain was incapacitated, his skull split open by a cutlass. *HMS Shannon's* first lieutenant had been killed, leaving second lieutenant Wallis as the senior officer in charge of two crippled frigates. Over the next six days, Provo Wallis remained on deck to coax his two wrecks along the entire enemy coastline, constantly expecting to be intercepted, till at last they reached Halifax.

It was the first major British victory, a critical morale booster, and young Provo was hailed as a hero. Promotion was rapid. From captaining ships, he became aide-de-camp to Queen Victoria, then a rear admiral. A special directive permitted any officer who had commanded a ship during the Napoleonic wars to remain on the 'active list' and so receive full pay. Thanks to his six days in charge of *HMS Shannon*, Provo Wallis enjoyed this benefit and, in his nineties, spurned all suggestions that he retire, insisting he was ready for active service if called upon. A tall, erect, leonine-looking man, Sir Provo died at his home near Portsmouth two months short of his 101st birthday.

The longest journey

A smudged, 65-year-old letter to my grandmother Trixie, *née* Beatrice Wallis, in South Africa from her niece Gwen in Australia informs her that in Sydney they have the seal ring of 'your late great uncle

Provo Wallis in old age

Provo Wallis'. Gwen remarks that Sir Provo bears a 'great likeness' to Trixie's fine-whiskered father, William Moncur Wallis.

For while James Wallis had boldly sailed with Captain Cook, his son Joseph – my great-great-great-grandfather – remained in Kent all his life, persevering in the traditional family craft as a naval shipwright at Deptford. Then, in the mid-1830s, there was an abrupt change.

It was a time of social ferment in England. The Swing Riots had begun in Kent and spread swiftly throughout the rest of the country. The aim was to oppose the brutal increase in rural unemployment, alongside drastic cuts in agricultural wages due to growing mechanisation.

Farmers and landlords began receiving threatening letters from the fictitious 'Captain Swing'. In 1834, six farmworkers met at Tolpuddle in Dorset to create The Friendly Society of Agricultural Labourers, an early form of trade unionism. One local landowner, Squire Frampton, the ancestor of a cheery rural lad that I went to school with, wrote to complain to the Prime Minister, Lord Melbourne, and the men were hastily arrested, tried and sentenced to transportation to Australia.

At the same time, the southern hemisphere exerted its pull on half of Joseph Wallis' eight children. A quartet of brothers emigrated to

Australia, then primarily known as a penal colony. Voluntarily they took the same protracted sea voyage to New South Wales as thousands of convicts.

The first to arrive in Sydney was William Wallis in 1834, followed later by his brothers – Joseph, Henry and Nathaniel. The most successful by far, however, was my great-great-grandfather, William, who within 20 years became immensely, ostentatiously wealthy.

3
+

THE UTTERMOST SHORES

Exit to another life

CHARLES DARWIN ARRIVED in Sydney in January 1836 aboard the *Beagle*, during its epic voyage around the world. 'In the evening I walked through the town,' recorded Darwin, 'and returned full of admiration for the whole scene. It is a most magnificent testimony to the power of the British nation.' This is the boisterous settlement, not yet 50 years old, that the Wallis brothers first encountered. Sydney, with a population of roughly 23,000, was expanding rapidly. 'My first feeling was to congratulate myself that I was born an Englishman,' remarked Darwin. 'Upon seeing more of the town afterwards, perhaps my admiration fell a little; but yet it is a fine town.'

It is unlikely that the newly migrated William Wallis would have shared Darwin's social scruples. 'On the whole, from what I heard, more than from what I saw, I was disappointed in the state of society,' sighed the young naturalist. 'Among those who, from their station in life, ought to be the best, many live in such open profligacy that respectable people cannot associate with them.'

Darwin also recoiled from being served by convict servants. 'The female servants are of course the worst, hence children learn the vilest expressions and …', he feared, 'equally vile ideas.' Consequently Darwin concluded with an imperious sniff: 'My opinion is such that nothing but rather sharp necessity should compel me to emigrate.'

No such qualms restrained the Wallis brothers, all of whom profited from opportunities that they could never have enjoyed in England.

Six days after Charles Darwin sailed out of Sydney, my 23-year-old great-great-grandfather married Susannah Moncur from Scotland, the orphaned daughter of Captain James Moncur of the East India Company. Susannah, 21, and her younger sister were 'bounty immigrants', a loan system devised to boost skilled migrants. On arrival the sisters had bought a dress-making business.

In Sydney, William Wallis started out as a carpenter and undertaker, became a builder and eventually acquired land and properties. Social mobility in this fledgling colony proved immeasurably more flexible than in Britain. In 1842, Wallis sued a client for handing over designs he had drawn for a row of terraced houses to another builder. Wallis demanded an architect's fee. The rival builder dismissed Wallis as 'a mere journeyman carpenter'. But the judge ruled in Wallis' favour: that he had been an architect, however briefly. 'The labourer,' affirmed His Honour with biblical wisdom, 'being worthy of hire.'

By 1851 Wallis was commissioned to build the first section of the Sydney to Parramatta railway line. But soon most of his labourers absconded to Australia's first gold rush, 200 kilometres away, and he relinquished the contract. By now Wallis owned considerable tracts of land in what is today the fashionable district of Woollahra, where there remains a street named after him.

In 1854 Wallis sold 346 plots by auction, and shortly afterwards sailed out of Sydney. He had accrued enough funds to enable him to visit the mother country in style. He, his wife Susannah and their two sons remained in England for nine years, and both young men studied at Cambridge University.

In May 1863, the eldest, my great-grandfather William Moncur Wallis, married Frances, daughter of the London publisher John Weale, and that same year the entire family returned to Australia.

The immigrant made good

When Charles Darwin had visited Sydney 27 years previously, he had remarked, with some surprise, on the existence of various 'beautiful villas'. One was now owned by the patriarch William Wallis. His imposing stone mansion, Moncur Lodge, stood on the prestigious promontory of Potts Point. Surrounded by extensive grounds, it boasted five bedrooms, servants' quarters, stables, a coach house and, as a later newspaper advertisement boasted, 'frontage on the waters of Port Jackson'.

By the time he died in 1885, aged 72, William Wallis had amassed a fortune, sired two grown sons and outlived two wives, the second of whom was 36 years younger than him. Then: my shock.

William Wallis, I discovered, had a breathtaking art collection. Three months after his death a notice in the *Sydney Morning Herald* trumpeted: 'GRAND SALE BY PUBLIC AUCTION', at Moncur Lodge, 'of the whole of the MAGNIFICENT COLLECTION of VALUABLE OIL PAINTINGS contained in the well-known PRIVATE GALLERY of the late W. WALLIS, Esq.' What? Family lore had relayed many unhappy tales of his vanished fortune, but a dazzling art collection? No one ever told me that.

The auction catalogue reveals that this emigrant had somehow assembled almost certainly the most valuable classic art collection in the southern hemisphere. The roll call is stupendous: Titian, Velásquez, Dürer, Holbein, Bruegel, Caravaggio, Canaletto, Raphael, Van Dyck, Rubens, Gainsborough and Turner.

The missing masterpieces

This was thrilling. No one had ever mentioned our family had once owned Renaissance masters, let alone a Titian. Were we such philistines that such a superlative art collection could vanish from our collective memory over the next three generations?

Judging by the provenances identified in the auction catalogue, the paintings were bought during William Wallis' nearly decade-long stay in England. The first one is recorded as 'Charity' by Rubens. 'Formerly in possession of Louis Philippe'. This refers to Louis Philippe I, the king of France from 1830 until he had to flee to England in 1848 disguised as 'Mr Smith'. An art collector, the exiled king died only four years before William Wallis arrived in London flush with money. Other works are listed as 'Formerly in the possession of Lady North' and 'From Lady Beresford's gallery'. Another two – 'From the Duke of Palma's Gallery' and 'From the Marcellino Palace, Parma' – suggest he also travelled to Italy in search of art.

What really grabbed my attention was the comment of the art critic of the *Sydney Morning Herald*, picking out one particular work that Wallis had loaned for exhibition in 1872: 'The same gentleman also sends from his well-known collection: the 'Gamblers' by Caravaggio (No.44), a large painting of great value.'

Could this be the artist's masterpiece, also known as 'The Cheats'? The painting shows, with Caravaggio's customary panache, a game

42

of cards: an older man, pretending idle curiosity, leans over to check the hand of a naïve dupe – while signalling to his accomplice, who reaches behind his back to pull an illicit card from his breeches. This is the work which paved the way for Caravaggio's brilliant but turbulently brief success, and the painting passed through the hands of some of the most powerful cardinals and princes in Rome.

This work, intriguingly, was said to have disappeared in the latter part of the nineteenth century, only finally resurfacing in 1987 in a private European collection. With mounting excitement I speculated: was it possible, during those lost years, that Caravaggio's innovative masterpiece could have been lurking obscurely in Potts Point, far from the influential centres of art dealing and connoisseurship?

Ungentlemanly double dealing

The painting, now known as 'The Cardsharps', was acquired by the Kimbell Art Museum in Fort Worth, Texas, in 1987: aha, I exulted, yes: the very year that it had apparently reappeared from mysterious obscurity.

My hopes were high that I had solved the mystery of the missing Wallis masterwork. The Texas museum responded to my eager query with elegant understatement, 'We do not believe this work has ever been in Australia.' They provided a more complete history from the time of Cardinal del Monte, showing that the painting had been in the possession of Don Maffeo Barberini Colonna di Sciarra, the eighth Prince of Carbognano, until 1925. So the existence of the genuine Caravaggio was now accounted for, not only during Wallis' lifetime, but for 50 years after his death as well. The Moncur Lodge 'Gamblers' was not the original.

'Damn,' I groaned, 'there goes our private Caravaggio.'

There are other possibilities. It could have been a copy, either from the sixteenth century or later. Or Wallis' oil painting could have been a fake. There were plenty of art dealers in London eager to palm off dubious 'Old Masters' to naïve millionaires. The most famous dealer of a later generation, Sir Joseph Duveen, who made a fortune out of selling European 'Old Masters' to American robber barons, observed 'Europe has a great deal of art, and America has a great deal of money.' The same cynicism would apply to a newly rich émigré from Australia seeking to raise his social status by buying classical art.

Wallis clearly thought that his art works were originals. In 1875 he wrote to the government offering to sell his collection, 'in consequence of failing health'.

His proposition was not well received. Parliament had recently voted £1,000 to the Academy of Art, precursor of the current Gallery of New South Wales, so it looked as though a council member was trying to cash in on this sizeable public grant. Minutes for the next council meeting record a ministerial reply, 'expressing the dissatisfaction of the government ...', the Minister evidently believing Wallis had been caught out in a blatant conflict of interest.

Early the following year, the Minister recommended the appointment of Trustees for voting on the grant, and pointedly excluded Wallis. A few days later Wallis scribbled a one line note to the Academy: 'Gentlemen, I beg forthwith to tender my resignation as a member of your council.'

The colonial imitation

William Wallis' paintings were almost certainly copies; very good copies. Before the advent of cheap travel or reliable colour reproduction, replicas of old masters were the only way people in distant colonies could gain an idea of the European originals. William himself believed his works were original and press reports accepted that his Titian, Velásquez, Caravaggio, etc., were the real McCoy.

It was only after his death and the great auction that the grandiose claims began to unravel: slowly but relentlessly.

Today only three of Wallis' paintings remain in the possession of the Art Gallery of New South Wales, though none have been on display for years. One sunny morning my daughter Julia and I travelled to a distant Sydney suburb, where the trio of remaining Wallis' art works are stored in a cavernous warehouse.

Towering stacks of retractable shelving were manoeuvred to locate the downgraded paintings. Finally they were ready for our inspection. The 'Spanish Beggar' ('after Murillo') is dark and brooding, but forlorn without a frame. In contrast, the 'Adoration of the Magi' ('after Ugolini') is an enormous canvas in an imposing gold leaf frame. Bubbling at the bottom suggests that this huge oil painting could have been placed above the fireplace in the drawing room at Moncur Lodge: a bravura status symbol.

'You should ask the gallery if you could take it home,' suggested the helpful assistant.

Julia seemed intrigued. 'But where would we put it?' she mused.

The final painting, bought at the 1875 auction, was sold to the gallery by a later owner. This is 'Storm and Wreck', which my great-great-grandfather had promoted as by the eighteenth century

French artist Claude-Joseph Vernet, celebrated for his seascapes and lauded by Denis Diderot, who enthused 'He has stolen Nature's secret; what she produces, Vernet can recreate.' But as a forlorn finale to all those lavish claims of genuine Old Masters, 'Storm and Wreck' is neither signed nor dated, and consequently now carries the proviso 'attributed to' Claude-Joseph Vernet.

And the Wallis 'Caravaggio'?

Eventually archive records revealed that when in 1902 the Gallery of New South Wales accepted the loan of this painting – by then renamed 'The Gamesters' – it was no longer identified as 'by' the great artist, but downgraded as 'attributed to'. Even that cautious rider was soon discarded, and all pretentions to be by the daring hand of Caravaggio were definitively, disappointingly, severed.

Losing the family treasure trove
William Wallis' fortune dissipated within a decade.

Aside from his art collection, what happened to all those properties and his baronial mansion with sea-fronted parkland? Discovering his second wife was only 28 when he married again at 64, I thought: aha, *cherchez la femme*. But Jessie died four years before her husband.

Valuations show that his assets were still sizeable, and his will stipulated most of the estate was to be divided equally between his sons, my great-grandfather William Moncur and his younger brother James. At least on my side of the lineage, there can be no doubt: my great-grandfather lost all his inherited prosperity.

In a note to my daughter Julia, my mother tried to clarify what happened. William Wallis Senior, she explained, 'bought him a large sheep station in Australia. In the 1880s there was one of the worst droughts in Australian history. More than half the nation's sheep died. The sheep station couldn't survive, so the family moved to Sydney to live with William's father at Moncur Lodge till the father's death in 1885. After his death, the Lodge was sold and they lived off the rents from properties his father had left. But, as a result of the great depression, their tenants didn't have the money to pay rent. Bit by bit most properties had to be sold off for a quarter of what they were worth.'

There had indeed been a catastrophic financial collapse, leading to soaring unemployment, strikes and social unrest. My great-grandfather appears to have been utterly unsuited to the tough life of Australian sheep farming. Scraping through a 'Natural Sciences Tripos' degree at Cambridge

William Moncur

had not prepared him to deal with one of the worst economic crashes in history. He also had nine children. Given the combination of financial crisis, drought, numerous dependants and a Cambridge education which did not equip him for those challenges, the handed-down family version claimed that it wasn't so puzzling that his large inheritance evaporated.

My mother also maintained that William Moncur, her

grandfather, was a gentle man, too kindly to press distressed tenants for rents they did not have.

But was this true?

Baba black sheep

In fact, my great-grandfather's problems had begun much earlier. But this embarrassing detail was not something that my grandmother told my mother. Possibly Granny Trixie didn't know herself. In 1877 she was 18 months old when a local newspaper reported, 'We now learn that the authorities have issued summonses against Mr James Henry Wallis and Mr William Moncur Wallis (both of whom have resigned their commissions as Justices of the Peace), in which they are charged with having, on the 18th of April, unlawfully and fraudulently combined, conspired, confederated, and agreed together by certain false pretences and subtle means and devices to procure a grant by purchase without competition ... of 200 acres at Tumbleton, in the name of Nathaniel Wallis the younger.'

The Wallis brothers pleaded not guilty, farcically claiming that they didn't know Nathaniel Wallis or even if he was a relative. They were released on bail and committed for trial the following month. An affidavit from Nathaniel Wallis confirmed that they were his cousins, but swore that he'd never authorised William Moncur to obtain land for him, and that the signature on the document was not his. Despite the incriminating evidence, the two former Justices of the Peace were acquitted.

Perhaps their father's wealth, plus the fact they had been JPs, bent the law in their favour. The Wallis brothers were clearly close.

As young lads both had briefly attended Sydney College, but the archives of the renamed Sydney Grammar School record for William, 12, and James, 11: 'Removed, a change being desirable on account of their intractableness.'

Ten months after the trial, a notice in the *Sydney Morning Herald* disclosed that William Moncur had applied for insolvency. His debts were enormous. My great-grandfather simply couldn't manage money. The list of creditors makes dismal reading, from banks to wine merchants, yet he still ordered luxury items from London.

He was 41 years old, and was forced to move into his father's mansion at Potts Point with his wife Frances and nine children. They remained there until the patriarch died. My great-grandfather didn't pursue any other career. They lived off rents from his inherited properties until those funds also dwindled, compelling his widow and two unmarried daughters, Ethel and my Granny Trixie, to live with various relatives in genteel dependency.

When Frances Weale of London had married my great-grandfather, the handsome, Cambridge-educated son of a wealthy immigrant 42 years previously, this cannot have been how she had imagined her future in Australia.

Taking tea with the Empress of China

'Auntie' Alix was born in China in 1895. Her mother Isabel was the younger sister of my great-grandmother Frances in Sydney. Frances and Isabel had grown up in London, where their father John Weale was a publisher of scientific, engineering and architectural works. Their mother Sarah was American, granddaughter of General Israel

Putnam, a flamboyant hero of the American War of Independence, commonly called 'Old Put'.

Alix's father, Charles Lenox Simpson, was a commissioner in the quasi-colonial Chinese Imperial Maritime Customs Service. After two wars to compel the decaying Qing dynasty to accept British opium imports from India, the British government also forced the Chinese to accept foreign trade and European residents in what were known as 'Treaty Ports'. The Customs Service, created in 1854 to collect duties from this trade, was staffed by foreigners, mostly British, wielding enormous power. By 1900 the department employed 20,000 staff and collected one third of all Chinese revenue. For British, French, German, American and other Westerners in their enclaves, life could be a parody of colonial frivolity.

This may account for Alix's imperious manner. As my mother explained to my daughter, Julia, in another of her concise notes, 'In those days the various districts were ruled by warlords who constantly fought each other. However, life for the Simpsons was extremely pleasant with a large house and a mass of servants. Alix's older sister Esmé was taken to tea with the last Empress of China, Tzu-hsi (1835–1908).'

For expatriate wives and daughters in the foreign legations, life was circumscribed but leisurely: a round of lunches, picnics, teas, tennis, card games, musical *soirées*, amateur dramatics and cocktail parties.

When the anti-Western Boxer Rebellion broke out, most of the Simpsons were in Tientsin. But Alix's older brother, the raffish Bertram Lenox Simpson, had followed his father into the Customs Service and was based in Peking, where he lived through the famous siege. Later he gained notoriety with the publication of *Indiscreet Letters from Peking*, which gives an unflattering portrait of the legation leaders in contrast to the accepted heroic version. Bertram was particularly scornful of British officials, accusing them of being more afraid than the women.

The siege so galvanised Europe, he wrote, 'in England the South African war was temporarily forgotten'.

Over sixty years later in London, when a teenager, my mother and I were asked by Alix to accompany her to the cinema to see a newly released film, *55 Days At Peking*. In this epic, Chinese insurgents lay siege to the foreign legation, where the US marine commander (Charlton Heston) has a torrid liaison with a shady Russian Baroness (Ava Gardner). The phlegmatic British Ambassador (David Niven) keeps everyone's spirits up as they wait for the Great Powers to dispatch an expeditionary force to save them.

Kaiser Wilhelm II addressed German troops setting out from Bremerhaven, and his ferocious words present a chilling foretaste of the policy of genocide soon to be implemented in German South West Africa. The official, published version of the speech suppressed the Kaiser's chilling exhortation: 'Prisoners will not be taken! Whoever falls into your hands is forfeited. Just as a thousand years ago the Huns under their King Attila made a name for themselves, one that even today makes them seem mighty in history and legend, may the name German be affirmed by you in such a way in China that no Chinese will ever again dare to look cross-eyed at a German.'

Looting in Peking

In *Indiscreet Letters*, published six years later, the German military attaché in Peking is portrayed as distinctly effeminate, wearing bracelets – and, most suspiciously, 'plays a vile game of tennis'. The description by Alix's brother of the Europeans under siege bears no resemblance to the valiant conduct of Charlton Heston or David Niven in *55 Days in Peking*.

The Boxers, mostly young, wore red bandannas. Their proper name, 'The Fists of Righteous Harmony', was derived from the martial arts they practised. It was a nationalistic movement in response to the encroachment of the white 'barbarians' or 'big-nosed hairy ones', particularly the British, who were expanding into China, 'as stealthily as silkworms nibbling at mulberry leaves'.

As the siege of the diplomatic quarter tightened, Bertram Simpson thought of Rider Haggard's character Umslopogaas, adding, 'We of Peking are, unfortunately, not on the mettle of the Zulus.' What most shocked contemporaries, however, and led to Bertram being treated with disdain forever after by the British, were his claims that once the siege was lifted many of the most respectable Westerners went on a wild looting rampage.

Bertram cheerfully admitted that he joined in, entering the Imperial City and penetrating as far as the imperial seraglio and the Emperor's bedroom, where he acquired an ornate silver chamber pot. 'It was organised plundering, and everyone winked at it,' he confessed. This was not the authorised version as reflected at the time, or even 63 years on with Charlton Heston as the gritty Major Matt Lewis. Bertram cynically concluded, 'Yet history is only made to be immediately forgotten.'

Indiscreet Letters appeared under the pseudonym of Putnam Weale, linking the names of his American and British grandfathers. The book caused a huge scandal. *The Times* correspondent dismissed him as a 'social pariah'.

Bertram, however, launched a maverick career in China as 'Putnam Weale'. He became a journalist, author of books on China, a novelist and eventually personally involved in the increasingly factional nationalist politics.

By 1930 Bertram was advising a northern warlord when he was shot and critically wounded. The motive remains unclear, though undoubtedly it was linked to his role in local power struggles. Six weeks later headlines around the world announced: 'Putnam Weale Dead'. My mother, aged 18, was visiting Paris with her great-aunt when Alix received news of her brother's assassination. Perhaps Alix had yet to develop that facade of patrician *froideur* which I later experienced, as Barbara, 17 years her junior, recalled trying to comfort a distraught Alix, who hadn't seen her older, disreputable brother for years.

After their father's death in 1909, Alix and her sister Esmé were taken by their mother back to Europe. A widow's pension from the Customs Service was modest, but Isabel Simpson primed her two girls – or 'gels' in Alix's throttled articulation – for advantageous marriages.

Staying in cheap *pensiones* on the Rivera, the sisters took part in fashionable tennis tournaments where they met eligible young men. Esmé first married an urbane Italian aristocrat, then a wealthy Roman industrialist.

Alix lived in London, having married Major General Wulff Grey who had made his money in West Africa. In the days when adults might slip me sixpence with the stern proviso, 'Save that in your piggy bank', the Major General – a splendidly upright old gent – always secretly pressed something metal into my hand, and on the way home in the back seat of my parents' Austin A30 I'd discover this to be a half crown: an act of unimaginable largesse, and by far the wealthiest I have ever felt.

Over the sea from Skye

Forty years later, in several long-neglected suitcases in the cellar at my mother Barbara's house in London, I found scattered pages of blanched typescript. It took weeks to assemble. To my astonishment, it was a memoir by her father, Lewis Rose Macleod, written in the 1930s when editor of the *Rand Daily Mail*. My grandfather was only ever referred to as Lewis Rose, which is what I shall call him.

The Macleods were from the Isle of Skye in Scotland. His father Donald was offered a job as an engineer in New Zealand, so he sailed there with his wife and two older sons in 1865. Lewis Rose was born ten years later. The family soon moved to Sydney, but my grandfather had to leave school, aged 13, on his father's death. Lewis Rose worked at many jobs, from office boy to dairy farming.

He recalled comparing youthful memories of Sydney many years later with the former seafarer Joseph Conrad: 'the wharves of Circular Quay, where the greatest liners would berth, and where all the famous wool clippers – the *Cutty Sark*, the fastest ship that ever sailed – waited to be loaded with a cargo of wool with which they would race one another to the London wool sales.'

Conrad had paid his first visit to Sydney in 1888 on the *Otago*, a three-masted iron barque, his first and only command. Over lunch in London with my grandfather, by then a literary editor, the novelist lamented that on his last visit all the clippers had been replaced by steamships. And 'with an eloquent gesture of the nervous hands', Lewis Rose records, 'he smiled reminiscently across the long avenue of years.'

Once the family finances improved, Lewis Rose was sent to Moore College Grammar School to continue his education. After a few weeks a family acquaintance arrived at the school and offered him a job. 'I went into the school building and got my hat,' wrote Lewis Rose, 'and walked away with him, there and then.'

After working on railway construction, he began contributing to Sydney journals and magazines. In 1900, aged 25, he published a lengthy pamphlet, *For Queen and Empire!*, extolling the contribution of New South Wales to the Boer War. 'Sport – and they say that Australians think of nothing else – is now a minor interest,' declared the fired-up loyalist. 'Our thoughts are all of war; the one thing of interest to us now is the great and momentous drama being enacted in South Africa.' Patriotically he proclaimed, 'We are fighting for a principle which we have been taught to hold sacred – the principle of right and justice for men of our breed wherever they may be.'

That, he stated, is 'the apotheosis of the Imperial idea'.

In December 1900 he published another partisan trumpet blast, *The Glory Roll*, with even greater jingoistic bombast. 'Of all the great events and crises recorded in the History of the building of the British Empire, none will rank of greater importance than the War in South Africa, now practically over, in which the great outlying

Colonies voluntarily joined their forces, and achieved fame fighting with the grand Old Mother Country.'

Before ever setting foot in South Africa, there's no doubting my grandfather's strident imperial credo: 'It is therefore evident that our destiny as a race is to "bear the White Man's burden" of Empire.'

Macleod's anti-Boer diatribe

Playing the paramour

By 1902 Lewis Rose had established himself sufficiently for a magazine to describe him as 'a well-known Sydney journalist, who devotes his leisure to the production of short stories, light verse, and occasional playlets'. The magazine complimented the amateur production of his comedy, *The Artistic Temperament*, which it judged 'went with a "snap"'. There is a photograph of the author with his small cast in costume. The caption identifies 'Mr Macleod and his artistic friends'. Apart from 'Mr L.R. Macleod as the choleric old general, Sir Andrew Blood', the article singles out 'Miss Wallis, as his sympathetic young wife, being quite commendable'.

Lewis Rose wrote a simple poem 'To BLW' (Beatrice Louise Wallis, my Granny Trixie):

'I've never wooed you in a play,
Nor have you harked to me,
Yet … somehow … dearest … well-o-day!
On one dear night not far away …
The moon was there to see!'

Their daughter, Barbara, con-
scientiously preserved the trim,
rectangular card on which this
romantic poem was written.
But the lower right-hand corner
is torn, so that the final words
of the last three lines in Lewis
Rose's meticulous handwriting
are missing. Nevertheless, the
sincerity of his proposal shines
through:

Beatrice, far left, Macleod, centre

'I've played the husband too, while you
Have played the loving wife.
Oh, little love, so sweet and ----
Whom only moonbeams saw ----
We'll play those parts for ---

That last line almost certainly ended, as, in fact, it was to be:
'We'll play those parts for life.' But to get married, Lewis Rose and
Beatrice had to wait three more years, until – and then separately –
they landed on a distant, far stranger shore.

4
✠
THE STRANGEST SHORE

Where the sun never sets

THE BOAST OF AN EMPIRE so boundless that somewhere under its dominion it is forever daylight is associated with a Governor of the Cape Colony, the colonial administrator George Macartney. Similar claims have been traced back to the Old Testament. Ultimately the British appropriated this assertion, along with much of the world, hence George (later Earl) Macartney was able to celebrate, 'a vast empire, on which the sun never sets'; adding ominously, 'and whose bounds nature has not yet ascertained'.

The first person to use the term 'Brytish Impire' was the protean Elizabethan scholar, Dr John Dee. One of the outstanding sages of the sixteenth century, Dee was a philosopher, mathematician, scientist and cartographer. An adviser to Elizabeth I, in 1570 John Dee published *Brytanici Imperii Limites* (the Limits of the British Empire), which he presented personally to the Queen. Dee argued that Britain had territorial claims well beyond its borders, and indeed had the right to colonise much of the northern hemisphere: a direct challenge to the might of the Spanish Empire.

Dee was the complete Renaissance man. Yet science was not enough. Dee longed to push his knowledge beyond all known bounds. He wished to communicate with the angels. Dee had a frustrating time with various mediums, until Edward Talbot turned up at his door in 1582, offering his services. To Dee's joy, Talbot proved to be fluent in the angelic language.

On my shelves I have an old quarto-sized volume which contains transcripts of hundreds of 'sessions' with various angels. After Christian invocations and sacred rites ('Three days before, abstaine from Coitus and Gluttony'), Talbot would peer into the crystal ball and summon *'Angeli boni'*. The angelic tongue was called Enochian. Only Talbot could speak Enochian, and only he could see or hear *'Angeli boni'*, particularly a chatty spirit called Madimi. Talbot's real name, though, was Kelley. He wore a black cowl that covered his ears; probably because one ear had been lopped off for forgery.

Dee and Kelley also experimented with alchemy, the art of transforming base metal into gold. But as gossip spread of heretical séances at Dee's Mortlake home, Kelley received an urgent angelic instruction that they should flee England. It was after they were expelled from Prague for practising 'prohibited arts' that the fey Madimi issued the shocking challenge. They were to swap wives.

Dee's patrician third wife Jane, 28 years his junior and a former royal lady-in-waiting, was aghast. But the wily angel revealed, via Kelley, that this constituted the ultimate trial of their faith in God. Passing this supreme test, Madimi promised, would ensure what Dee had always craved: 'the way of knowledge and understanding'. The following day only two words appear in Dee's diary, *'Pactum factum'*; the deed is done.

This outlandish tale of a great and foolish scholar could be taken as a parable for that 'incomparable Brytish Impire' which Dee had predicted: a struggle over the following centuries between avowed idealism, ruthless duplicity and crass materialism, where missionaries vied with charlatans, conquerors and capitalists.

Globalisation and its discontents

Dr Dee's forecast of a great empire must have appeared vainglorious at the time, as England was a relatively minor power. Dee had urged that imperial ambitions could only be achieved with a substantial navy. But as his passion for angelic séances grew, his influence at court waned. Subsequently Dee's eccentric spiritual experiments have diminished his historical reputation. His home in Mortlake, however, which housed one of the greatest libraries in Europe, should be acknowledged as a crucial incubator of British territorial expansion. All the foremost Elizabethan navigators (including Sir Francis Drake and Sir Walter Raleigh) were sent to take instruction from him.

The magus proved to be an imperial prophet. Yet now Britain appears to have regressed to a status similar to Dee's time: a middling power, deeply distrustful of other European nations. And judging by the boasts of modern British jingoes, many in that small isle are addicted to mystical notions of a new dawn of global influence.

While Dee had advocated a massive ship building project, due to Britain's relative weakness, much of the initial maritime jousting with the Spanish Empire was conducted by 'privateers'. Pillaging Spanish galleons for treasure, often with a semi-official status, these freebooters were a cheap way of filling government coffers. In many ways, such 'freelancing' continued with the expansion of empire, regularly driven by private enterprise, first in the Americas, then in India, later in Africa.

British expansion eventually created a vast network of trade and migration across the world. The ensuing astonishing exodus of many millions from the British Isles included most of my forebearers. Thus, shortly after the turn of the twentieth century, significantly more momentous for me, all four of my grandparents emigrated to South Africa.

That transplantation of my grandparents brings us full circle back to Dr Dee and his alchemical experiments: the dream of turning base mental into gold. But by then, there was no need for Dee's sacred rites ('Three days before, abstaine from Coitus and Gluttony'). In South Africa, huge deposits of that desired metal lay underground.

The widow's glory roll

The discovery of gold in the Boer republic of the Transvaal in 1886 triggered the birth of the turbulent mining city of Johannesburg. It also led in 1899 to Britain forcing war on two tiny Boer republics in order to assert control over this bonanza. Far away in Sydney, my empire loyalist grandfather furiously repeated British propaganda.

'A very large British population had settled in the Transvaal. Fair play had been denied to them. The arrogance of the Boers was increasing,' growled the 25-year-old Lewis Rose Macleod in his bellicose pamphlet, *The Glory Roll* (December 1900). 'Mr J. Chamberlain, Secretary of State for the Colonies, seeing danger in view, made some very reasonable demands, but before there was time for proper negotiations, the Empire was shocked to learn that, on 9 October 1899, the British Government had received a most impudent and unreasonable ultimatum from the Presidents of the Orange Free State and the South African (Transvaal) Republic.'

The conduct of these petty Boer Republics, huffed my grandfather, 'staggered humanity', but the incensed Lewis Rose immediately proclaimed 'Then it was our turn to "stagger humanity" and teach the world ... that who so offends against the "Widow of Windsor" offends each and all of her three hundred millions of faithful subjects.'

Not everyone shared the outrage of my grandfather. A month after his diatribe the Widow of Windsor died, and on my wall hangs a framed Government Gazette, edged in black, revealing the arrival in Pretoria of a telegram from Joseph Chamberlain: 'It is with profound regret that I have to inform you of the Demise of Her Late Most Gracious Majesty Queen Victoria. Her Majesty expired at Osborne House at 6.30 in the afternoon on the 22nd instant, to the great affliction of the Royal family and all classes of Her Majesty's subjects.' At the bottom of this yellowing poster is the reply from His Excellency the High Commissioner.

'News has been received here with profound sorrow,' cabled back Sir Alfred Milner. Then with reference to the fact that Victoria's ageing son had been proclaimed King Edward VII, Milner concludes, 'I beg to add the expression of my own humble duty to their Majesties of the deep sympathy which, together with thousands of loyal subjects in South Africa, I feel for them and the Royal Family in their great loss.'

In referring to 'thousands of loyal subjects in South Africa', the haughty Milner had been scrupulous in his choice of words. For Boer commandos were still fighting a desperate rearguard action. Nor could he presume to pledge any devotion to the British royal family from millions of black South Africans – soon to be cynically ignored in the post-war settlement, though Sir Alfred had cited the abhorrent Boer treatment of Africans as one of the primary reasons for going to war.

Yet once the might of Britain finally prevailed the way was clear for the gold frenzy on the Witwatersrand to resume. Among new migrants that flocked towards this promise of a new life and dreams of Ophir-like riches were my four grandparents.

The ghostly avenue

Lately, walking purposefully though the beautiful old Dutch East India Company Gardens in Cape Town, I have been accompanied by three generations of family ghosts. The Gardens were started in the mid-seventeenth century to provide fruit and vegetables for Dutch crews on their long voyage to the East Indies, and – in what is now a shaded botanical retreat – lions, leopards and elephants once roamed. My destination is the graceful National Library, opposite the nineteenth-century Parliament building, at the city end of the Gardens. I have been straining to read old newspapers on scratchy microfilm, or hunting for footnotes in neglected books for the tale of my two grandfathers. Since I knew neither of them, this has meant disinterring mysteries kept secret from me.

On my way I pass three imperial statues. Cecil Rhodes stands at the centre of these Gardens, stubby and streaked with verdigris. He gazes north with arm upraised, exhorting 'Your hinterland is there.' He is urging white settlers to cross the Limpopo River and seize as much of Africa as they dared. Close by Parliament is Queen Victoria, chubby but serene. For Britain to remain a great empire, she told her Prime Minister Disraeli, 'Be prepared for attacks and wars, somewhere or other continually.' Victoria regularly received plunder as an imperial tribute on the defeat of yet another distant enemy. In 1860, after the Summer Palace of the Chinese Emperor had been ransacked and destroyed, a Pekinese dog was shipped to Her Majesty, who perkily christened her new pet, 'Looty'.

Nearby is the frock-coated Sir George Grey, Victoria's cultivated mid-century Governor of the Cape. Gazing toward Table Mountain, he has his back to the National Library – first funded by a tax on wine – which Sir George endowed with his own superb collection of rare medieval and Renaissance manuscripts.

At the time, even though the empire was expanding rapidly, the Colonial Office was housed in a decrepit building in Downing Street that was slowly subsiding. Built above a sewer, whose noxious fumes caused the colonial office staff to suffer constant headaches, the basement had to be pumped out twice a day. It was feared the edifice might collapse at any moment. By 1862 a mere 48 staff were housed there to pilot Britain's distant realms. Most were unqualified, having been appointed through useful connections or outright nepotism, and even then, they worked only in the afternoon.

Today, my walk to the library takes me past the cobbled district near the top of the Gardens where I lived in 1970 before leaving South Africa. It was a slum back then. There were fathers and sons who snuck in the back door, while wife and daughters entered by the front because they were a different colour. One 'coloured' prostitute with two blond sons used to hire a white prostitute to take them to school every day. It was a racially-mixed neighbourhood, before the apartheid zealots moved in and separated every family according to their officially allotted category.

If I walk down that side of the Company Gardens, I often make a detour via Spin Street: to a spot behind the old Slave Lodge where slaves were once auctioned. On other days I take the opposite side,

Queen Victoria Street, and pass the grey stone building where a committee used to meet in Room 33 to adjudicate whether someone needed to be reclassified to another 'race group'. Nowadays, both sites have plaques, but almost everyone of every colour now hurries past without a glance.

So much, over so very long, has been forgotten. But right now, heading to the library archives, my mission is to disinter my own family's role in our fraught history.

A tale of two grandfathers

William Rostron was the first to arrive, in 1903. A working-class printer from the Lancashire town of Stockport, he disembarked at the provincial Indian Ocean port of East London. He was 28 years old. Two years later the enterprising Australian journalist Lewis Rose Macleod arrived, landing further north at the larger port of Durban in the Colony of Natal. He was 30 years old. At the time neither of them would have needed passports to sail across the world, one from Liverpool and the other from Sydney; nor was such documentation expected of their respective future wives, who dutifully came later.

This was the golden age of emigration, at least for white folk. They could simply board a boat in search of a better life. Between 1815 and 1914, 22 million people left the British Isles, while since the turn of the twentieth century, nearly half a million Britons – including William Rostron – elected to try their luck in South Africa. But with the outbreak of war in 1914 all that changed: the use of passports became obligatory.

The advent of steamships over sail had also radically cut the time required to travel from England. In 1850, it took an average of 42 days to reach Cape Town; by 1890, it entailed only 19 days under steam. When William disembarked in East London, it was a small but busy river port. Half a century before, the town had been described by a customs official as a 'mud-hole' of quarrelling and bankruptcy. But in the wake of the Boer War of 1899–1902 it was enjoying a minor economic boom. The town now boasted electricity and a tram system.

Not long after his arrival in 1903, William sent word back to Lancashire for his fiancée, Annie Maguire, and when she arrived in East London, Annie later recalled having to be lowered from the ship to the quayside in a wicker basket. William and Annie married in 1904.

Not much is known about them. Unlike my other grandfather, the prolific journalist, there are only fragments recalling this working-class couple. Though devoted to his mother Annie, my father barely mentioned his parents, having fallen out with his father. In the National Archives in Pretoria, Annie's death notice records her birthplace as Ireland, but states that both her mother and father were 'unknown'. This suggests that Annie may have been what used to be referred to as a 'foundling'. A friend of hers in Johannesburg told my father that Annie had once confided that her own mother had died in childbirth and that her father had committed suicide shortly afterwards, so she had been sent to Stockport in Lancashire to be cared for by relatives. Otherwise she never talked about it.

Annie also suffered from tuberculosis, though at what point or whether she recovered is not known. My mother once told me, trying to explain and excuse my father's emotional distance, that owing to this tuberculosis his mother never permitted herself to kiss him.

Only a single small photograph of William has been passed down: as a scrawny Lancashire lad. Two of Annie survive; one snap shows a stout, middle-aged lady alone in the sunshine on the narrow balcony of an inner-city Johannesburg block of flats. The sole memento of William to be found among my father's effects is a rectangular card advertising the business he started after his arrival in South Africa: 'Whittington & Rostron', it trumpets. 'Commercial & Artistic … Printers, Bookbinders and Account Book Makers. Argyle Street'.

Rival twists of fate

Two years later, the local economy slipped into recession. By late 1905, *The South African Typographical Journal* recorded that in East London some print union members had been forced to take up alternative trades. In January 1907, the month my father was born, the *Typographical Journal* reported that Whittington & Rostron had begun printing a supplement called *The Daily Guide* for the local newspaper, the *East London Daily Dispatch*. For the Rostrons this didn't prove auspicious, especially now that they had an infant son. Almost immediately *The Daily Guide* closed down, and its proprietor vanished: 'much wanted'. By April the *Journal* noted that although the firm had started printing a new paper, *Town Topics*, it was being sued. The plaintiff was awarded £25 and, crucially, 'the Judge held that the printers, Whittington & Rostron, were responsible for the libel, as well as the writer'.

This libel action left my grandparents penniless. The partnership in the printing company broke up and William sold his share to Whittington. In February 1909 the *Typographical Journal* had a brief paragraph noting 'the purchase of the printing office of R. Whittington & Co. by the *Border News*, Whittington having decided to return to the "Old Country"; Rostron had evidently severed his connection with the firm some time previously'.

In fact, my grandparents retreated a short way inland to King William's Town, at the foot of the Amatola Mountains. Having been at the centre of successive frontier wars with the Xhosa nation, this former garrison town had experienced both advances and retreats due to vacillating British policy in the Eastern Cape. It had been the hub of Queen Adelaide Province, which lasted barely a year. A decade later King William's Town was declared the capital of the short-lived colony of British Kaffraria. As with so much of the Rostron's lives, there's no trace left of their few years in the town now named Qonce.

There is a great deal more information about my other grandparents. In a sketchy note to my daughter, Julia, my mother wrote, 'They had decided there was no future for them in Australia. Lewis Rose took a ship bound for Durban where he was going to try and produce a shipping paper. The plan was for my mother Beatrice to join him as soon as he had earned enough to support them both. In 1905 your great-great-grandmother, Frances Wallis, decided to take her two daughters to England to see relatives that she hadn't seen since her marriage. The ship sailed to England via South Africa. The night before they reached Durban, Beatrice broke the news to her mother that she intended to get off the ship & marry Lewis Rose Macleod. As she was then aged 29, her mother couldn't stop her &

had to sail off without her.'

There is a curious photograph of their small wedding group after the ceremony at St Cyprian's Church in Durban. The formality of their stiff, studio-like poses is offset by the tropical fecundity of a grove of palm trees behind them. Lewis Rose is seated, slim and dapper, his dark hair parted exactily down the middle, while his new bride stands demurely at his side, appearing

My maternal grandmother,
Beatrice ('Trixie')

remarkably like my mother. Beside Lewis Rose sits a tense-looking woman in ruffles and white hat staring sternly back at the camera. This is his older spinster sister, Florence, whom my grandfather must also have 'sent for' from Sydney once he had established himself in Durban. Florence remained unmarried and lived with my grandparents until she died in 1934, her dependency and brittle temperament the cause of many unhappy domestic scenes.

The call of Mammon

The booming excess of the goldrush city of Johannesburg soon proved an irresistible lure for both grandfathers. This time it was Lewis Rose who made the first move.

Despite my grandfather's outraged anti-Boer claims regarding the causes of Anglo-Boer War in his diatribe, *The Glory Roll*, the truth was the exact opposite. An unholy triumvirate of Joseph Chamberlain, Cecil Rhodes and the High Commissioner for South Africa, Sir Alfred Milner, set out to provoke the Boer republics into a war which they were convinced would secure the gold reefs of the Witwatersrand for British interests. It did.

The aftermath of that war witnessed a roller-coaster period of fabulous, sometimes overnight fortunes offset by spectacular failures and, for Africans, a new chapter of industrial degradation and urban miseries.

In 1907 Lewis Rose was offered the editorship of the Johannesburg *Sunday Times*. Only one year old, this pushy new newspaper already had the biggest circulation of any weekly in South Africa. The first editor was the swashbuckling New Zealander Hugh Kingswell. The fact my grandfather had also been born in New Zealand may have helped, although a more credible reason is the reputation which he carried from Sydney, having written for many of Australia's leading journals. Lewis Rose had one other crucial qualification: he had already edited a gold-rush newspaper.

In 1903, two years before he sailed for South Africa, he had been appointed editor (and sole staff member) of the *Wyalong Advocate*, a bi-weekly paper in the New South Wales goldfields. It was a rough, hard-drinking town riven by sectarian and frequently violent politics. The rival paper was avowedly Roman Catholic, so by default the *Advocate* was regarded as Protestant.

'The "Protestant" storekeepers and hotelkeepers advertised in my journal, the "Protestant" miners and farmers and professional men professed to read it,' explained my grandfather in his unpublished memoir. 'The religious views of many of the folk were not very pronounced in relation to their social and moral conduct, but in regard to politics and business they were glaringly obvious.'

Sporting events and election campaigns routinely degenerated into fist fights. Drinking binges, when a miner stuck lucky, could start early in the morning, continue through the night and into the next day. As a local editor, Lewis Rose was required to join the celebrations. His other major expense was that readers would drop into his office expecting to hear all the latest local gossip as often it was the first time the subscriber had ridden into town for months.

'It was a social event of considerable importance,' he wrote. 'Obviously you had to rise to the occasion. You asked him out to lunch – no matter what time he arrived in the afternoon … and obviously the only drinks appropriate to such an occasion were expensive drinks.'

As editor, manager and sole staff member Lewis Rose wrote all the copy. In his opening editorial, he promised that 'Its news columns will be entirely free from scurrility, in any shape or form, and untainted by any suspicion of bias.' While the *Advocate's* front page was still dominated by advertisements, he introduced regular, sassy short features, no longer than a paragraph, in which he could insert gossipy barbs and jokes, as well as indulging his lifelong penchant for light verse and doggerel:

'I've just been down to Sydney
And a lively time I've had
I've seen the sights and all the fights
And found them not too bad.'

He reported news from Parliament of a 'resort to fisticuffs', with one MP yelling 'You are a diseased cur!' On the same page, under the rubric 'From All Quarters', Lewis Rose repeated an old barroom joke, 'Absence makes the heart grow fonder. It's a bit cheaper than a wedding too.' This seems like a mischievous reference to Beatrice Wallis, 500 kilometres away in Sydney, who – to judge from the previous magazine article about 'Mr Macleod and his artistic friends' – was already his sweetheart.

But late in 1904 he decided to pack in his rambunctious life in Wyalong. 'After a couple of years of this sort of thing I sat down with the traditional wet towel round my head and, with difficulty, did a simple sum,' he recalled. 'I divided the price of a bottle of champagne (thirty shillings) into the annual subscription to my paper (165 pence) and found that it wouldn't go. So I went instead.'

It had been ideal training, however, to edit the brash Sunday paper in the volatile El Dorado of Johannesburg.

The muck of gold

Looking back on his arrival in Johannesburg, Lewis Rose claimed that 'It is one of the most cosmopolitan towns on earth. All the people of the world are represented here.' He lists various other names that it was known by: 'the Cess-pool of the Universe', 'the New Sodom and Gomorrah', 'The Capital of Hell', 'Judasburg', and a presage of the more virulent anti-Semitism to come in South Africa, 'Jewburg'. Smart districts were so elegant that they mimicked those of Paris or Bond Street, while other areas, he sniffed, 'are squalid almost beyond description, white and black being herded in distressing promiscuity into tin hovels with an almost bewildering variety of folk of intermediate shades of colour.'

Whites, he lamented, were vastly outnumbered by blacks ('raw natives a few days removed from complete savagery'), yet Johannesburg also represented 'a goldmine for the man who caters for the vanity of women'.

The city proliferated with call girls, criminals and conmen. So many foreign women lived in one area, drawn by a city full of newly affluent bachelors, that it was known as Frenchfontein. 'Adventurers from all the world had flocked there, attracted by the lure of gold,' confirmed Lewis Rose, adding that the flourishing underworld of Johannesburg swarmed with swindlers offering bogus shares in fictional mines. The High Commissioner Milner, he recalled, had hired as the head detective an 'astute and handsome Greek' named Mavrogordato, whom Milner had known in Egypt. 'Mavro', as he was known, ('a ruthless – and, I believe, unscrupulous man') achieved some success, but the city has never quite managed to shrug off that chancy reputation.

'Life in Johannesburg has never been dull,' concluded Lewis Rose. 'The fever of speculation has always raged in its veins. It has been a place of quick "ups" and just as rapid "downs". And it has always been a place of sudden alarums, from the days of the Jameson Raid downwards. Beneath the surface too, there has always been a strong undercurrent of violence ready to boil up and seethe over on very slight provocation. It is a city of many smouldering hates which are easily fanned to flame.'

Robert Service, the hugely popular Lancashire-born poet of the Yukon gold rush in California, had already written a poem from

LOST ON THE MAP

afar about the end of the Boer War ('There was triumph, triumph, triumph down the scarlet gleaming street') that abruptly turns to dread ('it's the Army of the Dead'). In his most famous verse, Service described a Yukon prospector as 'A half-dead thing in a stark, dead world, half mad for the muck of gold.'

Service wrote the kind of folksy ballads, usually in the earthy voice of a roughneck that Lewis Rose liked to affect in his humorous ditties. But of all the gaudy characters that flocked to Johannesburg, Service's description of a miner 'half mad for the muck of gold' fitted Jacques Lebaudy, 'the Emperor of the Sahara'.

The son of a powerful French sugar baron, young Lebaudy inherited a fortune and set off on incessant travels on his yacht. On the coast of southern Morocco, he landed five men in the desert to establish the capital of his 'Empire', and returned later to find they had all been abducted by tribesmen. A dapper, nervy and brilliant man, Lebaudy sailed to South Africa and soon became a successful mining magnate in Johannesburg. He gambled wildly at the races and filled his swimming pool with champagne. He imported a troupe of Oriental dancers from Baghdad. The horses for his carriage had solid gold harnesses. Then he disappeared as suddenly as he had arrived. Lebaudy turned up in New York. Enraged that his wife gave birth to a daughter rather than a son, he beat her for years. They separated and he was often seen on the streets of New York, sometimes dressed in rags, followed by a gaggle of messengers and stenographers.

He was committed to a sanatorium, but escaped by diving through a window. One night, in 1919, Lebaudy broke into his own home, having decided that as Emperor he was entitled to take his daughter as a wife, in order to provide him with a male heir. Madame Lebaudy, defending her daughter, shot the 46-year-old 'Emperor of the Sahara' four times.

Lebaudy represented only a crazed extreme among flamboyant adventurers and staggeringly wealthy 'Randlords'. The intrepid and imperial-minded *Times* journalist Flora Shaw, herself previously suspected of a role in the Jameson Raid, defined such exhibitionist and kitschy Johannesburg displays as 'classless excess'.

Johannesburg was a cauldron of social pressure and racial tension. Into this combustible metropolis stepped my grandfather, the 32-year-old Lewis Rose Macleod.

The magnet of the mines

Gold was the sole reason for the brutally sudden birth of Johannesburg. 'You must, if you can, visualise a continuous line of these great mines extending for 60 miles from east to west, each mine a town in itself,' explained Lewis Rose in his memoir. 'On these mines work went on unceasingly. By night great arc lights cast their spluttering beams on the huge heaps of tailings – the accumulated residuum after the gold had been extracted from the rock – and the towering heaps of white sand that looked like miniature Alps. Night and day the stamps of the great mine batteries thundered unceasingly.'

The mines had been forced to close during the Boer War, and there had been an exodus of black migrant mineworkers to the rural areas. Afterwards most were loath to return to the infernal underground working conditions at reduced wages. To get the gold mines running again at full profit, mine owners did not wish to employ unskilled white labour, which would involve paying higher wages. The solution, energetically endorsed by Alfred Milner – by now, having been made a Viscount, the administrator of the two defeated Boer republics – was to import Chinese labour.

Between 1904 and 1906, over 63,000 Chinese workers were transported to the Rand as indentured labour. They were penned into compounds and subject to flogging or prison for even minor infractions. Despite their pay being negligible, these trapped conscripts still had to refund the costs of their own recruitment and passage to South Africa. It was a profitable solution for the Randlords, and this expedient soon returned the mines to full production.

Nevertheless, it led to an outburst of xenophobic hysteria, the result of a powerful alliance between Boer leaders and white miners who were fearful that the imported Chinese were not only lowering wages, but threatened to encroach on their monopoly of skilled work.

There were scare stories of rampant Chinese crime and sexual outrages. The *Sunday Times*, under the editorship of George Kingswell, published a poem on its front page that began:

'Ten little Chinamen working in a mine,
One tasted dynamite and then there were nine,
Nine little Chinamen sat up rather late,
One smoked opium and then were there eight …'

It continued to work gleefully and hideously right down until there were no little Chinamen at all.

By the time Lewis Rose took over the *Sunday Times* the crisis had largely been resolved, though with dramatically unintended results. White mineworkers who vehemently opposed Chinese labour had been supported in Britain by trade unions and the Labour Party. In South Africa, partly in response to Milner's aggressive 'Anglicisation' policy, Boer leaders founded the *Het Volk* party which exploited the emotive Chinese furore by portraying them as thieving heathens and pitiless rapists.

On the other hand, the British Liberal Party, which had been divided over the Boer War, was united in opposition to what they denounced as 'Chinese slavery'. In 1906 the Liberals swept to power in Westminster and, eager to be of rid of this distant dilemma, granted the Orange Free State and Transvaal responsible government. Milner's replacement as Governor of the defeated Boer Republics, Lord Selborne, promptly announced the end of all Chinese recruitment on the mines.

Dip your pen in gall

When the *Sunday Times* was launched in February 1906, it had been shrilly denounced for desecrating the Sabbath. Sixty churches across the Rand pinned admonitions to their doors demanding that congregants shun this organ of the devil. Naturally the first edition sold out and by the time my grandfather took the helm, it was selling over 35,000 copies a week.

Lewis Rose was rapidly filling out, still dapper but no longer looking like a skinny bohemian. Now he wore a waistcoat even on the hottest day. A sepia photo of the first Macleod home in Johannesburg shows a gracious sandstone mansion, grandly called

'Bishopric', set in a large garden with neat hedges and Cyprus trees. A smart automobile waits nearby. Walking towards the porch with faux Greek columns are my grandmother in a wide straw hat, her husband in a dark suit and Homburg hat, and between them, a small girl in white frills and bonnet, presumably my mother's older sister Betty.

Being editor of an influential newspaper instantly put Lewis Rose in a position to mix with British Governors, leading politicians and millionaire grandees. The place where the powerful met and socialised was the plush Rand Club: from high-ranking officials and mine managers, to Randlords and 'men who were rich yesterday and hoped to be rich tomorrow,' observed Lewis Rose. 'In the Rand Club at eleven o'clock in the morning, and also at the aperitif hour before luncheon, at lunch itself, and again in the late afternoon you met everyone and heard everything. Indeed, if you wished to keep abreast of the news, it was essential that you should be there at all those hours.' It seems that the new editor of the *Sunday Times* rigorously kept to this demanding routine.

The other club he frequented was the Athenaeum, 'established by Lord Milner after the war with money advanced by the British government to provide a suitable English atmosphere for administrators condemned to "exile" in a "foreign" country.' The ethos, clarified my grandfather, was supposed to be strongly imperialistic, though the conduct of members reveals a less publicised aspect to the recreational pursuits of empire builders.

'I have never seen so many club rules broken in one night as we used to break them almost every night in the week and twice on Saturday,' he wrote. 'Our polo matches in the hall, with chairs for ponies, were worth going a long way to see, and the casualties were enormous. The Athenaeum was a pioneer in the matter of providing a "ladies room", and the number of scandals it succeeded in providing ought to have proved sufficient to prevent any other club from ever following its example in this respect.'

Such riotous behaviour is in dramatic contrast to the later image of Lewis Rose as sedate and avuncular. Various colleagues described him as courteous, though occasionally intimidating, and yet – often remarked on – unfailingly kindly. As his girth expanded and hair receded, peering forbiddingly through owlish glasses, he increasingly resembled a rotund establishment gent in a three-piece suit, winged-collared shirt with a natty bow tie. Most remarked on his wit. This could also be wielded to frightening effect. My mother's oldest friend recalled being terrified as a teenager when momentarily left alone with my grandfather. After an awkward silence, she timidly enquired, 'And how are you today, Mr Macleod?' He turned, glowered and growled, 'I believe all is in order, thank you. I am merely waiting for Mr Hopkins to make the necessary arrangements.' At the time, Hopkins & Sons were one of Johannesburg's leading undertakers.

At the *Sunday Times* he daringly placed cartoons on the front page. There were regular anonymous columns, such as 'The Passing Show' which allowed for sharp comments on local personalities, and he indulged his taste for lampoon under titles like 'Letters that were never sent' and 'Things they say in their sleep'.

The Dictionary of South Africa Biography credits Lewis Rose with initiating improvements in newspaper layout and news presentation, describing him as having 'a forceful pen' and being 'bold in controversy'. On handing over the editorship of the *Sunday Times*, George Kingswell had advised the new editor 'dip your pen in gall', while Lewis Rose declared his own journalistic credo to be 'No damned cheek from anybody.'

The major political question of the time was the proposal that the four separate British colonies in South Africa (the Cape, Natal, Transvaal and Orange Free State) should unite. If so, was it to be a unitary or federal state – and, decisively, who would have the right to vote?

The divisive subject of the franchise came down to a clear choice: ought the new constitution permit only white men to vote, or could it incorporate the existing provision in the Cape which allowed for a limited, qualified black and coloured franchise? In racially obsessed South Africa, only a few years after the Boer War, this was a mightily emotive subject: one on which everyone had a passionate opinion, and about which the editor of the increasingly influential *Sunday Times* was expected to weigh in.

And pontificate he did; pen dipped in gall.

Resorting to biblical bile

It begins relatively mildly by the standards of the day. In January 1909, as the debate about the franchise heated up, the *Sunday Times* carried a prominent article, 'The Cape boy: A curious product' by 'One who knows him'. This character is a mystery to most Europeans, laments the anonymous author, 'It is said that he possesses all the white man's vices and none of his virtues.' In a tone of ostensible scientific detachment, the writer asserts that the varying bloodlines of the 'Cape boy' explain his baffling characteristics: his belligerence (Bushman), passion for music (Hottentot), addiction to high-flown language (Malay) and love of ostentation (Bantu). 'The Cape boy displays extreme gullibility', concludes the article, 'and exposes the folly of broad-minded Europeans who in an excess of radicalism desire to give a Coloured man political equality whilst they deny him economic equality.'

It is unlikely that my grandfather, not yet a frequent visitor to the Cape, would have written the article. But in a lecture, he once confided the art of writing editorials: 'You hold yourself in reserve till the best possible writing subject comes along and then you seize it all for yourself.' So it is likely that Lewis Rose penned most *Sunday Times* editorials on the franchise himself, for they now surfaced with increasing vehemence. In the very next issue, the unsigned editorial exhibits all the traces of the Macleod style: 'The "guileless native" is a phrase which frequently invades the columns of the daily press, but – like the Scotsman in the famous story – "we hae oor doots" about the local son of Ham's complete freedom from guile.'

This is a reference to the biblical story of Ham, the outcast son of Noah, and its exploitation in theological justifications for racial discrimination. The Book of Genesis chronicles how Noah, aged 500, produced three sons: Shem, Japheth and Ham. But when the flood finally subsided 120 years later, Noah celebrated by planting vines and getting drunk. Ham, entering Noah's tent, saw his ageless father naked (which may have been a euphemism for something more risqué), and for this outrage Noah cursed Ham's son, 'Cursed be Canaan: a servant of servants shall he be unto his brethren.'

On emigrating to South Africa, Lewis Rose left behind a massive

Bible given to him by his mother. Published in New Zealand in 1873, as a frontispiece it has a full-page illustration of Noah's ark. The queue of animals confirms that Noah had obeyed the divine directive: 'Every living thing of all flesh, you shall bring two of every kind into the ark.' Along with the expected elephants, bears, tigers, camels, horses, sheep, snakes and monkeys are (not usually logged) a pair of wallabies and two duck-billed platypuses (or platypodes). Lewis Rose was clearly aware of Noah's supposed 'racial' curse, which would have needed no explanation for white South African readers.

The Book of Joshua goes further: 'Now therefore you *are* cursed, and there shall none of you be freed from being bondsmen. And hewers of wood and drawers of water for the house of my God.' Today there are websites which still maintain, with no textual proof, that Ham was black, supposedly either singed by Noah's fury or that the name means 'hot' or 'brown'. This twisted interpretation of hewers of wood and drawers of water had been used in the American South to lend scriptural justification for slavery. It was quoted in South Africa throughout the nineteenth century, often thundered from the pulpit, and was cited well into the latter half of the twentieth century to justify crude racial tyranny under apartheid.

The naming of names

As the National Convention to decide on the nature of the Union of South Africa drew to a tense conclusion, the escalating sense of panic over the franchise becomes palpable. Shortly after the 'local sons of Ham' jibe, a *Sunday Times* editorial titled 'The Coloured

Vote' demanded 'An emphatic expression from the Colonies that have not become hypocritical negrophilists.' An all-white front was vital, it argued, as in the Cape, 'Dependent as they are on natives and cross-breeds, the Progressives and Bond will assuredly put up pledges to maintain the status of the kaffir and the Cape boy.'

This, huffed the editorial, would lead to demands for the vote by 'their coffee-coloured brethren in the northern colonies' and 'a dangerous degree of kaffir and coloured discontent'. If that were to happen, 'the scandal of the Cape would be repeated here, and the balance of the parties would be determined by the coloured man'.

The fear was that if this issue was fudged, a final decision would soon be made in London by liberal 'faddists at Westminster'. The editorial proposed a temporary compromise: that the northern colonies stand firm, but permit the Cape to keep its current franchise arrangements with the stern proviso that 'no coloured man, who is not on the register at the time of the first election, shall ever be enrolled there'.

The rising fervour of a 'pen dipped in gall' suggests that Lewis Rose was writing the editorials himself. For me, as his grandson, these diatribes make for exceptionally uncomfortable reading. My distress is all the greater, because although Lewis Rose died seven years before I was born, my mother always told me that her father, whom she adored, was gentle and thoughtful, usually adding that I seemed to have inherited many of his characteristics. I imaged so too, not least in his trajectory as a journalist, a writer of fiction and plays. In fact, before I came across Lewis Rose's racial invective, I deeply regretted never having known him, convinced that my grandfather would have proved to be, for me as a young man, an

Sunday Times *editor Lewis Rose Macleod*

understanding and encouraging fellow soul.

With my previous strong sense of identification, it became increasingly disturbing to read on as my grandfather raged ever more indignantly against voting rights for 'cross-breeds', 'half-castes', 'niggers' and 'kaffirs', seeing any dilution to an all-white franchise as 'a grovelling and subversive fear of the inferior races'.

This, for me, is no longer impartial history. It's become intensely personal; alarmingly, extremely close to home. So this, too, however inconvenient, must be included in my reckoning with our chequered, often hidden story.

Facing the *****facts

Should we even be allowed to repeat such bile today, printing the offending words in full? The approach today of newspapers, reporting on the use of such abusive terms, is to replace the offending letters with asterisks, as in 'K*****'. It is a thin disguise. The eighteenth-century German mathematician and aphorist Georg Christoph Lichtenberg pithily expressed his reservations about such transparent expurgation: 'There are people who always write the word Devil with a D and a succession of dots. They likewise render

84

this mark of respect to certain parts of their own body. The cause of this is hard to discover. Even Fielding writes Kiss my a--- instead of Kiss my arse. Presumably in this case it amounts to the same thing as putting on a pair of trousers.'

So, no *****. It dilutes the offence.

While at university in the heyday of apartheid, I wrote an exposé for the student newspaper of the abuse and underpayment of African staff. The story began with an incident of a white female supervisor yelling at an elderly black female cleaner, 'If I say shit here, you shit here. And if I say eat it, you eat it. Understand?' The printed edition came back with an amendment by the decorous printer. Now the supervisor's diatribe read 'If I say defecate here, you defecate here …'.

The sting had been replaced by absurdity. There's no escaping bigotry by wrapping it in gentility. It should be confronted head on and the insult named.

With six weeks left before the decisive vote, the *Sunday Times* spelled out its stance on the franchise crisis. 'There can be no temporising with this all-important subject,' growled Lewis Rose, adding about the proposed Cape compromise. 'If the constitution is accepted as a working compromise today, that must not be regarded as a guarantee that it will not be revised tomorrow in the interests of the racial purity of the white people. And any agitation among the natives must be repressed by a corresponding and unflagging political resistance among their white rulers.'

So tragically it came to pass.

5

⊹

FOR A WHITE SOUTH AFRICA

A voice in the wilderness

HAVING CREATED EVERY beast and every fowl, says *Genesis*, the Lord took them to Adam: 'and whatsoever Adam called every living creature that was the name thereof'. It took many centuries, however, before man presumed to label people of other colours by a legion of derogatory names; 'the sons of Ham' being relatively mild.

So what is meant by the formula 'standards of the day', often used to justify the prejudices of the past? In deploying racial epithets, my grandfather was reflecting conventional contemporary European attitudes regarding white racial superiority. Yet it is also important to ask: was there no other yardstick, or expressions of different opinion, against which to measure such bigoted ideas?

'Racialism' was widely understood then by most white South Africans to refer to animosity between English-speakers and Afrikaners. Faced with what it called 'The black peril', the *Sunday Times* pleaded with the Dutch and English to unite and 'in the name of common sense let us make an end of "racialism"'. For the majority of whites terms like 'kaffir' or 'half-breed' were entirely acceptable, even respectable: a usage that mirrored their blinkered 'common sense', permitting them the biblical privilege of classifying different people. Some, however, were more blinkered than others.

Cecil Rhodes was altogether cruder. 'I prefer land to niggers', was one of his boasts. As a politician he promoted racial segregation; as a mining magnate, he said of Africans 'it must be brought home to them that in future nine-tenths of them will have to spend their lives in daily labour'; and as an ardent imperialist he encouraged slaughter, ordering his officers in Matabeleland not to take prisoners: 'You should kill all you can, as it serves a lesson to them.' When I was young my father often told me, approvingly, that Rhodes' motto was 'Equal rights for every civilised man.' What he actually said was 'Equal rights for every white man.' But confronted with press reports of this remark during an election meeting in the Cape, where there was the 'Coloured franchise', Rhodes hastily tailored his own slogan, substituting 'civilised' for 'white'.

Everything about Rhodes was inflated: size, ambition, ego, chicanery and racism. He was admired, even idolised, by many contemporaries, but also harshly criticised. Consequently, for anyone who was literate there was in fact another index by which to measure racial attitudes. Olive Schreiner, the visionary writer and thinker, had at first hoped for great things for South Africa from the energy and enterprise of Rhodes, 'the Colossus'. But his greed, corruption and contempt for black Africans soon became apparent to her. Rhodes, she said, had looked good and evil in the face – and chose evil.

Olive Schreiner had soared to fame with her novel *The Story of an African Farm*. My grandfather would certainly have read her trenchant criticisms of white prejudice. The black peril, wrote Olive, was actually a white peril hanging over every black man. The year before the decisive Act of Union, she published a booklet, *Closer Union*, which argued that 'no distinction of race or colour should be made between South Africans'.

She was, after Cecil Rhodes, the most famous person from South Africa, where her ideas were widely known, if unpopular, among literate whites. Consequently, there was certainly a forceful contemporary gauge against which to measure the 'standards of the time'. As Olive once remarked (an observation that still holds true): 'Strange that people can live in a land and understand so little of its people and problems.'

The dawn of dark days

Yet Olive Schreiner, despite her far-sighted vision and humanity, also casually used the word 'kaffir'. In fact, the term was still used after World War II on the London Stock Exchange to refer to gold shares, with newspaper headlines referring to a 'Kaffir Boom'. Before the Boer War it had been estimated there were as many as 600 'kaffir' jobbers trading in shares on the London Stock Exchange. Nevertheless, the man who had got the mines working again after the war, the arch-imperialist Lord Milner, was dismayed when the *Het Volk* party won the 1907 election in the Transvaal.

'They have given South Africa back to the Boers,' he lamented.

The German-born Milner's views on Anglo-Saxon superiority were uncompromising. 'I am a British (indeed primarily an English) nationalist,' he trumpeted. 'If I am also an Imperialist, it is because the destiny of the English race, owing to its insular position and its long supremacy at sea, has been to strike fresh roots in distant parts of the world. My patriotism knows no geographical bounds, but only racial limits. I am an Imperialist and not a Little Englander, because I am a British race patriot.'

My grandfather, though a dutiful imperialist himself, found such stridency absurd, being a consistent advocate of an end to 'racialism' between Boer and Briton. Describing Lord Milner and his 'kindergarten' – the coterie of Oxford graduates recruited to help administer the post-Boer War economy – Lewis Rose scoffed that 'Imperialism to these people meant briefly, do not trust the Boers in any shape or form … keep a military garrison in South Africa, and collar, if possible, the whole of the political power in the country for the mining industry.'

In contrast to Milner's pugnacious imperialism, the *Sunday Times* maintained that in order to avert 'the black peril' it was vital for all whites to unite. A week after the National Convention finally wrapped up, Edward VII died, and the paper carried a conciliatory message from General Louis Botha, shortly to become the first Prime Minister of South Africa. Botha diplomatically asserted that the Dutch 'will feel his loss no less profoundly' than the English. Two weeks later, on 31 May 1910, unification was officially inaugurated, and the *Sunday Times* greeted it gleefully with the banner headline, 'The Dawn of Union'. The Cape non-racial qualified franchise, for men only and based on educational and property criteria, was retained, but restricted to the Cape. Over the next half century that was remorselessly whittled way.

Olive Schreiner, again a lonely voice of dissent, had called the Act of Union 'a speculator's dream', and prophesied it marked 'only the beginning of dark days …'.

89

At the crossroads

My father Frank's first memory of a public event was the sensational police chase after the violent Foster gang when he was seven years old. The Rostrons had moved from King William's Town to the mining town of Boksburg on the East Rand. In July 1914 the Foster gang attempted to rob the Boksburg North branch of the National Bank, and when surprised, they killed one man and wounded another. On the run, the gang embarked on a robbing and shooting spree across the Rand which seized the public's imagination. The police circulated a poster offering a £500 reward with photographs of three men: 'Robert Ward Jackson, alias Foster, alias Bailey, alias Capt. White'; 'John Maxim, alias Maxwell, alias Milton Maxim'; and 'Carl Mezar, alias George Smit'.

William Foster, the handsome son of an Irish immigrant, was the leader. He had met John Maxwell, a Texan, when Maxwell or Maxim was performing in a circus as 'Cowboy Jack', displaying his remarkable shooting skill. Carl Mezar was described as 'Dutch, gives his age as 22, but looks younger'. Their brutal rampage across the Rand was chronicled breathlessly by local newspapers, and the apocalyptic finale two months later was to have an unexpected and bizarre impact on South African history.

It was a time of economic boom on the Rand. My grandfather William, now that he had moved to the industrial centre of the new Union of South Africa, became deeply involved in trade union activities on behalf of the influential Printer's Union. He also signed on as a printer at Johannesburg's main daily, *The Star*.

Meanwhile my other grandfather, Lewis Rose, had moved on. In the penultimate issue before leaving the *Sunday Times* in July 1910, he had welcomed the formation of the South African Labour Party, recognising that it represented white workers against any encroachment from black labour. In his final edition as editor, there was a comment on the front page about the recent, racially-charged 'fight of the century' in Nevada between Jack Johnson, the first African-American world heavyweight champion, and James J. Jeffries, who had been lured out of retirement as 'the great white hope' by a huge financial offer. Jack Johnson won, and the *Sunday Times*, which had never before put sport on the front page, felt obliged to offer an explanation for the triumph of a black boxer: 'Given a certain amount of science, a coon – any old coon, not to put too fine a point on it – would be a mighty tough proposition to put to sleep, because of his superior ability to stand punishment.'

Lewis Rose had been enticed to found a new enterprise. *The Observer* aimed to be, unique for its time, a national newspaper. Most of the capital was put up by mining magnates, including Sir Lionel Phillips, and Lewis Rose had been offered a considerably higher salary and, unusually, a quarter share of profits. The policy of the new paper was vague. A torn two-page 'Memorandum of Agreement' for the new weekly merely records, 'The policy of the said newspaper shall be generally to support the Unionist Party in South Africa at present constituted under the leadership of Dr Jameson.'

Phillips, the major force behind this venture, had played a prominent part in organising the raid led by Leander Starr Jameson ('Dr Jim'), and had been sentenced to death for his role. But both had survived and prospered: Jameson as a politician, Phillips as a Randlord. The memorandum is signed, however, by another shareholder: Geoffrey Robinson, originally recruited from England to serve in Milner's 'kindergarten'. When Lord Milner left South Africa, he arranged for Robinson – who, according to Lewis Rose, worshipped the lordly High Commissioner 'with a passionate idolatry' – to become editor of *The Star* in order to back the largely English-speaking Randlords and propagate Milner's evangelistic imperial creed.

Shortly after his agreement with my grandfather, Robinson returned to London to join *The Times*, where Lord Northcliffe soon appointed him editor. In 1917, in order to inherit a family estate in Yorkshire, Robinson changed his name to Dawson. Two years later he resigned from *The Times* due to His Lordship's 'anti-Hun' views, but was reappointed after Northcliffe's death. From 1923 to 1941, while Dawson again edited *The Times*, he was a leading proponent of appeasement with Nazi Germany. Today Geoffrey Robinson/ Dawson is mostly remembered for confessing in 1937, 'I do my utmost, night after night, to keep out of the paper anything that might hurt [German] susceptibilities and dropping in little things which are intended to soothe them.'

Meanwhile, Lewis Rose's manifesto for *The Observer* stated that 'A New Nation needs a new newspaper.' South Africa's first national newspaper lasted seven months. 'Its life story may be told in one word – <u>failure</u>', confessed its ex-editor, cheerfully admitting that they had not foreseen all the problems in trying to print simultaneously in different cities. But most of all, he acknowledged, 'the main interests of a very large section of the population of South Africa are in Great Britain', so rather than informed local news, many readers wished for the results of British football or cricket matches.

White miners strike back

Had the middle classes been less set on news from England, they would have grasped that there was mounting tension along the Rand. In May 1913 a dispute at a mine near Boksburg quickly spread to other mines. Phillips saw this as an opportunity for the Randlords to face down demands from the better paid white miners. 'A general strike would, of course, be a serious matter from a dividend-paying standpoint,' he wrote to colleagues. 'I do not think, however, that it would last very long and, if it does happen, we must make up our minds once and for all to break the unions here.'

In response, 18,000 white workers answered the call for a general strike. The railway station and offices of *The Star* were set alight. The next day a huge crowd massed outside the Rand Club, the haunt of the city's plutocrats. It was a Saturday morning. Lewis Rose, the inveterate clubman, was inside. 'Ugly-looking mobs gathered outside its door,' he wrote. 'A shot was fired somewhere in the vicinity, a striker was hit, and the sinister rumour spread that the man who fired was a well-known civil servant. The crowd was clamorous for his blood and determined to get it. A number of members hastily garrisoned the building and occupied it effectively until the military got the position well in hand. But it was an unpleasant situation while it lasted.'

This is a very evasive account. There is no mention of troops firing at the crowd. Perhaps 25 people were killed. Another member present that day was the London-born, Oxford-educated solicitor Sidney Bunting, then on his long political odyssey from mild English liberal to become the first leader of the Communist Party of South Africa. Appalled by the wild violence of the troops that day,

Bunting resigned from the Rand Club.

In all, during the strike, it is estimated that at least 100 civilians were shot. Eventually Prime Minister Botha and the more ruthless Jan Smuts, Minister of both Finance and Defence, negotiated an end to the strike, reluctantly consenting to investigate the white miners' grievances. But eight months later, in January 1914, a railway strike rapidly escalated to a general strike, and this time Smuts determined to crush it. He declared martial law and called in troops. Soldiers surrounded the union leaders, forcing them to surrender. Smuts ordered the deportation of nine leading unionists, an illegal act; they were taken to Durban by train under armed escort led by Major Trew, the father of one of my mother's lifelong friends. 'A smashing blow had to be struck at syndicalism in South Africa,' claimed Smuts. 'I gave that blow.'

A major reason for the strike, and others that followed, was the desire to protect skilled white labour. They feared that mine owners wished to relax the colour bar in order to hire cheap black labour. It was a widespread attitude across the 'white' empire, and in Britain too. On 1 March 1914 there was a colossal demonstration in London at Hyde Park, sponsored by trade unions and socialists, in support of white workers in South Africa. *The Times* stated that it was the biggest workers' rally ever seen in the capital, with a marching column seven miles long and an estimated crowd of half a million. Several of the deported unionists spoke, and warned that the aim of mining magnates was to drive down wages by employing far cheaper black labour. Mahatma Gandhi, who was having his own tussles with Smuts, remarked 'To the socialists of South Africa the brotherhood of man means the brotherhood of white men.'

But the contest between white workers and bosses had yet to reach its bloody climax: a violent insurrection eight years later in which William Rostron, the emigrant printer from Lancashire, was to play a subversive role.

Distant drums of war

My other, grander grandfather, within days of the collapse of the short-lived *Observer*, launched a new weekly – in opposition to the *Sunday Times*: 'the most prosperous paper in South Africa, whose fortunes I had done as much as anyone to establish,' wryly remarked the ever-resourceful editor. *The Sunday Post*, despite being financed by mining magnates, never took off, though it staggered on for another four years.

'The main problem was that the paper had the "magnate taint",' admitted Lewis Rose. In an attempt to broaden the paper's popular appeal, he resorted to publishing lurid crime stories and 'tell-all' series by swindlers and robbers. The most successful were the reminiscences of the retired hangman of Cape Town, under the title 'The man who hanged a hundred men.'

These gruesome revelations led to an immediate jump in circulation: 'particularly,' gloated the editor, 'in District Six, the poor quarter of Cape Town largely populated by Malay "Cape boys" and "poor whites", a district which had provided Blake with a good many of his clients.' But the series lasted only three weeks before Lewis Rose was summoned to Pretoria by the Attorney-General, who warned that the hangman was bound by the Official Secrets Act, and that any further publication risked a term of imprisonment for the editor.

The Sunday Post's staunchest supporter proved to be the wife of its proprietor. 'Lady Phillips took a great interest in the paper,' said Lewis Rose, 'an interest that was apt at times to become a trifle embarrassing.' An Afrikaner by birth, Florence Phillips (*neé* Ortlepp) was conspicuously self-assured; or 'domineering' according to Lewis Rose: 'She wanted to take Johannesburg by the neck and shake it into (a) a proper appreciation of all that she and her husband had done for the place; (b) a right way of political thinking – that is her way; (c) a proper appreciation of art; and (d) the possession of a general South African spirit.'

Lady Phillips had founded the Johannesburg Art Gallery with money from her Randlord husband. Naturally, she also attempted to meddle in Sir Lionel's newspaper, leading its editor to admit, 'I disappointed her grievously many times by keeping out of the paper things which I considered it would be bad policy to print.'

In 1913, with impeccable timing, the formidable Lady Phillips published a book entitled, *A Friendly Germany: Why Not?* In the preface, Her Ladyship explained that her mission was to demonstrate that 'alarmist reports' of an impending war between Britain and Germany were a dangerous folly, and that 'for the sake of Western civilisation' the two 'should not be parted by artificial agitation'. What was actually at stake, Lady Phillips warned, was nothing less than 'Black and Yellow perils'.

Clouds on the horizon

The solution, declared Her Ladyship, was simple: listen to Germany's demand for 'a place in the sun' and sensibly hand over some disposable colonies. 'There are vast expanses of territory now in the hands of effete Europeans who would gladly shelve their responsibilities,' she argued. 'There are Mohammedan countries in a state of decay, but of real potential wealth.' If that was not enough, she listed other options: Angola, the Congo, or countries in Asia Minor or South America.

Within months the book had been reprinted three times. The *New York Times* carried a supportive report under the headline, 'Remarkable book written by the wife of Sir Lionel Phillips', closing with the observation that 'The book gives little opportunity for current gibes about women who dabble in politics.'

One great benefit to Lewis Rose was that Lady Phillips hired his spinster sister, also called Florence, as her social secretary. Florence Macleod was known by all as 'Cloudie', though it is unclear if this was to resolve any confusion with her imperious employer or because of the turbulent upsets she unleashed in the Macleod household. It was one of Miss Macleod's jobs to file in a large scrapbook the many reviews of Lady Phillips' *A Friendly Germany*. Not many months later, however, the advantage of being a first-time author married to a rich man proved invaluable. As the European situation deteriorated, recorded Lewis Rose, employees were dispatched to buy up 'in hot haste all the copies of that unfortunate book'.

But even the editor of the *Sunday Post*, it seems, was not too apprehensive about any brewing European crisis. He had been busy writing the lyrics for South Africa's first musical comedy, *The Girl from Springfontein.* Performed by an English touring company, the musical opened in November 1913 with considerable fanfare at His Majesty's Theatre in Johannesburg. *The Girl from Springfontein* is a frothy burlesque of mistaken identity, English snobbery, buffoonish Afrikaners, unexpected entrances and hasty exits, misunderstandings in love and police bungling.

In the final act Reggie, on the point of being arrested as 'Mr Brown', is revealed as none other than the son of Lord Hamfordhurst. The comely Gracie passionately informs her dim uncle, the High Commissioner: 'You can't arrest him, I love him!' Critics were complimentary. The lyrics were 'witty and clever', applauded one, while another commented that 'Mr Macleod has employed his wit and satire to good purpose in creating food for laughter out of South African idiosyncrasies.' The musical ends with a reprise of the patriotic chorus: 'Old England breeds a restless race, / Her sons are scattered wide', closing on the romantic finale, 'And it is each man's pride, / A home to make where he may take, / His young colonial bride.'

Meanwhile the newspaper that Lewis Rose edited had been fatally hobbled by its association with mine owners. The paper was losing £5,000 a year. It was doomed. Early in 1915, the *Sunday Post* was amalgamated – flattery of a sort – into his old newspaper, *The Sunday Times.* Perhaps he should have taken the cue from one of his own lyrics in *The Girl From Springfontein*, where the chorus sings:

> 'Society gossip! Society news!
> Oh, ladies who write for the press
> We like what you write, but 'twould give us delight
> To read all the things you suppress.'

A desperate last stand

In August 1914, when war broke out in Europe, my grandfather forecast in the *Sunday Post* that Britain and her allies would triumph within a year. Johannesburg newspapers were equally gripped, however, with accounts of a final, homicidal spree by the Foster gang: a brief circulation boost for the failing *Sunday Post*, while the drama of the frantic police chase was avidly followed by the seven-year-old Frank Rostron.

William Foster's serious criminal career had begun the previous year when he and his accomplices robbed a jewellery store in Cape Town, getting away with a haul worth £5,000. William and his younger brother Jimmy were tracked down and sentenced to 12 years' hard labour. Outraged that Jimmy was not treated more leniently, William Foster's fury turned into a murderous vendetta against all authority. While awaiting trial he married Peggy Korenico in Cape Town's Roeland Street Prison and, following sentencing, he was transferred to Pretoria Central Prison. After only nine months, William escaped. Teaming up with the Texan cowboy John Maxim and Carl Mezar, the trio rapidly became notorious across the Rand as the violent Foster gang.

Their botched raid on the bank in Boksburg, near where the Rostrons lived, led to the gang's first murder. Over the next two months in a series of armed raids the gang, also known as the 'motorcycle bandits', killed four more, three of them policemen. The fourth victim was Detective Sergeant Charles Mynott, who went to a house in the south of Johannesburg after a tip-off. In the yard, Mynott saw two men by a large black touring car and recognised them: William Foster sat on the running-board, while

Carl Mezar leaned against the bonnet softly playing a mouth organ. Peggy Foster sat in the back holding a baby.

The detective didn't see a third man working underneath the car. Drawing his pistol, the Detective Sergeant shouted, 'Hands up!' Foster appeared unperturbed and denied that he was the wanted man. From under the car, unseen by Mynott, the Texan cowboy passed a pistol to William Foster, who shot the policeman.

Roadblocks were immediately set up all round the city, and more than 1,000 policemen were deployed in the hunt. The house the Foster gang had abandoned was discovered to be packed with stolen goods, as well as hair dyes and false moustaches.

Foster drove at speed east to Germiston, another mining town near Boksburg, and left Peggy and the baby with friends, then raced back to Johannesburg. The gang talked their way through one road-block, but shortly afterwards their car was found abandoned, stuck in a ditch, having veered off the road. It was night and they were now on foot. Sniffer dogs were brought in.

That night, at a roadblock further west, occurred the fatal shooting that may have prevented the outbreak of a full civil war, or another Anglo-Boer War. The decision by Prime Minister Botha, the former Boer general, to send troops to German South West Africa to aid the British war effort angered many Afrikaners. Thousands were prepared to take up arms once again, rather than side with Britain against Germany. The potential rebels looked for guidance from their former commandants, the most admired being the brilliant guerrilla leader, General Jacobus ('Koos') de la Rey. His loyalties were split between his former comrades: Generals Botha and Smuts, and the rebels. What followed remains highly ambiguous.

Another former Boer general, C.F. Beyers, had resigned in protest as commander of the South African armed forces in order to join the 1914 rebellion. There are conflicting accounts of the role played by De la Rey.

The final show down

My grandfather, as editor of the *Sunday Post*, was contacted by an informant who claimed that General de la Rey had summoned a meeting of former commandoes, 'all the men to be fully armed and to have eight days' provisions and horses'. Not wishing to alert rival newspapers, Lewis Rose waited till the last minute to call General Smuts on his farm at Irene, near Pretoria.

'His replies,' wrote Lewis Rose years later, 'were cast in cryptic form for fear of eavesdroppers. "There has," said Smuts, "been a false prophet abroad, and what you have heard is true to a certain time. Since then, certain things have happened. De la Rey has been here. The meeting will take place, but it will not have the result you expect. Believe me, that is so. You will do us a great service if you withhold your information from publication."' The scoop was ready for publication, but the dilemma of whether to heed Smuts' request was overtaken by events. As dark fell, De la Rey was shot when the car he was travelling in failed to stop at a police roadblock.

General Beyers and General de la Rey had set out earlier for a meeting of potential rebels. The previous year in *The Girl From Springfontein,* Lewis Rose had lampooned Beyers as 'General Brink', a pompous Boer commander who had been flattered by an audience with Kaiser Wilhelm, as indeed had Beyers on a European tour. But while Beyers had chosen to side with the rebels, General de la Rey's role remains murky. Though Smuts had hinted that De la Rey had been convinced to remain loyal, it seems more likely that he had agreed to travel with General Beyers in order to join the rebellion. Deneys Reitz, one of Smuts' closest confidants – who as a teenager had ridden with Smuts' commando on daring raids during the Boer War – was convinced De la Rey had been swayed to join the rebellion by the mystic Afrikaner prophet, Siener ('Seer') van Rensburg. Reitz had met De la Rey only days before his death and wrote 'I saw that his mind was affected, for his talk was of Christian science, spiritualism, and the dreams of Van Rensburg, his tame prophet.'

The notoriously elusive Smuts had mentioned 'a false prophet'. He may have hinted at the Siener van Rensburg, whose apocalyptic visions convinced many Afrikaners that an uprising would succeed and herald the destruction of the British Empire. But when the car carrying the two Boer generals sped through a cordon set up to trap the Foster gang, police fired and killed De la Rey. Many believed, and some still do, that the government assassinated a potentially charismatic rebel leader.

The next day a police search party discovered the Foster gang's hideout: a cave, screened by bushes, in a rocky ridge of the Kensington hills, not far from where my father was later to go to school. News spread rapidly, and a large crowd gathered to witness the bloody finale.

The police planned to starve the gang out. The trapped men, though, had agreed they would never go to prison again. The next morning, Foster shouted that if he could speak to his parents and see his wife and child, they would surrender. But as his father and the family were about to leave the cave, Peggy handed over her baby and announced that she was staying with her husband. After that the crowd outside heard several shots. The Foster gang had turned their guns on themselves. 'When the police entered,' wrote Lewis Rose, 'they found Foster lying across the body of his wife …'.

Your (mother) country needs you

The Afrikaner rebellion fizzled, public attention turned back to the war in Europe, and the *Sunday Post* folded into the *Sunday Times*. My grandfather immediately started another weekly with the ill-omened title *Truth*. In the first issue of September 1915, he predicted that the European war would be over by the end of October. The following month, in a review of *The Rainbow* by D.H. Lawrence, *Truth's* literary critic predicted a very bad end for the novelist, 'Unless Mr Lawrence takes himself firmly in hand.' *Truth* had a pink cover. It couldn't last. After only three months, the next issue was the last.

Early in 1916 Lewis Rose sailed for England, visiting the mother country for the first time with the aspiration of offering his services to the British war effort. Accompanying him on the *Balmoral Castle* were his wife Trixie and two daughters: my mother, Barbara, three, and her older sister, Betty, five. Also on board were many Englishmen, 'who, shocked to find that the war had not ended in a few months, were hurrying home to enlist'. There is a photo of Lewis Rose, aged 41, hair receding, waist expanded, reclining on a deck chair in jacket, tie and sweater despite the blazing sun.

'My first aim was to do something in a non-combatant role for my country, but nobody appeared in need of the only kind of assistance I was in a position to offer,' he lamented. Before me now are curt notes of refusal from the Ministry of Munitions and the Foreign Office. After several dispiriting months, the recently eminent South African editor was hired as a lowly sub-editor at the *Daily Mail*. He hated it. His salary 'did no more than pay my taxi fares for the week, with perhaps a slight contribution towards the heavy cost of alcohol I found necessary to consume each day to nerve myself for the ordeal of entering the sub-editorial room at Carmelite House every day'. It was, he admitted, 'a revolting and soul-searing experience'. Fortunately, it did not last long.

Lewis Rose was soon appointed literary editor at the *Daily Mail*, a role he found extremely congenial despite the bullying of its proprietor, the dazzling but capricious Lord Northcliffe. Formerly Alfred Harmsworth, Northcliffe had essentially invented the popular press. He also owned the *Daily Mirror* and *The Times*. Northcliffe was the greatest, later certainly the maddest, of all British press tycoons. He was called 'The Chief' by employees, whom he by turns tormented and flattered, often signing himself 'Lord Vigour and Venom'.

His splendid motto was 'News is what someone, somewhere is trying to suppress; the rest is just advertising.' He also boasted that 'God made people read so I could fill their brains with facts, facts, facts – and later tell them whom to love, whom to hate, and what to think.'

Being literary editor, my mother told me, was the job that my grandfather loved most. *The Daily Mail* was the highest circulation British newspaper, and this gave Lewis Rose access to most of the leading literary figures of the day. He corresponded with Kipling,

J.M. Barrie, Somerset Maugham, Arthur Conan Doyle, E.M. Foster – who was later to stay with him in South Africa – as well as H.G. Wells, Aldous Huxley, Rider Haggard and John Buchan. Above all, he became friendly with Joseph Conrad.

Love, literature, torment

Lewis Rose admired Conrad enormously. They lunched together when the novelist travelled to London, while Conrad invited my grandparents to his Kent home for 'a sort of sit-in-the-garden and dream (if not exactly doze) day'. Born Józef Korzeniowski, English was his third language after Polish and French. Conrad's spoken English was erratic and his heavy accent deteriorated with age. Once, when his son was hurt, the novelist recommended the application of 'iodine', but the terrified lad thought that his father had said 'You are dying.'

Lewis Rose commissioned articles from the writer, then at the height of his fame. But Conrad distrusted any editorial tinkering, requesting, 'if by chance the exigencies of space demand the elimination of a few lines I beg I may be given the job myself. I will know best where to strike.'

Gentlemanly correspondence was only part of Lewis Rose's job. Lord Northcliffe returned from an extended visit to the battlefields of France, and demanded to see the 'Page Four Editor'. This was the page for opinion articles, and my grandfather was deputising for an executive who was 'on war duty in Mesopotamia'. Unfortunately for Lewis Rose, The Chief took an intense personal interest in the leader page, and for the next few years proceeded to persecute him.

'If you were in constant close association with Lord Northcliffe it was impossible not to hate him,' confessed my grandfather. 'But your hatred was never long-lived. You hated him violently at one moment, and you loved him just as violently the next. If he liked you he took an almost fiendish joy in hurting you. If he didn't, he hurt you all the same – but only once or twice as a rule.'

The Chief must have liked Lewis Rose, because he tormented him constantly.

One day Northcliffe circulated a memo stating that Macleod 'needs watching and driving'. The next day Lewis Rose received a scribbled note: 'Will you and your lady please me by coming to lunch on Saturday?' Cables arrived from distant realms. 'You don't say where Solomon Islands are fullstop. You are getting vague fullstop.' His Lordship loved to threaten the sack. 'Mr Macleod has bucked up a good deal since he knew someone was waiting for his job,' he gloated. More mildly, The Chief rebuked his literary editor 'I do not like the notepaper which you use for letters to contributors. There is nothing of the literary about them. They look like memorandum forms which one expects to receive from Harrods.'

Lewis Rose continued to write light plays and publish humorous short stories. He joined both the Garrick and the Savage Clubs: the former famous for its theatrical flavour, the latter for literary and artistic patrons. Lewis Rose was in his element.

His wife, Trixie, hated London. She found it cold and snobbish. My mother Barbara, 11 by the time they left, was so unsettled by this that she had developed St Vitus' Dance – a nervous affliction that in her case involved rituals like tapping on a door 20 times before she could enter a room. She was judged far too anxious to attend school.

Northcliffe became increasingly unpredictable, prone to fits of rage. He sent Lewis Rose a postcard from Monte Carlo: 'I'm watching you.' Like many autocrats, The Chief had strange dislikes. One was the name William. He changed the Christian name of a young journalist, William Heriot, to 'Heriot' and when Mr Heriot saw his new byline (Heriot Heriot) in print, he objected, so never appeared in the *Mail* again. His Lordship was incensed by the word 'Colonial', insisting instead on 'the Dominions'. A curt note sighs, 'My dear Macleod, for the two hundredth time I ask – will you desist from speaking of "England" and "Englishmen" when "Britain" and "Briton" should be used.'

Later, a fading memo from The Chief barks: 'I do not like the look of a queue. Every queue is the basis for a possible riot.'

His Lordship goes mad

Perhaps all powerful press magnates go mad in their own way. Alfred Harmsworth, Lord Northcliffe, however, had to be certified.

He spied on his staff, then became worried they were spying on him. Once my grandfather was accompanying Northcliffe on a stroll round his grand country mansion at Broadstairs in Kent, when he felt a poke in his ribs and His Lordship hissed 'Look at him!' 'Who?' 'My valet,' whispered Northcliffe. Lewis Rose still couldn't see him.

'He's not there now,' murmured The Chief. 'He knows I'm watching him!'

Northcliffe wielded huge power. His newspapers conducted a

LOST ON THE MAP

vendetta against an obscure solicitor due to some imagined slight against Lady Northcliffe until the man's livelihood was destroyed. Not that His Lordship was faithful to his wife. Always sensitive about the subject of exam results, some wags joked that the only examination Northcliffe had ever passed was the Wassermann test for syphilis.

In 1922, clearly unwell, The Chief embarked on a world tour. Daily telegrams were sent from the *Aquitania* of the ship's menus, with instructions they should be printed in the *Daily Mail*. From New York, Northcliffe cabled George V, 'I am turning Catholic', to which the King replied, 'I cannot help it.' The tour lasted seven months, and on his return my grandfather noted a dramatic deterioration. His Lordship was furtive and nervous, more suspicious than ever. Lewis Rose was summoned to his home, No.1 Carlton Gardens. 'Does anyone know you've come here?' demanded Northcliffe. He explained that people were following him. Instructing Lewis Rose not to tell anyone where he had been, Northcliffe confessed, 'It's awful – awful, I'm having everyone watched.' Shortly afterwards The Chief appointed Glover, the porter at Carmelite House, as head of the *Daily Mail* advertising department.

He told Lewis Rose that he was embarking on a secret trip to Germany under a false name: 'taking my life in my hands'. If the Germans discovered who he was, he confided, they would poison him. At Boulogne, Northcliffe informed the station master there had been an attempt to assassinate him. In Paris, the editor of *The Times* found his boss in his hotel room waving a Colt pistol at a dressing gown hanging on the door, which The Chief had mistaken for an intruder.

He was eventually persuaded to travel in a darkened carriage to Evian, where the famous surgeon Sir Frederick Treves and the editor of *The Times* decided to consult a neurologist. Northcliffe agreed to see this specialist only when assured that he was an expert on German poisons. The neurologist certified His Lordship as insane.

The French president sent his private railway coach, and Lord Northcliffe was accompanied to Calais, then back to London. My mother recalled her father coming home having spent the entire afternoon driving around London in a taxi attempting to calm His Lordship down. The Chief died at his Carlton Gardens home in August 1922. Lewis Rose wept. Life as literary editor was no longer the same.

When he was offered a job in South Africa, Granny Trixie announced, 'I shall die if we don't go back!'

They went.

Workers of the world

In 1920 the Rostrons moved from Boksburg to a tin-roofed bungalow in a white working-class neighbourhood, La Rochelle, south of Johannesburg. When I visited 11th Street in the late 1990s there were burglar bars on the windows and razor wire on the outside wall. When my mother saw the photos, she remarked, 'It's much smarter than it used to be!' By then the street was mostly inhabited by young black families.

At the end of the road, you could just see Turffontein racetrack. This was particularly poignant, as one of the few things my father confided to me about William Rostron was that he regularly spent the housekeeping money at the racetrack. Frank even told my mother that his father would take him to the races perched on his shoulders, and once he'd placed a bet on a horse Frank could feel William's body quiver with uncontrollable excitement. That, though, must have been before they moved within walking distance of Turffontein racetrack, because by then my father was 13 and breeding bulldogs to make some pocket money to help his mother Annie.

However, long after my father's death, an entirely different picture of his father William has emerged from the letters of long-dead socialists, and even from police archives. I never met either grandfather, but there is a large volume of material both by and about Lewis Rose Macleod. About the printer from Lancashire there are only scraps. Yet combined, those hints and clues suggest a parallel story; an opposing explanation to the one I had been brought up to believe. The question is: why was this kept a secret; was it shame, filial anger; or something else?

The first shock came as I thumbed through a rare copy of *Printers Saga*, the official history of the South African Typographical Union. On page 510, covering the year 1920, was this: 'It is of interest, as here recorded, that *The Star* office has become 100 per cent trade union mainly as a result of the *missionary* (or should we say "undercover") work of a member who … may now be revealed.' The next page records that 'At the annual general meeting in February, a presentation was made to Bill Rostron in recognition of his services as a "missionary" at *The Star* office during the previous three years …'.

Good grief, a printer at *The Star*, where my father started as a reporter – and Frank didn't think to mention that? William might even have helped him get his big break as a reporter at *The Star*, which later led to Frank covering both the 1932 Los Angeles and 1936 Berlin Olympic Games. Even the name William appears suddenly misleading. For the persona who emerges from the shadows is 'Bill', the union man.

There was more, much more: perhaps far too much and scandalously so, even years later, it now seems, for my ambitious father, who must have known that I would have been riveted by Bill Rostron's other, dissident life.

Bolshevists in our midst

Buried in the National Archives in Pretoria, among bulky files of dust-coated police dossiers, is the carbon copy of a report in July 1919 by Acting Inspector A. Trigger. The previous evening he had clandestinely attended a meeting in Johannesburg of the International Socialist League. 'The usual speeches in favour of a Socialist Revolution were indulged in,' recorded Inspector Trigger. 'At the meetings reference is constantly made to the coming Social Revolution …'. The undercover Inspector identified a sinister development. 'Assisted by one Ross,' he reported, 'the International Socialist League have now secured printing machinery and intend to establish their own printing press with the least possible delay.' It would have been easy to skim over Inspector Trigger's spelling mistake or mishearing; in fact, the suspect proved to be not 'Ross' but Rostron.

This was the start of a long association for the emigrant from Lancashire with the left-wing South African press, feared by the police despite its miniscule size.

Bill Rostron flirts with the Bolsheviks

The International Socialist League (ISL) had been formed after a split in 1915 from the segregationist Labour Party. The direct cause of the rupture was that the Labour Party, along with many socialist parties in Europe, abruptly dumped its long-standing anti-war stance in order to support their country's war effort. The dissidents called themselves the 'war on warites', and their new journal aimed to 'propagate principles of International Socialism and anti-militarism'. The fact that Bill associated himself with this degree of radicalism shows that he was more than a loyal trade unionist, though it wasn't till after the war that he managed to find a printing press for the weekly ISL paper.

The police proved to be dedicated readers of *The International*, as well as spying on ISL meetings. In another report, Inspector Trigger reported that 'pious wishes were expressed for the establishment of a Socialist Government in South Africa in order that a general equality might ensue…'. Trigger added with evident distaste: 'After the usual speeches were finished at about 11 p.m. dancing was indulged in by the bulk of the gathering, comprised largely of the youthful element of both sexes.'

Inspector Trigger was kept extremely busy. That same month he alerted his superiors to a cutting from *The International*, noting that it contained 'an alleged report from the CID'. This suspicious article claimed that a police report to the Minister about a secret ISL meeting 'has fallen into our hands'. It would seem that the zealous Inspector Trigger was unaware that this was an overblown parody. The spoof article states that the meeting began with a collection for 'St Lenin and St Trotzky', then revealed that the Treasurer announced Moscow had wired 50 million roubles, diverted from Ireland to South Africa, as 'it was thought more blood could be shed in less time'.

The natives, the report continued, were to be incited to massacre white women and children just as the Allies were doing in Europe, and concluded with a rousing flourish that 'every woman present was nationalised'.

There's another cutting in the 1919 police files, this time a real one, obviously included because the CID Deputy Commissioner thought it contained important views. Headlined 'Bolshevists in our Midst: The Danger of Stirring up the Natives', it is a letter to *The Star* by Captain I. de M. Overbeek MC. 'Awake! South Africa, awake,' urges the Captain. 'Do you realise that with the preponderance of black over white in this country, if the International Socialists, alias Bolshevists, alias war-on-warites are allowed to influence black against white, that they will have attained their end, namely the overthrow of law and order.' The military man's conclusion was to be repeated over many years in many other 'Letters to the Editor': that encouraging ideas of equality would only end with 'the massacre of women and children'.

The natives are restless

Exactly 50 years later, during a university vacation, I worked as a cub reporter on the now defunct *Evening Post* in Port Elizabeth. Occasionally on a slow day the letters editor begged me to provide something for his page the next day. With relish, under a burlesque *nom de plume*, I concocted preposterous views similar to the above letter in *The Star*, so asinine that I imagined anyone who read them would collapse laughing at the insanity of apartheid – with the happy result that, in Port Elizabeth at least, the tyrannical system would implode. Alas, invariably my lampoons were taken literally, and replies to the editor (with pseudonyms like 'Common Sense') congratulated the paper for publishing such prudent opinions.

What emerges from those old police reports is the terror that was to haunt white South Africa for so long (and, in some quarters, still does): panicky rumours, mainly from outlying areas, concerning 'native unrest'. Police are sent to investigate and regularly find 'no signs of unrest'.

In a 1919 telegram to the Minister of Justice about a meeting of '1,500 natives in Pietersburg Dist.', the CID Deputy Commissioner warns: 'Certain section of European population obsessed with belief that meeting would end by massacre of whites and our officers told me that idea was prevalent throughout districts.' In a follow-up letter, the jittery Deputy Commissioner states, 'It is clear that everything possible is being done to work up the natives, and the chief plank in the platform of the International Socialists is to unsettle the natives.' He frets that faced with 'large bodies of semi-barbarians' his men do not get enough support, and so he concludes, 'It seems an extraordinary thing to me that in a freedom-loving country like South Africa the government should hesitate to tackle it.' At the end of this tetchy letter the Minister of Justice scrawled, 'What on earth does he mean by this?'

In 1920, *The International* boasted on its front page: 'Among its most sedulous readers are the heads of the police, who rightly see in it a danger to the social system they protect.' By now Bill Rostron was the foreman in charge of printing the weekly ISL 'organ', as communists the world over still prefer to call their party newspaper. By various accounts Bill was a reliable and skilled printer, but everyone agreed that he was difficult to deal with.

The subversive 'organ' consisted of only a few pages of tightly packed print. Below the title, with an insignia of a rising sun — oh, those lost optimistic days! — was the strap-line: 'The World's Co-operative Commonwealth'. After the jibe about their devoted police readership, an article on the following page borrows for its title the old Biblical slur, 'Hewers of Wood', in order to confront, it says, 'that besetting problem — the "native problem" — which the ISL alone in South Africa has set itself to face and to tackle.'

The anonymous author admits that even among Socialists it can be difficult to discuss this, due to a 'lynch law' attitude to any whites suspected of 'tampering with Kaffirs'. The article poses the dilemma which, it laments, white workers do not wish to face: 'Yet do what we will, we white workers cannot eliminate the black worker.' In fact, it was the vast majority of white South Africans, capitalists and politicians too, that tried to duck this reality for the next 74 years: 'We may ignore him, combine against him, scab on him, bully him, shoot him; and he may hate us, fear us, scab on us, combine against us; but there he is, not merely indispensable to production, but doing all the dirty work, most of the heavy work, most of the unskilled work, some of the skilled work, really the great bulk of all the work in this country.'

This peroration closes with the fundamental question: 'What is a workers' movement without him?'

The brutal answer came two years later.

Raising the red flag

Strikes broke out at coal mines in January 1922, then spread to the gold mines, after mine owners attempted to cut costs by replacing semi-skilled white workers with cheaper black labour. The strikes rapidly escalated into a rebellion with a uniquely South African confusion of class conflict and racial terror. By February this was no longer a mere trade union dispute, but a white working-class uprising, involving women, families and communities right across the Rand. Rebel commandos were hastily formed and armed. It had become an insurrection.

One of the rare snippets my father imparted to me about William Rostron is that he had printed pamphlets for the 1922 Rand Revolt. 'Bill' was still in charge of printing *The International*, but that weekly was now the official organ of the Communist Party of South Africa

(CPSA). The CPSA had been formed the previous year, absorbing the tiny International Socialist League. The outbreak of white working-class fury presented both a revolutionary opportunity and an ideological dilemma for the fledgling party. The press were calling this upheaval 'The Red Revolt', yet the armed rebels were clearly attempting to establish white working-class supremacy – fuelled by their dread that if the mine bosses got their way many whites would sink into an undifferentiated proletariat, with the lowly social status of 'black'.

Their skin colour guaranteed white miners not only skilled jobs and higher wages, but bequeathed them a bizarre sense of pride and rank. Many white coal miners even retained a black servant. Famously, right across the Rand, workers and their families marched under defiant banners that appealed: 'Workers of the World Unite and Fight for a White South Africa'.

In addition to its weekly journal, the Communist Party rushed out pamphlets and manifestos, all of which would have been overseen by Bill. The prominent and cultivated Marxist, Sidney Bunting, did his best to sway white rebels against their racial exclusivity. There had been increasing instances of attacks on blacks by white strikers. Again and again, Bunting urged in print that the only way to fight capitalism was through the unity of all workers, irrespective of colour. He exhorted, 'The people who do the work of a country eventually inherit it.'

East to west across the gold reef, hastily armed white rebels controlled whole neighbourhoods, including the Rostron's modest borough of La Rochelle. Many of those insurrectionary commandos were ex-WWI servicemen.

The dogged CID officer Alfred Trigger, now promoted to Major, warned the Boksburg police there would be 'Sinn Fein-type attacks on barracks and stations'. By the middle of February, Major Trigger declared that the situation was 'definitely revolutionary', and he was certain that this uprising constituted 'an armed rebellion against the authority of the state'.

Jan Smuts, Prime Minister for just over a year, responded ruthlessly. Martial law was declared, tanks deployed. Artillery shelled insurgent positions. Rebel strongholds were bombed from the air. The revolt lasted three months. The estimated death toll was 200, with 153 being strikers. Over 1,000 white workers were arrested and four mutinous leaders were executed, three of them going to the gallows singing 'The Red Flag'.

Enter the bogeyman

Far away in London, Lewis Rose Macleod wrote an article which was syndicated round the world. 'The rattle of musketry in the streets of Johannesburg is no new thing,' he began, explaining that 'the great gold city … was always more or less a storm centre.'

From his affable clubman's perspective, he portrayed another aspect of the gold rush metropolis: a benign climate, pleasant living conditions for white miners in 'company homes'. 'The present epidemic of violence is due to several causes,' he stated. 'One is that the character of the white mining population has changed a good deal during recent years. Many Dutchmen of a low order of intelligence have taken the place of the old type of British miner, and the attempt to reduce their pay and employ more natives has roused the spirit of race antagonism.'

Viewed from the blinkered citadel of Carmelite House, Lewis Rose spectacularly misjudged what had occurred. He failed to see that this was not merely yet another violent strike, but an enraged white insurrection where English and Afrikaner workers had combined. The 1922 revolt may have been crushed, but it marked the start of a new and powerful alliance, linking rural Afrikaners and urban white workers. In the election two years later, Smuts was bundled out and in came the Pact Government.

This coalition between Afrikaner nationalists and the segregationist Labour Party firmly entrenched the colour bar, speeding up the litany of crude racial legislation that was to sustain white supremacy in South Africa till nearly the end of the twentieth century.

My grandfather, though, had sounded a note of alarm that was to persist into my own adult lifetime. Lewis Rose concluded, 'But there is another fact which must not be lost sight of, and that is that Johannesburg, with its many opportunities for speculation and a large native population upon which to prey, has always had a very strong attraction for Russian refugees of the basest sort.'

The communist threat from Moscow was a rich seam that was mined for many, many years to come, even if those Bolshevik bogeymen never quite materialised.

The 1922 Rand insurrection had nevertheless witnessed a startling display of bravado. For the first time in this gold-dazzled city of Mammon – and most likely for the very last occasion too – a red flag had been hoisted over Johannesburg City Hall.

6
☩
GRANNY GETS HER GUN

Narrow chested specimens

THE FAR-FLUNG GRANDEES of the British Empire tended to be a tight-knit coterie: educated at select public schools, followed by Oxford or Cambridge, and invariably bound by cosy family ties. In South Africa, Lewis Rose's 'dullest' High Commissioner, Lord Selborne, was the son-in-law of Lord Salisbury, a (three times) former Prime Minister. Lord Milner, Selborne's predecessor had an affair with (and later married) Lady Violet Cecil, the wife of Lord Salisbury's soldier son, Major Edward Cecil (while the cuck-olded Major was trapped during the siege of Mafeking). And Lord Selborne's successor in South Africa, Viscount Gladstone, was, of course, the son of Queen Victoria's serial (four times) Prime Minister.

Amongst this colonial cronyism I discovered a patrician personal connection. My 'Auntie' Alix's son George Grey was elected to the House of Commons in 1942, aged 22, but resigned to join the army and was killed in Normandy in July 1944. My mother would occa-sionally accompany Alix to visit his grave in the village of Le Repas. Recalling that George had represented Berwick-upon-Tweed, and that his father, Major General Wulff Grey, had been a financial backer of the Liberal Party, I contacted the then MP: yes, he replied, Alix's husband had been a cousin of Sir Edward Grey, an earlier MP for the constituency – and Britain's longest-serving Foreign

Secretary. Sir Edward had been part of the 'Liberal Imperialist' faction during the Boer War, but on taking over as Foreign Secretary in 1905 he completed a sharp about-turn. The only way of escaping the outcry over Chinese labour on the Rand, he concluded, was to grant responsible government to the former Boer Republics of the Transvaal and Orange Free State.

Sir Edward is mostly remembered today for a remark on the eve of the First World War. Gazing down from his window at the Foreign Office as dusk fell, Sir Edward watched lamps being lit along Whitehall and murmured, 'The lights are going out all over Europe; we shall not see them lit again in our lifetime.'

Meanwhile, for a decade or more, another more vaporous spectre had haunted Britain. At the very moment of Britannia's greatest reach, Edwardian Britain was stalked by a dread of national physical, mental, even moral decay: a foreboding of potential imperial decline. This came into sharp focus after the Boer War, when it became known that 40 per cent of recruits had proved unfit for military duties, many suffering from poverty-related diseases like rickets. Rudyard Kipling, Conan Doyle and Rider Haggard all expressed alarm that the industrialised proletariat of the world's most powerful nation had declined into racial enfeeblement.

Baden Powell, the hero of Mafeking, founded the Boy Scouts precisely in order to beef up 'pale, narrow-chested, hunched-up, miserable specimens' emasculated by city life and, he believed, self-abuse. Instead, the colonies were viewed as an antidote, producing sturdier and more self-reliant specimens of white manhood.

In 1910 Alix's older brother Bertram, still in Peking, sounded a shrill alarm. Under his pen name Putnam Weale, Alix's opinion-ated brother wrote a widely read book, *The Conflict of Colour: The Threatened Upheaval throughout the World*. This was a voluminous and doom-laden résumé of his view of world affairs, stating his belief that contrasts of colour constitute history's fundamental driving force. Weale listed estimates for the 'World According to Colour' and concluded that 'when every living being in the world is counted, the odds against the white man may be said to remain roughly two to one'.

A crisis of colour

This is the spectre that has always haunted colonisers.

During the Edwardian era 'whiteness' was seen to be under threat: undermined from within by physical degeneracy, and from without by a massive discrepancy in demographics. This anxiety was tersely expressed in a letter to the *East London Daily Dispatch* in April 1907, when William Rostron was still printing a supplement for the newspaper. 'Sir – It is curious and sad, but undoubtedly a fact, that the white races in South Africa show a marked tendency to degeneration, not in physique, but in grit and moral attitudes. This is undoubtedly due to the contact with an inferior race, and in this way the influence of the kaffir is profoundly modifying the character of the white race in South Africa.' The letter, not surpris-ingly, was signed 'Pessimist'. The prognosis of 'Pessimist' was bleak: 'No, South Africa is a black man's country and to savagery it will return, it and its population, white and coloured.'

Bertram was aghast at the idea of miscegenation, asserting that it produced 'dreadful hybrids'. But in *The Conflict of Colour*, he argued that for Britain to hold its position in the world it would eventually have to cede equal status first to China (yellow), then India (brown), as it had done with the white Dominions. 'The secrets of supremacy have been revealed; and other countries, led by what England has done, are beginning to accept in their extra-European affairs what may be called by the same clumsy doctrine of *pis-aller*,' he fumed; *pis-aller* being translated roughly as 'a solution of worst or last resort'. Bertram's criticism of British foreign policy, under the pseudonym Putman Weale, was unremittingly caustic, charging that it was one of drift and denial.

Ironically, this foreign policy was guided by Sir Edward Grey, the cousin of Bertram's future brother-in-law – and who, as Foreign Minister, admitted to an intense aversion to foreign travel.

The big blip in Weale's global theory was Africa. His chapter headings introduce 'The Yellow World', 'The Brown World', finally 'The Black Problem'. Chapter IV begins 'There is perhaps nothing quite so cruel in the whole world as the strange law which has given to so many scores of millions of human beings coal-black faces and bodies, thus so distinguishing them from the rest of the human family that this singular colour – together with the unalterable odour which accompanies it, and the simian features which accentuate it – is held to be the mark of the beast.'

In 1910 Weale articulated the sexual terror which was to drive ever-greater racial repression. 'How to keep races pure,' he fretted, maintaining that 'the black man is a great breeder of men'. For Alix's brother it was a nightmare of numbers in South Africa: a mere one million whites, he calculated, set among six or seven million blacks. Having totalled up his arithmetic, Weale spelled out the cataclysmic dread that was to be the recurring nightmare of so many European colonists for so long: 'The white man, where he is entrenched in strong communities, can only be conquered by other races by total extermination.'

Solving that riddle, counselled Weale, lay far beyond rational white men, 'who, born and bred in temperate climes, can never know more of men's thoughts and ambitions in such mysterious lands than they do of the thoughts and ambitions of the possible men of Mars. And with that one must end.'

A fearful return to Africa

During her lonely years in London, Granny Trixie grew particularly close to her cousin Alix. So perhaps it is not surprising that my mother, aged 11, should announce to her friends that by returning to South Africa in 1923 she would be living in a very dangerous country – though she was referring to wild beasts rather than Weale's wild 'breeders'.

Nevertheless, after the Great War British fears had increased dramatically that an end might be nigh for the millennia of white ascendency. The slaughter of so many Europeans had even led some to refer to that conflict as a form of 'racial suicide'.

The 1924 election in South Africa was fought over precisely that anxiety: a bitter contest over competing claims about who would best guarantee the preservation of white primacy. Lewis Rose arrived back in Johannesburg to take over the editorship of the *Rand Daily Mail* in time to offer vigorous editorial support for the re-election of

Prime Minister Jan Smuts and the South African Party.

Before departing London, he had been presented with a cartoon at a farewell dinner at the Savage Club. Over the caption, 'The Savage Macleod begins editing in South Africa', it depicts a grotesquely caricatured black man with the round features of Lewis Rose, dressed in grass skirt, bow tie and spats, a bone tied to his head by a wisp of hair. A bubble commands: 'Boy! Bring me the literary editor. I want to hit him with a lot of assegai.' Now his editorial assegais were aimed at the coalition between Afrikaner nationalists and the segregationist Labour Party. This odd alliance of rural and urban working whites, he suggested, was bound to lead to economic stagnation.

On election day Lewis Rose argued that General Smuts stood for continuity: for prosperity based on boosting profits from gold mining and strengthening the British connection. The voters were not swayed, and General J.B. Hertzog formed the Pact Government, committed to entrenching and reinforcing South Africa's colour bar.

Two months later Joseph Conrad died at his home in Kent, aged 66, and Lewis Rose composed a long and appreciative obituary for the paper he had recently left. Conrad had celebrated his previous birthday with my grandfather. 'The last time I saw Joseph Conrad was in March of this year, a few days before I sailed for South Africa,' wrote Lewis Rose in the *Daily Mail*, 'and his last words on that occasion were in the nature of a wistful half-promise that he would pay me a visit in Johannesburg. "I would come, my dear" – the habit of saying "My dear" to his intimates, instead of "My dear so-and-so" is one of the tricks of speech which indicated his foreign birth – "I would come with pleasure, but how can I answer for her?'" The novelist glanced at his corpulent, invalid, devoted wife, Jesse, on a nearby couch, to explain why he'd never be able to visit.

An abyss of class

The social gap between the Rostrons and Macleods was stark. While Lewis Rose edited an influential daily paper owned by mining magnates, Bill was printing the financially-strapped Communist Party 'organ' which struggled to come out each week. It was also regularly raided by the police.

The Macleods soon had a large two-storey home with an enormous garden. Lewis Rose sentimentally called this house Dunvegan after the castle in Skye that had been the home for chiefs of the Macleod clan for over 800 years. The Johannesburg Dunvegan was featured in a local magazine with the caption: 'Mr L.R. Macleod's new residence, Auckland Park'. The photo of the expansive living room is flooded with sunlight and looks as spacious as the whole of the Rostron's bungalow in La Rochelle.

Shortly after his return to Johannesburg, Lewis Rose received a letter from the executors of Lord Northcliffe's estate informing him that, along with all other employees, His Lordship had left him a bequest. Lewis Rose's share was £333. That was about half the sum that Bill Rostron

My father Frank with his mother Annie

had paid to buy his small tin-roofed house on the other side of Johannesburg. There is a faded snapshot of my father Frank, fresh-faced and probably in his late teens, sitting on a motorbike outside that house, his mother Annie perched on the back, posing: dark-haired, thin, smiling uncertainly.

There are no adult photos of Bill Rostron, not even at the nearby racetrack of Turffontein where he supposedly lost much of their housekeeping money. In contrast, there are stiffly formal photo-graphs of Mr and Mrs Macleod at horse racing events, Trixie in elegantly sweeping hat and Lewis Rose in dark morning suit and topper, alongside high-ranking dignitaries, including two Governors-General of South Africa.

Lewis Rose and Trixie (centre) at the races with Governor-General,
Lord Clarendon

Then there was Lewis Rose's sister Cloudie, still acting as social secretary to Lady Phillips. Though born in modest colonial circumstances in Australia, Cloudie adopted all the snobbery of her rich employer and the affectations of parvenu Johannesburg society. My mother Barbara said that as a young girl she often heard Cloudie, after a soirée she had organised for Lady Phillips, remark of some moneyed but unsophisticated guest, 'not quite out of the top drawer'. Baffled, Barbara would sneak into Cloudie's bedroom to rummage through her top dresser drawer, but all she ever found were hairpins, a hair brush, face cream and powder puffs.

Barbara, who till then had been deemed too 'nervous' to attend school, was now sent with her older sister, Betty, to Roedean, Johannesburg's most exclusive girls' school; like so much else, an imitation of the British original. She was 12 years old.

Five years older, my father was already helping Bill Rostron after school at the printing workshop and, while still at school, he began writing a sports column for a local paper, the *Commercial Advertiser*. Frank's name now also appeared in the sports reports of other papers as he won amateur boxing bouts. After one contest against provincial rivals, the *Cape Times* judged, 'The best boxer on

My father, Frank Rostron

128

view was undoubtedly Rostron. He is a great all-round boxer, using left and right impartially, with a splendid upright stance. He goes his own way, quite calm and unperturbed.' The 1926 programme for a gala contest against a combined Oxford and Cambridge touring squad records that by the age of 19 he had fought 68 bouts, winning 61 of them, and in the process had become the South African junior middleweight champion.

Lumping the proletariat

There was, however, a great deal of tension at the Rostron home in La Rochelle. Bill and Annie had long periods when they refused to speak to each other, and so as a young boy Frank was employed as the go-between. My father never talked about this, but according to my mother, Annie Rostron would, for example, instruct her son, 'Tell your father dinner's on the table.' Frank would dutifully convey this information, to which his father might reply, 'Inform your mother that I'm not hungry.'

Like most children with torn loyalties, Frank tried to placate both parents. He was devoted to his mother, but his father shared his interest in sport, encouraged him to box, and let him help in the printing works after school. Bill also secretly sent some of his son's attempts at writing sports reports to newspapers, and as a teenager Frank was astonished to discover his own byline in the *Sunday Times.*

Bill Rostron was still in charge of printing *The International.* The weekly carried regular paeans of praise for Revolutionary Russia: 'the most wonderful thing in the world today'. But six months after the explosive 1922 Rand Revolt, which had soaked up much of the party's funds, *The International* announced that due to a financial crisis it would now be published only fortnightly. Nevertheless, on the front page the party paid tribute to 'the able and conscientious management of our foreman printer, Mr Rostron'.

If Annie was sickly and tubercular, Bill by several accounts could be difficult and cantankerous. A leading communist of the time, Eddie Roux, described many years later the constant crises in keeping the party press and publications going, and specifically recalled that 'The manager of the press was a reliable fellow and a good printer; but he was said to suffer from lead poisoning, he had an uncertain temper and had to be handled carefully.'

As with all small left-wing publications, the financial difficulties were unrelenting, requiring constant appeals for help ('Rent, rates and other running expenses must be met …'). Having commended their 'conscientious' printer Mr Rostron, the newspaper added reproachfully 'but there is a limit to the burden-bearing capacity of even the best-managed office, and that limit has been reached …'.

In 1923, the leading Communist Party member Sidney Bunting – a music-loving, Oxford-educated lawyer – wrote to his wife, 'Dearest Girl, our CE meeting last night got through a lot of work and we have given Rostron leave to carry on business in the name of "The Commercial Printing Co." concurrently with our own business of the ISL Press, on certain terms of course.' Bunting, who had remained in South Africa after volunteering for the British army during the Boer War, does not spell out those conditions. But it was clearly a way to allow their foreman to take on extra work in order to make up the wages that they couldn't afford to pay in full.

Astonishingly, one of the contracts Bill accepted, as he moonlighted with the Communist Party's printing press, was to produce the rival publication of the segregationist Labour Party. The first issue of *Forward* in December 1924 pledged its adherence to a rigid 'white employment' policy. When *Forward*'s inaugural manifesto resoundingly proclaimed 'We look forward to a future of bright and useful work for the betterment of mankind ...', what it meant was: the betterment of white man and womankind. This was in direct contrast to the ethos of the Communist Party, on whose press the weekly was being printed. In the second issue, *Forward*'s editorial was headlined 'Towards a White South Africa'. On the front page was a message of support from D.F. Malan, the Minister of Interior and Education, who in 1948 became the first National Party Prime Minister, implementing the policy of apartheid.

In fact, to disguise the true ownership of the Commercial Printing Company, which would have put off potentially more lucrative business, Bill posed as the proprietor. My father certainly thought that Bill was the boss. 'My father had a small printers and publishers business and printed among other things, the Labour weekly *Forward*,' he recalled, 'and during school holidays I used to potter around correcting proofs and talking to the linotype operators.'

Though masquerading as the proprietor, Bill was not a party member. This was spelled out in a long letter from Sidney Bunting to the Comintern, the powerful Communist International in Moscow. 'Our press has for a number of years past been obliged to conceal from the public its communist identity,' he wrote. 'Our manager, who has been in charge ever since the press started, has appeared before the world as the proprietor of the business, although actually only a wage earner. He has brought in a good deal of work, indeed the bulk of the work, from customers who would indignantly refuse to give it if they knew it to be a communist press.'

Bunting explained to Moscow that Bill had also lent £300 towards the cost of a new printing plant, and together with outstanding unpaid wages, the Party at that point owed him about £400 – which casts a completely different light on my own father's belief that Bill Rostron squandered the housekeeping money on horseracing, leaving Frank and his mother Annie to struggle.

Betting on the wrong horse

The Communist Party, with Bill's help, had bought a new press in the hope of enticing further outside contracts. The gamble did not pay off. Within 12 months the party's debts stood at £750, and the aim of Bunting's letter to Moscow in November 1926 was to beg the Comintern 'very urgently' for a large loan. Apart from debts incurred in acquiring the new press, Moscow was also informed that my grandfather was partly to blame for the party's deepening financial woes. Under considerable financial stress himself, and harassed by creditors as the supposed owner of the press, the strain was beginning to show. Bill's testiness was now driving away business.

Moscow was informed that he had 'served the interests of the party on the whole very faithfully'. However, 'bearing the brunt (and discredit to himself) of dealing with creditors,' Bunting explained, 'he is to a certain extent suffering from nervous strain, often resulting in extreme irritability.' This, 'coupled with the usual white worker's antipathy to blacks, has resulted in extreme friction between him and the representatives of the I.C.U. (Native General Workers Union), who brought their paper to be printed at our press.' He had 'very seriously insulted them on a number of occasions …'. Bill ended by throwing the union's copy out of the window.

The party was in a bind, Bunting informed Moscow. They could neither refund Rostron, nor fire him. The latter would expose the true Communist ownership of the printing business, which 'will mean at present the loss of most of our custom …'.

The following month Bunting wrote to his comrade Eddie Roux confiding the party's mounting financial crisis. 'In spite of all our efforts,' he confessed, 'it remains impossible to raise funds to pay out Rostron, and as that is still as necessary a step as ever, a sale may occur at any moment …'. There is no evidence that Moscow responded to the request for a generous loan, so by September 1927 the crisis had hit.

Bunting wrote to another leading communist, James La Guma, to confirm that the party newspaper – by then renamed *The South African Worker* – had been closed down. 'The Printing Press has eaten itself up, i.e. it has been carried at so heavy a cost in the last few months, especially since Weinstock took away *Forward*, and has lived on money borrowed from Rostron (about £500) from me (about £900) and latterly from me almost exclusively, so that my little fortune is almost gone …'. He continued, 'We expect to get at most £1,000 net for the plant, out of which Bacharach and Rostron will probably expect to be paid first, and I shall take what is left, and there will certainly be nothing over for the Party.' There was a lesson to be learned, Bunting felt: 'Well, we have come to the conclusion that the Party can't run such a business…'.

Two months later Julius First, a founding member of the Communist Party of South Africa and the father of Ruth First (who was assassinated by an apartheid letter bomb in 1982), tried to sell the Commercial Printing Company to the Industrial and Commercial Workers Union (ICU). This was bad timing. Exactly one year earlier the ICU had expelled all its communist members. Nevertheless, Julius First ended his letter with this qualification: 'The only reason for wishing to sell is the fact that the writer has been unable to devote the necessary time the business demands, and further the irritability of the foreman not permitting harmony in the conduct of the business.'

It is staggering to think that though not mentioned by name, only as the 'manager', the otherwise obscure printer Bill Rostron and his much noted 'irritability', charitably ascribed to lead poisoning, was seriously discussed by the Executive Committee of the Communist International in Moscow. Above all, this presents a startling alternative explanation to my father's grievance that Bill had squandered most of their housekeeping money at the racetrack. Instead, it seems that the metaphorical horse his father had disastrously bet on was, in fact, the Communist Party of South Africa.

The likelihood is that, unable to pay Rostron his £500, a deal was struck whereby Bill took over the company. Eddie Roux's 1944 biography of Sidney Bunting was printed by the Commercial Printing Co., and when it was reprinted half a century later, Bunting's son, Brian, stated that by then the press was owned by Bill. Bunting's other son recalled that as a boy, 'We often visited a linotype shop and there was an old-timer called Rostron who set type by hand.'

All the evidence suggests that Bill inherited the Communist

Party press by default. Either that, or with nearly 100 years' added interest, the current South African Communist Party – successor to the original CPSA – owes me, as his sole living relative, a huge sum of money.

Fight over the flag

Compared to Bill Rostron, my maternal grandfather earned a fortune. Yet despite an annual salary of £2,500 at the *Rand Daily Mail*, Lewis Rose also ran into debt. His lordly style of living forced him to approach the board of directors for a loan of £2,000. It was not long before the board had raised concerns after their editor commissioned a series of articles from the London *Daily Mail*'s roving correspondent George Ward Price for what they regarded as a spendthrift £500. Ward Price was soon to become world-famous as the only foreign journalist with direct access to Germany's new Chancellor, Adolf Hitler – and later, but slightly less infamously, as my godfather.

All the board's complaints were forgotten, though, when Lewis Rose played a central role in resolving a crisis that contemporaries feared might rip the new nation apart. In retrospect it vividly reveals the utterly piffling concerns of white South Africans: a stark contrast to their blindness over the country's real racial problems.

The cause of this strife was a ferocious battle over the national flag. Enmities from the Boer War appeared to revive when Afrikaner nationalists began to demand a new flag to replace the Union Jack. In 1926 the Interior Minister D.F. Malan introduced a bill proposing a radically different design, removing all imperial symbols and the

Union Jack. Festering hostility between Afrikaner nationalists and empire loyalists exploded. There was even talk of war. *Die Volksblad* sermonised, 'It is an inexorable law of nature that there must be sacrifice, and in some cases even death before life can appear.'

Proponents of retaining British symbolism were equally partisan. The province of Natal threatened to secede. Lewis Rose leapt into the fray. 'If this question of the flag is not promptly removed from its present atmosphere,' he pontificated, 'it will not be long before the whole country is again flooded with the poison gas of racialism.' Once more, 'racialism' did not refer to pigment but rivalry between Afrikaners and English-speakers. The furore crystallised mutual fears, and proposals for a referendum were quietly shelved when both sides realised that this dispute split their own ranks.

Surreptitiously, my grandfather began an intrigue. When the Prime Minister backtracked and suggested a commission to consider another design, Lewis Rose endorsed the proposal in the *Rand Daily Mail*, using his editorials to prod Smuts into a more conciliatory position. At the same time, he exploited rivalries in the Cabinet by secretly making contact with Tielman Roos, the ambitious Deputy Prime Minister.

The crux of the matter was whether the Union Jack should be included in the new flag, and if so, precisely what size it would be granted. The Minister responsible, D.F. Malan, refused to back down, so Roos deviously outflanked his colleague.

Writing a letter to the *Rand Daily Mail*, which was blazed across the front page, Roos suggested a compromise. Known as the 'Roos Manifesto', he proposed that all symbols be accorded equal status. The banality of his proposal highlights the pervasive lack of vision among white South Africans. But his letter caused a sensation. The fact Roos had written at all was surprising, but that he chose an English-language paper to go public was astounding. The Deputy Prime Minister had not only broken cabinet ranks, but audaciously undermined his National Party rival Malan.

Events moved fast. As fights broke out, faced with what Smuts now called the biggest crisis the Union had faced, he and Hertzog met and a compromise was reached: the Union Jack was to be given the same size as the emblems of the two old Boer Republics. The *Rand Daily Mail* trumpeted: 'Happy Ending to the Flag Controversy'.

Roos wrote a congratulatory note to Lewis Rose: 'The outcome must have made your keenest critics your greatest admirers, owing to the far-sighted vision directing your efforts.'

Ironically, the African National Congress had held a series of protest meetings to demand that the Union Jack be retained. But the opinions of the black majority were barely noticed by either side. A columnist for the newspaper *Ons Vaderland* asked scornfully of the opposition, 'What notion have their kaffir friends about a flag?'

Roos' success was only temporary, however, as was the humiliation of the rival that he had so comprehensively outmanoeuvred. Malan, who had originally blustered that the rancorous flag furore represented South Africa's 'last great racial question', became Prime Minister 20 years later, ushering in the long calvary of apartheid: that monstrous blueprint for another 'last great racial question'.

A cradle of horrors

For centuries, Africa had dredged up manifold terrors in the European imagination.

Once it was thought that white people who ventured south of the equator might turn black or deliquesce. Early maps, which frequently represented almost the entire continent as Aethiopia, made up for lack of detail with warnings of cannibals and the monstrous Cyclops as well as depictions of naked men with dogs' heads.

Yet alongside such terrifying dangers were alluring depictions of other fictions, such as the whereabouts of the mythical Christian monarch Prester John, or the location of the untold biblical wealth from King Solomon's mines. For Europeans, Africa simultaneously represented a potent magnet of attraction and repulsion.

The climate initially presented a massive impediment to European penetration. Joseph Conrad remarked that the continent had much to thank for all those tropical diseases that decimated marauding Europeans; for if the climate had not been so hostile, and frequently fatal, the exploitation of Africa would have been even more extensive and ruthless. Earlier João de Barros, the sixteenth century Portuguese historian, had written: 'But it seems that for our sins, or for some inscrutable judgement of God, in all the entrances of this great Ethiopia that we navigate along, He has placed a striking angel with a flaming sword of deadly fevers, who prevents us from penetrating into the interior to the spring of this garden, whence proceed these rivers of gold that flow to the sea in so many parts of our conquest.'

The ghoulish chimeras imagined to inhabit the interior of Africa, which included ants the size of a mastiff and boiling rivers, are often more interesting than the facts, as they tell us what people were inclined to believe – and that otherwise perfectly sensible Europeans were capable of swallowing outlandish notions that defy common sense or logic. The cockatrice, for example, was a mythological creature believed to have originated in the deserts of Africa which could turn people to stone or kill them with one glance. Perhaps confused with the Egyptian crocodile, the cockatrice was pictured as a two-legged dragon with the head of a cockerel or sometimes a distorted human face. The Roman writer Pliny the Elder confidently asserts in his *Natural History* that 'Its touch and its breath can scorch grass, kill bushes and burst rocks.'

Church window: the imagined, terrifying cockatrice

Africa has long been a mirror to the European psyche, reflecting the darkest imaginings that bubble up from our unconscious – but which are, instead, swiftly projected onto a conveniently blank canvas. In South Africa this strange pathology culminated in apartheid, the masterplan to address that 'last great racial question'. As a result, white South Africans, with tyrannical laws and state violence, effectively created exactly the social monster that they had always dreaded: like the deadly cockatrice, manufactured out of their own ignorance and fear.

Granny protects her patch

As a teenager I was astonished by the lack of knowledge about their own country displayed by many well-travelled friends of my parents. Successful businessmen who had been at Jeppe High School with my father would testily deny the litany of repression and torture by the apartheid government, while denouncing those well-documented brutalities as malicious slanders from a liberal Western press duped by Soviet propaganda. They also recycled myths about black people and their aspirations: that 'agitators' employed a belief in witchcraft to whip up an otherwise contented black populace. A few even related terrifying reports that in remote areas white people were being systematically liquidated in a diabolic 'liberation' policy of white genocide. Then as now, anxious rumour-mongers usually had little or no understanding of African history, let alone of other languages or living conditions.

Their evidence was habitually as reliable as medieval maps showing a mysterious kingdom in the interior of the continent populated by one-legged men who cast no shadows.

My wonderful, sweetly daffy old Granny Trixie never had an opinion on any serious matter and would repeat beatifically, 'My late husband Lewis Rose used to say ...'. Though she remained delightfully cheerful, by the time that I was a teenager Granny was placidly doolally, once charmingly asking my father if he had met my mother, or when I had once again failed a maths exam informing me, 'My grandson is a mathematical genius, you know.' Granny used to sit on the shaded stoep of her tin-roofed bungalow in Rosebank, beadily watching over her dusty, heat-singed front lawn.

There had been repeated newspaper reports that a gang was

travelling round Johannesburg, cutting people's pristine turf into neat squares and making off with a saleable commodity for some new sub-urban garden. Apart from the deduction that they must have had a lorry to carry away their swag, the fact this gang could move so freely round Johannesburg in the late 1960s suggests that they were equally as likely to be white. But one day I discovered that Granny kept a small revolver tucked under her pillow. She in turn was surprised that I was surprised, and explained her pistol to me with a serene smile, 'Just in case the natives try to steal my lawn at night, dear.'

Firearms of all calibres, and for all pigments, remain conventional South African accessories. Nearly 30 years later, not long after our first democratic election and shortly before I was due to return to South Africa, I had a play performed in Johannesburg, and although the stage directions indicated the presence of a revolver, it was a very minor prop. Nevertheless the director, presumably in a quest for absolute South African authenticity, insisted that rather than a plastic replica the production required a real, functioning pistol. After only a few rehearsals this handgun was stolen, inducing acute nervousness in the producers that the weapon could be traced back to them – and that the production company might be charged as an accessory to a violent crime, perhaps even murder.

We still live with age-old fears.

7

+

DISTANT SKIES, FALSE GODS

You sent us the light

AS OPPOSED TO a conventional blackout, let's call it 'whiteout': an almost supernatural inability to detect in blazing sunlight what is right before your eyes. Such myopia did not end in 1927 with the flag fiasco. Eighty years later I walked into a small exhibition in Cape Town dedicated to a previously neglected black photographer. In a glass display cabinet were a number of knick-knacks, and on a lower shelf was a black and white photo with the caption: 'A Bantu poet. This is the native who delivered an oration to the Prince of Wales at King William's Town.'

Even 13 years after the establishment of non-racial democracy in South Africa, there was no attempt to identify the anonymous 'native', let alone record that he was original and distinguished; or that his influence, undetected by whites at the time, was considerable. This 'native' was Krune Mqhayi: a prolific poet, journalist and historian, credited with writing the first novel in isiXhosa. Mqhayi was also an *imbongi*, 'a kind of oral historian', explained Nelson Mandela in his autobiography, 'who marks contemporary events and history with poetry that is of special meaning to his people'.

The usual translation of *imbongi* is 'praise singer'. That is clearly what local white dignitaries thought they were getting when Mqhayi delivered his 'oration' to Edward, the Prince of Wales, on his visit to King William's Town during a royal tour in 1925. The vain and capricious prince, later briefly the King-Emperor Edward VIII but known after his abdication as the Duke of Windsor, must have imagined he was being showered with acclaim in unintelligible isi-Xhosa. The other colonial bigwigs were also doubtless charmed by this amusing display of a 'native' in a leopard skin; how gratifying, they must have congratulated themselves, that these local blacks wished to display such ardent loyal affection.

In fact, Krune Mqhayi was delivering a masterfully seditious performance that was understood by every Xhosa spectator present. Under the guise of sumptuous flattery and royal adulation, Mqhayi savagely flayed the Prince, all the suited white officials, and their flowery-hatted wives. 'Ah Britain! Great Britain! / Great Britain of the endless sunshine!', he began fairly conventionally:

> 'She has conquered the oceans and laid them low
> She has drained the little rivers and lapped them dry
> She has swept the little nations and wiped them away …

Then as the Prince of Wales and his entourage looked on with fixed, benevolent smiles, Mqhayi got into his stride. Strutting up and down the podium, his reedy voice rising in a crescendo, he listed all the imperial blessings dispensed by Great Britain:

> 'She sent us the preacher, she sent us the bottle.
> She sent us the Bible, and barrels of brandy.
> She sent us the breech-loader, she sent us cannon.
> O roaring Britain! Which must we embrace?'

More than a decade later, a similar fiery oration was to electrify the schoolboy Nelson Mandela. But for the benefit of the Prince of Wales, Mqhayi concluded:

> 'You sent us the truth, denied us the truth;
> You sent us the life, deprived us of life;
> You sent us the light, we sit in the dark,
> Shivering, benighted, in the bright noonday sun.'

A (Stalinist) native republic

Throughout the flag crisis, Bill Rostron was still in charge of printing the Communist Party newspaper, *The South African Worker*. When the compromise Union flag was hoisted for the first time in May 1927, most whites applauded it as welcome evidence of white unity. The Communist Party denounced this new national emblem as 'a symbol of the unity of Boer and British imperialism'.

Still small, the party had nevertheless grown. In a few years, under the leadership of Sidney Bunting, membership had risen from a mere 200 to 1,750 by 1928, 1,600 of them black Africans. But that was the year which saw an abrupt lurch in ideology, leading to doctrinal fanaticism, personal vilification campaigns, and finally the purging of some of the most dedicated party members.

Until then Moscow had largely left the local party alone. But in 1928, the Executive Committee of the Communist International (Comintern) in Moscow ordered the Communist Party of South Africa to adopt a new dogma, known as the 'Native Republic'. In fact, the slogan ordered by Moscow was not quite so catchy: 'An independent native South African republic as a stage towards a workers' and peasants' republic, with full, equal rights for all races, black, coloured and white.' This remains the official creed today of the renamed South African Communist Party, though now it trades under the slogan 'the two-stage theory of revolution'.

The directive from Moscow divided party leaders in Johannesburg. The majority, led by Bunting, objected that the new slogan represented a deviation from classic Marxist class struggle into an unpredictable form of black nationalism. Bunting argued that the 'Native Republic' policy would cause division within the working-class, as it did not appear to be directed against capitalists, but to be aimed at working-class whites – because they were white. A minority in favour of the Moscow line were led by an emigrant couple from England, Douglas and Molly Wolton. Douglas Wolton maintained that the black masses might not understand 'Workers of the World Unite', and so needed a slogan that would reach out to them as blacks.

The party decided to present both positions to the sixth conference of the Comintern. Bunting travelled to Moscow with his wife Rebecca to deliver the majority report in person. They were accompanied by their young friend Eddie Roux. The trio received a tremendous shock. Arriving in July 1928, the Buntings were informed by a high-ranking official, 'We are going to attack you!'

The Comintern congress was presided over by Nikolai Bukharin, the leading Bolshevik intellectual, who demanded that the role of national liberation and anti-colonial struggles now be accorded precedence. Yet even as he enforced this strategy ruthlessly, Bukharin knew that he was slipping from Stalin's favour himself. The following year he was stripped both of his position in the Politburo and of the editorship of *Pravda*. Ten years later, after one of the most outlandish of Stalin's show trials, Bukharin was executed with a bullet to the head.

Although Bunting thought this Moscow-imposed strategy was 'verbiage', returning to Johannesburg he determined to support the policy publicly. But the thoughtful, bookish Bunting was no match for Stalinist intolerance. Dissent, even if privately expressed, was to be crushed. This new 'Bolshevik' drive, led by the Woltons, aimed to exorcise all 'right-wing, social democrat elements'.

The doctrinaire Molly Wolton took Stalin's hypothesis so literally that she ended up endorsing a quasi-apartheid approach. Stalin contended that the nation is a community with a common language and culture. Loyally applying his logic, Molly concluded that with different tribal and linguistic groups in South Africa there was not one single nation in the making, but several. Accordingly, she proposed that their slogan should be modified to 'a Federation of Independent Native Republics'.

Faced with such convoluted dialectical diktats, the local Communist Party was not merely ideologically split, but began to unravel rapidly.

Smash the imperialist bloodsucker

In 1931 Sidney Bunting took part in a May Day march, which inevitably passed by Johannesburg's Rand Club. The following morning the *Rand Daily Mail* headline boomed 'Communists Rush Rand Club', reporting that club members watched from the upper floors as marchers tried to storm the entrance but that Mr Freeman, the hall porter, helped repel the mob. At the subsequent trial of a march organiser accused of inciting violence, Bunting appeared as a defence witness to deny that there any been any disorder. 'We got to the Rand Club, which has long been a stopping place for such processions,' he explained to the court. 'As far back as 1907, I can remember, they have always stopped at the Rand Club to give a boo or to offer execration.'

The *Rand Daily Mail* editorial the day after the protest had not taken such a jaunty view. 'It was a puzzled Johannesburg which watched a bedraggled procession in which dirty-looking natives of the lowest class marched shoulder-to-shoulder with Europeans, many of them of obvious low mentality,' growled the voice of the establishment.

My maternal grandfather may have been lunching in the Rand Club at the time of the fracas. The editorial denouncing the march echoed his orotund style: 'For some time past these "hot gospellers" have been allowed to preach their inflammatory doctrine without let or hindrance, and the question now arises whether decisive steps should be taken to put an end to their poisonous activities.'

Denouncing 'European mischief-makers', the editorial sounded a call to action. 'The breaking down of the social barrier between black and white is a serious development that cannot be lightly regarded,' it thundered. 'If the law as it stands is not adequate to deal with these people it must be amended so that they may get their just desserts. The white Bolshevik is bad enough. The black one is unthinkable.'

During his cross-examination, Bunting was asked if he was a

member of the Communist Party, to which he gave the dramatic reply, 'I understand that today I am not a member.' He had discovered that morning, from a newspaper account, that he had been expelled. The *Rand Daily Mail* report was headlined 'Not Red Enough'.

Now the sectarian Stalinists really poured their bile on Bunting, probably because he was widely admired in the party and among trade unionists. With cartoon-like glee they heaped ever more ludicrous abuse on him. The mildest slight was that he was a 'social democrat'. He was a reformist, they alleged, representing a 'right-danger' that almost amounted to 'counter-revolutionary' activity. To cover all bases, however, it was additionally charged that he'd been infected by 'left-wing danger' too.

The party newspaper, renamed *Umsebenzi*, unleashed a flurry of smears, among which was the suggestion that Bunting was a government *agent provocateur*. He was called 'a white chauvinist' and referred to as 'Lord Bunting', or the 'imperialist bloodsucker Lord Bunting'. To complete the absurdity, 'Lord Bunting' was also accused of being in 'alliance with counter-revolutionary Trotskyism'.

The party devoured itself with doctrinal ferocity. Before long, Bunting's chief tormentors, the Woltons, returned to England leaving behind a riven and irrelevant organisation whose membership had dwindled to a rump of 150. The dedicated and reflective Bunting fought back with reason and pamphlets, again printed by Bill Rostron. But Bunting's health deteriorated badly and, with his wife Rebecca, he ended his days as caretaker of a block of flats in central Johannesburg.

The stifling city

Ironically, it is the Marxist Sidney Bunting that is the link between my grandfathers: Bill the printer and Lewis Rose the editor. My mother told me that despite Bunting's revolutionary convictions and her father's denunciations of his party in the *Rand Daily Mail*, Lewis Rose respected Bunting, and in 1939 employed his son Brian, a prominent Communist himself, as a sub-editor. Earlier, when Bunting had published pamphlets to defend himself after his expulsion from the Communist Party, he had gone back to (in the words of his other son Arthur) 'an old-timer called Rostron'.

That the Communist Bunting and conservative Lewis Rose should know each other was not so surprising in the restricted white cosmos of Johannesburg. London-born Bunting had been to Oxford, and his father had been a prominent English editor and reformer. The divide in white society was class and snobbery.

As a young woman, my mother found it stultifying. For my father Frank, from a more flexible class, the city seemed exhilarating as he mixed with flashy entrepreneurs as well as boxers, gold prospectors and chancy characters lurking at the edge of the law.

'There was still a feverish gold-rush mentality,' he told me. 'Things changed with dizzying speed. Buildings shot up or were hurriedly torn down. Some made fortunes overnight, while a seemingly respectable businessman would vanish without trace and you'd discover that the police were after them.' Minor gold claims were established by marking out an area with pegs after a gun was fired; and as an athletic teenager Frank had been hired by an overweight, red-faced prospector to take part in just such a race – in order to stake the older man's claim within the strict time limit.

In more stodgy society, with cheap black labour so abundant, it was high status to employ white servants. My mother recalled the sniggering about women who had arrived from England as 'governesses' and married well. Her father, despite a modest pedigree of Scottish emigrants, scoffs in his memoir that touring theatrical companies 'were for many years a fine recruiting ground for the rich young men – and some of the rich old men too.' And he sniffs archly that 'One Governor-General, whose name in charity I shall suppress, threw his net rather wider than tradition demanded, and on one occasion caught the wife of a man occupying a public position, whose social life in London seemed to have been limited to the saloon bar of the corner pub.'

The Rostrons, in contrast, lived on a tight budget, and my father paid for the last years of his education with his freelance journalistic earnings. After Bill abandoned home, his relationship with Annie irretrievable, Frank refused to speak to him again. One day Bill turned up to see his son at the *Star* office, where Bill had once unionised 100 per cent of print workers, but Frank had him thrown out of the building.

Big, booming, boastful

The only domestic discord at the Macleod's grand home, it seems, was the insecurity of Lewis Rose's spinster sister. Though social secretary to Lady Phillips, Cloudie had to live with her brother and his family for the rest of her life as the eternally dependent, and thus perhaps resentful, relative. She threw tantrums and dissolved into histrionic tears at the smallest perceived slight. She made my grandmother, Trixie, so miserable that Granny later asked my mother 'Do you think I'm a bad person? When Cloudie died, I was so happy.'

Lewis Rose entertained royally at Dunvegan, which was inevitably a stopover for visiting dignitaries. In 1929 E.M. Foster stayed with them, but Barbara's only memory is that the bashful novelist locked himself in the lavatory and couldn't get out.

Lewis Rose indulged his own literary aspirations by writing doggerel. In a battered leather folder, I recently found sheaves of four-line rhymes, all meticulously dated. In these squibs he displays a less stuffy attitude. The first is called *Friendship*:

> 'I like Herbert, he likes me,
> Closer friends could scarcely be.
> I know enough to make him swing –
> Oh, friendship is a precious thing!'

Of *A Novelist*, he pronounces:
> 'He mucks about with people's lives,
> For him there are no faithful wives;
> His heroines must be seduced.
> For thus bestsellers are produced.'

And in *MP* he sighs:
> 'The politician – look at him
> Big, booming, boastful, full of vim.
> For me he always does the trick –
> That is to say, he makes me sick.'

The racial psychosis that haunted the country rarely punctured this privileged cocoon. When it did, the cause was usually a sexual phobia. Barbara and her mother were driving home through the countryside when, well away from the strip road, they saw a lone black man peeing behind a bush. A farm truck approached from the other direction and suddenly pulled over. 'It was an Afrikaans farmer with a very fat wife,' recalled my mother. 'The farmer leapt out and began beating the African viciously and when I tried to intervene, he kept screaming that this black man had insulted his wife.'

The *Rand Daily Mail* supported the United Party, which in 1936 introduced The Representation of Natives Bill, summarily eliminating the tiny quota of black Africans from the common voters' roll. They were displaced to an entirely separate electoral roll: one still restricted to males only, as well as educational and property qualifications, but now strictly defined solely by their colour. The bill stipulated that to represent them, this very limited number of black males could elect three whites to the House of Assembly and four whites to the Senate; ensuring, judged General Smuts in a blithe state of whiteout, 'the main elements of justice and fair play for all concerned'.

The Olympics of white supremacy

As Bill Rostron had forsaken home, Frank bought out his father's interest in the small bungalow at La Rochelle. He continued to win boxing trophies as a middleweight and, as a medium-fast bowler, played in the Transvaal cricket league. During his 20s my father covered almost the entire gamut of journalistic roles for *The Star*. Aged 25, he was dispatched to cover the 1932 Olympic Games in Los Angeles, where one night my mother told me (with what I thought was a slight tic of irritation) he danced with Norma Shearer, the leading Hollywood vamp of the day.

Two years later *The Star* sent him to London to report on the Empire Games. Both in Los Angeles and London, Frank had also acted as the manager of the South African boxing team. So when the paper selected him to cover the 1936 Olympic Games in Berlin, my father was again asked to manage the South African boxing squad – though this time with far more dramatic results.

These Olympics were designed as a showcase for Nazism. Special attention was lavished on the South African boxing team. 'Party invitations flowed like confetti,' Frank wrote. 'From Joseph Goebbels, the sinister Minister of Propaganda, from the Deputy Führer Rudolf Hess, and from the head of the Hitler Youth Baldur von Schirach, who showed me personally over one of his youth camps. Then came what subsequently proved to be a loaded bomb. I received a letter from a very high government official, a Dr Leibbrandt, who said that he had read an article of mine about a boxer/physical culture crank, Robey Leibbrandt, who dieted on charcoal, slept on hard boards, and rejoiced in similar austerities.'

Robey Leibbrandt was the star of the South African team. Of German-Irish extraction, he wasn't just a self-discipline zealot, but an ardent Afrikaner nationalist. The official who'd contacted Frank was Dr Georg Leibbrandt, a prominent Nazi. During the war, as a director in the Reich Ministry for Occupied Eastern Territories, he attended the 1942 Wannsee Conference: one of 15 Nazis gathered to coordinate a 'final solution' for the extermination of the Jews.

In his letter, wrote Frank, Dr Leibbrandt asked, 'Would I bring Leibbrandt to lunch as he, the Herr Doctor, had a long-lost brother who had emigrated to South Africa and he might be related. At the same time, he was authorised to say Joseph Goebbels would agree to a personal interview with Hitler – then most journalists' dream.'

My father's version that he 'smelt a rat' in this offer – an interview with Hitler to a young sports writer for a distant Johannesburg daily – was contradicted by my mother. She quietly said that Frank was furious when his editor cabled back to say that the Nazis clearly intended to use him to make propaganda for the return of the former German colony, then governed by South Africa under a mandate imposed by the Treaty of Versailles. Frank was tersely instructed to decline the proposed interview.

Unsurprisingly, Dr Georg Leibbrandt was not related to the South African boxer. He had been tasked to recruit the German-speaking nationalist to the Nazi cause.

Fight to the death

In the ring Robey Liebbrandt won his first two bouts, but during the quarter-final he hit his Czech opponent so hard that Leibbrandt broke a bone in his right hand. Frank tried to obtain consent for the South African to have a pain-killing injection for his next contest but with only 10 minutes to go, permission was withheld. Leibbrandt's right hand was so swollen that his glove had to be slit open for it to fit. Even so, it proved a close fight. Much of the crowd thought Leibbrandt had won. Able to punch only with his left, Frank's report in *The Star* recorded that Leibbrandt 'fought a remarkable one-handed contest against a moderately good Frenchman tonight. He was the victim of a doubtful decision.' The Frenchman went on to win the Olympic title.

The Nazis had meanwhile arranged for the former world heavy-weight champion Max Schmeling to 'drop in' on the South African team and chat to Leibbrandt. 'But the penny didn't drop till several years after the Games,' Frank admitted. 'When I went to Nuremberg to report on the stupendous *Reichsparteitag*, the annual rally of the Nazi Party, who should I meet by accident but a battered Robey Leibbrandt? He was living like a lord as an *Ehrengast* (honoured guest) on Hitler's special train.'

After this, 'Leibbrandt disappeared'. In fact, the boxer was study-ing at the Reich Academy for Gymnastics, and then joined the Germany army where he trained alongside Max Schmeling as a glider pilot and parachutist. Finally, Leibbrandt was also sent on a sabotage course.

On graduating he was assigned a mission to infiltrate South Africa, personally authorised by Hitler. He was to initiate a sabotage campaign to encourage Afrikaner nationalists to rise up against the contested decision, at the outbreak of the Second World War, for the Union to join the fight against Germany. The object of *Operation Weissdorn* was to assassinate Prime Minister Smuts, organise a *coup d'état*, and install a Christian National Socialist government.

A 22-metre racing yacht was requisitioned and after five weeks at sea, Leibbrandt was landed on the deserted shores of Namaqualand. 'Loaded with dollars, elaborate radio transmission equipment and explosives,' wrote Frank, 'for months, he led the authorities a dance, blowing up railway lines, pylons and bridges and transmitting information to *Zeesen*, the German propaganda radio.' After eight months, during which he recruited a small army of fighters, including dozens of policemen, Leibbrandt was captured and charged with high treason.

'The oddest twist of half a lifetime of reporting,' continued Frank, 'is that the *Daily Express* should have sent me in 1942 as a foreign correspondent back to South Africa – so I was able to attend his trial in Pretoria. Leibbrandt continuously gave the Nazi salute and howled Nazi propaganda from the dock. Suddenly, he spotted me in the press box. Despite his threatening me with violence at our last meeting, and with accompanying warders struggling to silence him, he shouted, "Hello Führer, what the hell are you doing here?" I was jokingly called "Führer" by the Olympic boxing squad because in Berlin my lapel badge read *Mannschaftsführer* (team leader).' My father concluded, 'I was deeply moved when this once glorious athlete, who posed for artists, was sentenced to be hanged, as to me he was plainly a mental case.'

On being condemned Leibbrandt gave a Nazi salute and yelled 'I greet death!' But he wasn't executed. On the basis that the boxer's father had fought bravely in the Boer War, Prime Minister Smuts commuted his sentence to life imprisonment.

London calling

In the summer that my father was covering the 1936 Olympics, my mother Barbara appeared in a season of Shakespeare plays in London. The disparity between their circles was vast. Just as Frank was mixing with prize-fighters and Nazis, a card for 'Miss Macleod' arrived from Buckingham Palace allotting her a prime viewing point on Horse Guards Parade for the funeral procession of King George V. This was organised by Alix, who after her marriage to Major General Wulff Grey had grand social connections.

Barbara, 18, 'presented' at court

There is a much earlier royal invitation, this time from the Lord Chamberlain, 'commanded by Their Majesties to summon Miss Barbara Macleod to a Court at Buckingham Palace'. That was when my mother and her sister, Betty, had visited London in 1931, and Alix arranged for them to be 'presented' at court: an arcane ritual whereby high-born 'gels', in Alix's strangulated diction, would line up and curtsy to the monarch. There is a formal photograph of my mother, aged 18, in a satin gown with a long, snowy white mantle cascading behind her, obeying the Lord Chamberlain's directive of 'Court Dress with feathers and trains'.

Most astounding, though, is that Barbara chose to be an actress at all. Having suffered so badly from 'nerves', she didn't go to school till she was 12. But despite being intensely private, my mother was determined and disciplined; into her 90s she learned a poem a day in order to keep her mind active. Looking back, I wonder if she resolved to overcome her own crippling shyness by going on stage.

Her father objected vehemently. Lewis Rose kept a pocket-sized notebook to jot down sub-Oscar Wilde aphorisms. His distinctly un-Wildean attitude to women on the stage can be gauged by his attempt at a breezy man-about-town epigram: 'All lost girls found wandering in a wood are beautiful, unless it happens to be St John's Wood, when of course they are merely actresses. Actresses too are beautiful, but not until they have appeared in the Divorce Court in the capacity of co-respondent.'

That was still the warped attitude of Lewis Rose's many respectable male friends in London, to whom he wrote introductory letters to help Barbara on her way. She was shocked when these apparently upright gents, all married, generously offered to take this lovely young colonial 'gel' to dinner or fashionable nightclubs, and then, almost to a man, brazenly propositioned their old friend's daughter, less than half their age.

In South Africa, after her father relented, Barbara's first acting contract, aged 19, was to play a 'maid' at His Majesty's Theatre, where 28 years before, Lewis Rose's musical comedy *The Girl From Springfontein* had been performed. But she was still desperate to escape the stifling social coop of Johannesburg. There was, too, that other South African contagion which she found increasingly unbearable.

Shortly before she died, aged 92, my mother seemed very shaken and confessed that she'd had a nightmare. It was a memory, and had so upset her that I wrote it down.

'When I was about 14 we had a servant called Jim who had a small Pomeranian dog,' she said. 'Jim used to make it sit up in the blazing sun for half an hour at a time. I cried. I begged him to stop.

But Jim shouted 'That's what white people do to us!'

A son's late reckoning

Soon after I began to burrow into our family's past, and pressing my mother for more memories, I became aware that she seemed increasingly reticent. Was I intruding too much, or was there some dank secret that Barbara feared I might discover? So I made my mother a

Frank, the stylish reporter

promise, 'If that's what worries you, and I do stumble on some appalling family outrage, I will abandon this venture.' Happily, it's a pledge I have been able to honour. Although I have exhumed secrets and mysteries, I've not unearthed anything horrendously or shamefully scandalous; at least not by today's garish exhibitionism. Only after her death, for example, did I discover the truth behind our founding family myth: rather than being eaten, as she herself told me, Captain Wallis had sailed away from Tahiti in *HMS Dolphin*, rendered almost unseaworthy as his crew had swopped nails for sex. Barbara would have found that, I'm sure, absurdly funny.

Or was she anxious in case I might uncover the caustic prejudices of her father? As Barbara had not yet been born when Lewis Rose was pronouncing his most virulent imprecations against 'niggers' and 'half-castes', it is unlikely that she knew the worst. By the time that she was an adult, her father's views had moderated. Also, my mother was never shy about facing up to awkward truths.

No, I suspect the reason for her reticence was that Barbara was an exceptionally private person, and had been brought up to consider that talking about oneself was appallingly boorish. Following my pledge, my mother demurred no further, and since her death there have been many days when I wished that I could confide my latest discoveries – such as the claim by William Moncur, her grandfather, that his brother introduced the crawl stroke.

After returning to Australia in 1863, the brothers heard that Fred Beckwith, an English swimming champion, was boasting that he had created the popular new 'side crawl'. William Moncur was so affronted that, as a magistrate, he had an affidavit drawn up insisting that his younger brother, James, had demonstrated this novel stroke to Beckwith during a visit to Kent in 1855. The row was summed up by the headline in a Sydney paper: 'A disputed honour; Australia's claim'. My great-grandfather's irate affidavit reveals, though, that they had copied this stroke, 'from a darkey … as far back as 1851'.

In fact, overarm strokes had been employed by the ancient Assyrians and Greeks. But if anyone could lay claim to spreading the 'side-arm' style to England, precursor to the crawl, it was an anonymous Aboriginal lad.

Barbara would have understood that this was a minor, but telling, illustration of the pervasive imperial sense of prerogative in 'appropriating' whatever they wanted from 'darkies'. Nevertheless, while that is a long time ago and verified in print, the original dilemma remains: what is the justification for invading the privacy of a parent?

In this, I resolved to follow the example of the overweight and middle-aged Marie-Henri Beyle, better known as the great French novelist Stendhal. In the 1830s, lonely and in bad health, Stendhal wrote an audaciously frank autobiography, the idiosyncratic *The Life of Henry Brulard*. Much of the early narrative concerns Stendhal's loathing of his materialistic lawyer father, Chérubin Beyle. But of his 'dearest mother', Henriette, who died young, and his much-loved grandfather, Stendhal jotted another note on the manuscript: 'December 1835. I alone think of them today, and with what tenderness towards my mother, who has been dead for forty-six years. So I can speak freely of their faults.' He adds, 'My right to put down these memories: what human being does not love to be remembered by someone?'

Adrift on the map

By 1937, when Frank resigned from *The Star* and made his way to London, Barbara had already played a number of small parts in the West End. For Frank, the major shock in London was the sight of the long queues of unemployed white men. 'In South Africa,' he admitted, 'the very fact of being one of the two and a half million whites, who rest as an upper crust on nine million blacks, made one a species of aristocrat.'

He was offered a job as a sub-editor on *The Times*, whose editor Geoffrey Dawson (formerly Robinson when he had edited *The Star*) was doing his utmost to never print anything negative about the Nazis. '*The Times* has the air of a cathedral, no voices raised, not even the clatter of typewriters,' recalled Frank. This was far too stuffy for the energetic young colonial, and he soon talked his way into a job at the *Daily Express*: brash, fast-paced, and then boasting the largest circulation in the world.

One of his first assignments was an audacious publicity stunt: an exhibition fight with the towering former world heavyweight champion Primo Carnera. The British boxing authorities were questioning whether the Italian was punch-drunk, and the *Express* spotted the opportunity of a marketing coup in promoting a 'try out'. Carnera's manager agreed to three rounds, and after being widely advertised, several hundred people paid one shilling to see this bout at the Blackfriars Arena, the only boxing ring in the world to have once been a church. Also present, to Frank's horror, were newsreel cameras and rival reporters.

'He knocked me sideways once or twice,' wrote Frank. 'But the big chap was never a fast thinker. I got cocky and impulsively let go a pivot punch. It was an ancient punch but had been banned as dangerous. This involved whirling in a circle and depended on split-second timing. If your opponent counter-punched while your back was to him, you'd only learn about it later. But if successful it can mean the delivery of a fearsome backhander. By sheer luck I caught my ponderous

Frank takes on former world champion Primo Carnera

target slap on the kisser, about my only solid punch of the affray. Carnera blinked, then joined in the crowd's laughter. But I heard his manager hiss, 'He's trying to make you look a mug. Go for him!' After that, I sprinted out of range till the third and final bell.'

This couldn't be more different from the stolid tempo at *The Times*. In April 1938, Frank described his 'helterskelter' routine: 'On Tuesday I flew back to London from Hamburg, and by eight the following morning raced back to Germany, this time to Berlin for Hitler's birthday party, to which I had received an invitation because I had been an official at the Olympic Games two years earlier.'

In the same year, Barbara returned to South Africa to star in a play. 'Miss Macleod played the part with a poise that was nearly perfect,' judged one review. 'She should not be wasting her time here.' But now, more than ever, she was finding the stultifying affectations of genteel white society in Johannesburg intolerable.

Towards the end of 1938 in the Eastern Cape, unnoticed by the outside world, there was another pivotal event. The *imbongi* Krune Mqhayi was invited to Healdtown, a Methodist school near Fort Beaufort. In front of the stern, extremely patriotic British headmaster, the Rev. Dr Arthur Wellington, he gave another bold and subversive display. One of the pupils, in his final year, was Nelson Mandela.

Mqhayi wore his leopard skin kaross

My mother, the elegant young actress

and carried a spear in each hand. The effect, recalled Mandela in his autobiography, was electrifying: 'It seemed to turn the universe upside down.' Mqhayi told the rapt Xhosa high school students 'For too long we have succumbed to the false gods of the white man.' Mandela could hardly believe his ears. 'His boldness in speaking of such delicate matters in the presence of Dr Wellington and other whites seemed utterly astonishing to us,' he confessed. 'We rose to our feet, clapping and cheering. I did not want ever to stop applauding.'

A call to arms

Days after war broke out in Europe in September 1939, Prime Minister Hertzog insisted that South Africa remain neutral. During a debate in parliament, however, he veered into what appeared to be a defence of Hitler, and as a result narrowly lost the vote. Jan Smuts formed a new government and declared South Africa to be at war with Germany. Smuts was soon invited to join the Imperial War Cabinet in London, and was made a Field Marshall. But the bitter political split in South Africa was to have lasting consequences. Many Nazi sympathisers among Afrikaner nationalists were interned for the duration of the war, but they subsequently emerged triumphant with the election of the National Party in 1948.

After the war my father was asked to write a book about his escapades as a war correspondent. My mother said that he never completed it because Frank always needed the pressure of a deadline to write. But the surviving fragments reveal a side to my father that had been kept hidden from me. Aside from a reporter's energy and guile, there was compassion and raw courage.

He crisscrossed the world, covering many of the major theatres of war: from North Africa and the Middle East, through to Italy and the Normandy landings. Frank was among the first to witness the release of emaciated prisoners of war from Japanese camps, and – most hair-raising of all – covered the mayhem of the independence war in Java (Indonesia), during which he was commended in dispatches as 'quite fearless'.

Early in his uncompleted memoir, my father mentions his discomfort as a journalist at the number of personal pronouns creeping into his account. 'Spare my blushes by not counting how many "I's" there are,' he pleaded, a misgiving with which I identify as I write now.

Nevertheless, Frank recounted that at first, shortly after the outbreak of war, he was seconded from the *Daily Express* to the BBC, and was on duty the night in May 1941 when Hitler's deputy Rudolf Hess parachuted from a Messerschmitt fighter-bomber near Glasgow. Hess, whom Frank had met in Berlin, was on his own bizarre (and still mysterious) peace mission from Germany. Frank was instructed to phone 10 Downing Street and have Churchill woken with the news.

In South Africa, my mother's photo was plastered up in posters all over the country with the slogan 'I joined up – why don't you?' She starred in a propaganda film about women taking part in the war effort, then enlisted with 'The Bandoliers', a South African army entertainment unit. Her diaries track their erratic travels, often on shot-up transport planes, to Egypt, Tripoli, Palestine, Lebanon, Damascus and Baghdad. One entry reads: 'So he's dead and I've lost another friend. I can't weep anymore, they're all going so quickly and I'm being left behind.'

On the other hand, another diary entry notes, 'Captain X has asked if he can come to our tent tonight. Oh God, not another bloody proposal!'

Her father, Lewis Rose, died in 1941 while still editor of the *Rand Daily Mail*. His funeral was attended by a huge crowd and most of the city's dignitaries. A front-page report noted that, 'There were also present representatives of the Indian and native communities.' There was no explanation for their unexpected attendance, but Lewis Rose's racial views had clearly softened and all who recorded memories of him remarked on his civility to everyone. Frank's mother, Annie, died two years later, virtually unnoticed. Frank had been briefly back in South Africa, but had been ordered abroad again. His mother reassured him she was fine and that he must go.

He did, and she died the next day.

A white man's indaba

In Cairo, Frank attended the trial of two Zionists, who in 1944 had assassinated Lord Moyne, the British Minister for the Middle East. On the first day he slipped out his Leica camera and surreptitiously took several snaps of the prisoners. Fearful that the quality would not be good enough for newspaper reproduction, Frank attempted another shot and was arrested. Pointing to his 'war correspond-ent' shoulder flashes, he convinced the court police that he was a VIP and should be taken to the presiding judge – who, not being informed that Frank had already taken half a dozen snaps, gave permission for one photograph to be taken during a court recess.

Frank raced to wire his photos to London and the next day received the verdict craved by every distant correspondent: a terse 'herogram' applauding, 'Splendid. Picture frontpaged.'

Both prisoners pleaded guilty, and surreptitiously handed Frank a handwritten 'confession' for publication. The pair were sentenced to hang and begged Frank, as the only person they knew in Cairo, to attend. The youngest came in first and, asked if he wished to say anything, replied, 'I want to make a protest about being hurried to a death sentence without being given time to put my best suit on.' (His companion, in turn, complained he had not been given time to shave.) As the noose was placed round the first Zionist's neck, he began singing in Hebrew until the trapdoor opened and 'a half-note strangled in the vocal cords as the vertebrae snapped, and in the silence there was only the gruesome flutter of the last twists of the sack-like body'.

At the outset of the First World War, a reader had written to the *East London Daily Dispatch*, for which Bill Rostron had done some printing, requesting that all white folk carefully explain to their servants and employees that the conflict was, 'A white man's *indaba*'. Any hint that they too might carry arms, he suggested, might give the natives 'ideas'. Although thousands of black and coloured South Africans served in wretchedly paid, non-combatant roles on the front lines during that war, suffering enormous casualties, the same standard was applied during the Second World War: no weapons.

By mid-1942, however, the situation looked desperate, and Prime Minister Smuts made a dramatic declaration in Parliament. 'Before Japan, before the enemy takes this country, I shall see to it that every coloured man who can be armed will be armed.' D.F. Malan replied that allowing 'kaffir soldiers' into a fight among white men threatened bloodshed in South Africa between 'white and non-white'.

In 1944, Smuts announced from London that the critical time had come to arm coloured soldiers, but back in South Africa his cabinet quietly resolved that his plan 'should not be proceeded with'. By then, 100,000 black and coloured South Africans were serving as drivers, batmen, trench-diggers, cooks and typists. None were allowed to bear arms: a prohibition for which I nearly paid with my life in Cape Town 25 years later, when a resentful, very stoned former member of the Native Labour Corps held a gun to my head, shouting angrily that he had picked up this German Luger from a battlefield in which 'you whities didn't even trust us to carry a bloody gun'.

But I have run ahead of myself. For such a threat to (eventually) galvanise me, my parents – as you will have guessed – must first meet.

A royal affair

Barbara was 35, Frank 40, when the *Daily Express* dispatched him to cover the royal tour of South Africa in 1947. It took place from February to April, at a time when drab, post-war Britain, with rationing still in force, was suffering an atrociously severe winter. Record snowfalls led to prolonged power cuts and devastating floods. In those grim conditions, the long, sunlit trip by George VI, his wife and two daughters, Elizabeth and Margaret, generated avid public interest, reflecting a late glow of imperial splendour. For although Britain was on the cusp of withdrawing from India, there was little domestic recognition that the sun was setting on the empire.

Instead, the regal visit was seen as an imperial reward for South African support during the war. Prime Minister Smuts, facing an election the following year, thought that a display of royal pomp might give him a boost. But unlike most English-speakers, Afrikaner nationalists were not impressed. When the royal cavalcade reached Pretoria, the sole mention in the newspaper *Die Transvaler*, edited by Hendrik Verwoerd, was that 'a certain Mr and Mrs Windsor' would disrupt the traffic.

Arriving in Cape Town, the Windsors boarded the sumptuous White Train for their 7,000-mile triumphal progress. Luxury carriages, ordered from Birmingham, had wood-panelled bedrooms, bathrooms and a dining car that could seat 24. Another train, not as opulent, travelled slightly ahead with the press corps, including my father.

The White Train stopped every night so that the sleep of the royal personages would not be troubled. Horses were brought to the train the next morning so that the princesses could enjoy a ride in the veld. At dawn one day, my father told me, two horses were brought to the White Train: the first for Princess Margaret, not quite 17, the other for the king's handsome equerry, the former fighter pilot, Peter Townsend. Meanwhile, a single horse was delivered to the other train for George Ward Price, the *Daily Mail's* correspondent who had gained fame for his access to Hitler. Ward Price waited to observe which route the teenage princess and her escort chose, then tactfully galloped in the opposite direction.

Such delicacy is inconceivable in this more intrusive age of celebrity gossip and telephoto lenses. What Ward Price deliberately missed was the stirring of a famous but ill-starred romance, which eight years later provoked a constitutional crisis when Princess Margaret was forbidden by her sister, by then Queen Elizabeth II, to marry the much older Group Captain Townsend, a divorced man.

At this point Frank received the cable that every far-flung correspondent dreads. Arthur Christiansen, the editor he revered, was blunt. 'Intense competition rival newspapers have unalternative but to send our best box office name James Cameron.' Cameron was already a star. The previous year his eyewitness dispatch of the United States' nuclear tests in the Pacific had shot him to prominence. A follow-up cable tried to mollify the disgruntled reporter in South Africa, reassuring Frank that the tour would be shared as a double act: 'Rely your magnanimity take it in good part.'

This uneasy journalistic two-hander reached a climax when the royal entourage returned to Cape Town at the end of their tour. For her birthday on 21 April, Princess Elizabeth planned a speech dedicating herself to serve 'our great Imperial family'. As heir to the throne, the *Daily Express* gave this special coverage. The canny Christiansen solved the problem of appeasing his egotistical correspondents by granting the right side of the editorial page to Rostron and the left to Cameron. My father wrote a straight news account: the presents to be opened at breakfast, a public holiday declared, fireworks and her speech to be broadcast live on radio to the empire.

Cameron, on the same page, produced the stylish pyrotechnics hoped for when he had been assigned. He began with a flourish: 'Princess Elizabeth today achieves her majority, a vote, £15,000 a year, and the congratulations of several million people who never saw her in their lives. It is quite a lot for one day.' He noted that in future she would be the nominal ruler of 100 million people across the globe – though never Empress of India. Then he listed other British colonies showing signs of restiveness, concluding that 'South Africa itself is a large and doubtful question mark.'

Love on the run

His remarks, swiftly relayed back to South Africa, caused a scandal. Cameron had dared to suggest that Elizabeth had been shielded from the country's racial problems. Yet despite being cocooned in the world's most lavish train for most of the epic tour, he wrote, the Princess was not a simpleton. 'She knows, for example, that of every five faces she saw in the procession of towns and villages throughout the Union four were black. She will have noticed that those four were always on the other side of the railings. She will have learned that the politics in South Africa are differentiated almost wholly by divergences of opinion on how to keep the native in his place.'

It was an unpardonable indiscretion to spoil this royal jamboree; to mention, as Cameron had done, 'racial problems, anti-monarchical propaganda, and the Ghost of Kruger'. He was denounced in the local press, which compared the cavalier Scotsman unfavourably with the locally-born Rostron – 'who', harrumphed one indignant Cape Town columnist, 'has forgotten more about South Africa than Cameron ever knew'.

With the tour drawing to a close, however, Frank had another worry.

In a souvenir 'Royal Tour' album, there's a photo of the King attending a reception at the start of the tour. George VI stands awkwardly on the garden steps at the Governor-General's Cape Town residence. A few metres behind is my mother, who had travelled from Johannesburg for the occasion. This is where Barbara first encountered my father. They soon met again in Johannesburg.

Finally returning to Cape Town on the accompanying 'royal' train, as the two-month tour drew to its conclusion, Frank's colleagues asked him what his plans were regarding the beautiful Barbara Macleod. One of them (perhaps my future, but entirely absentee godfather Ward Price) informed him that he would prove a bloody fool if he let such a wonderful woman escape. When they reached their destination Frank sent Barbara telegram.

'Please speed Cape Town soonest,' it requested. 'Important matters to discuss.'

Miss Macleod arrived the next day, with mother Trixie in tow as chaperone. Frank took Barbara, without her mother, to the grand Mount Nelson Hotel for dinner. 'He spent the next three hours telling me what an impossible person he was,' my mother told me. 'That he was egotistical, selfish, not domesticated, that he was married to the *Express*, travelled all the time – and was exactly the sort of man that no woman should ever consider marrying. Having made the position clear, he proposed.'

Consequently, as the great French novelist Stendhal remarks well into his own unconventional memoir: 'After all these general reflections, I'll proceed to get born.'

8

‭✝‬

OUTRIDERS OF EMPIRE

The inheritance of myth

MY MOTHER, BARBARA, liked to recount the dramatic story of how, when I was born in Johannesburg, a brief announcement about my modest debut had appeared in *The Star*, for which my father Frank had once worked as a young man. In response to the notice came a pitiful request from Frank's own father, to whom he hadn't spoken for over 20 years.

William Rostron was dying in a nearby hospital, said Barbara, and it was his final wish that my father forgive him and bring me to his bedside, so that William could set eyes upon his only grandchild before he died. My mother said that naturally she encouraged Frank to put aside all long-nursed bitterness and visit his father. But she put her foot down about him taking the new young Rostron.

'After all,' she would conclude indignantly, 'you were only a couple of days old!'

It's an affecting story. There's plenty of raw drama: a new babe, a dying man, the frantic plea for forgiveness. It was 1948, with a tense election in full swing, the result of which would change everything. Only Barbara's story isn't correct. In the national archives, years later, I discovered that William had died five years after my birth, in 1953. Indeed, in March 1952 there had been a court case against him. My notoriously cantankerous grandfather had bought a fish and chips shop called 'Benny and Phil's' – but failed to pay for it.

In April 1948, however, my mother had been lying in a hospital in Hillbrow, then a raffish, high-rise 'white' neighbourhood, which by the 1990s had become an unruly, poor, crime-racked black enclave. You can see why many years later Barbara might easily conflate in her memory all those emotive elements – my birth, a touching deathbed reunion – into one vivid scene. Most dramatic of all: a few weeks later the grim National Party swept to power, and ushered in the long nightmare of apartheid.

Entrances and exits

In May 1948 the National Party won the acrimonious general election, after campaigning on a vow of rigid racial segregation. Having emerged a pip-squeak before this calamity – a mere six weeks before the venom of apartheid entered the bloodstream of South Africa and the vocabulary of the world – I cannot be held totally responsible for it. Even so, I have most certainly benefited from the unearned privileges that flowed from a legislated righteousness imparted by my pigmentation.

The Nationalists' rise to power changed my parents' plans; not that long-term planning is the forte of newspaper correspondents. Their wedding had, in fact, been marked by the chaotic hithering-and-thithering that characterised their surprisingly successful marriage. At midnight, following his marriage proposal, my father had caught the 'King's flight' back to England to discuss his future with his editor. Two days later he hopped onto another royal flight back to Pretoria, having telegraphed his fiancée 'Please meet me for marriage appointment at Johannesburg Magistrates Court on

Saturday.'

But Barbara had not yet completed the return journey to Johannesburg. Overcoming bureaucratic hurdles, they married on the Monday. Frank forgot to book anywhere for their wedding night, and early the next morning he again caught a 'King's flight' back to England, leaving his new bride with her mother.

By 40, Frank had established a reputation as a swashbuckling correspondent. In September 1945 it had been extensively reported that the Japanese Admiral Shigeru Fukudome had attempted to surrender the Singapore naval base and Japanese fleet to Frank and another correspondent when they arrived an hour before the official British envoys. In 1947, of Frank's frenetic wedding schedule, the *Sydney Morning Herald* recorded that 'He recently established an air passenger record by making the flight between London and South Africa three times in 15 days, and thus flying a total distance of 19,500 miles.' A British Sunday paper also pointed out that he'd even made a profit from this huge mileage: for while royal flights were free for royal tour correspondents, Frank had won handsomely at poker during those long trips.

On one of his hasty visits back to London, the editor of the *Daily Express* offered Frank what had once been the job of his dreams: a daily sports column. But 'despising sport after an exciting war', he turned down this prestigious niche. With the prospect of marriage, my peripatetic father, deluding himself that he might be cut out for a more sedate life, resolved to return to South Africa and open a news agency. He was brimming with optimism.

The Johannesburg *Sunday Times* even commissioned a special feature ('A Globe-trotting journalist sees …') under the buoyant headline: 'South Africa as Land of Peace in a Discordant World'. 'What a country,' concluded Frank, 'if only we South Africans could stop making the most of our internal trouble ourselves.' And he was confident that this too was about to change for the better.

A change of plan

In pursuit of this dream my mother, who had followed Frank to London, sailed back alone on a cargo boat, heavily pregnant. The sea was rough, the ship's doctor drunk. He'd stare at her stomach and slur, 'Just keep the bloody thing in.' My iron-willed mother pulled off that feat as far as Cape Town, then conveyed her bulging freight by train to Johannesburg, just as my father flew in – as usual, at the very last minute. Six weeks later came the election of a political party many of whose leaders had hoped for a German victory. One of the first acts of the new government was to free the former boxer Robey Leibbrandt, condemned in 1942 as a traitor.

While racial segregation had been the policy of both main political parties, many returning servicemen, after fighting fascism, probably expected a gradual evolution towards black African rights. Yet having fought for 'freedom' in Europe, only a minority of whites thought at the time to apply the same standards in their own country.

Nevertheless my father was optimistic that South Africa would steadily become more tolerant. Mere pigmentation has made the white man an aristocrat, Frank had written the previous year, leaving blacks to take the strain of hard labour and menial tasks. But the victory of the National Party shocked him deeply. The brutal advent of apartheid, however, has largely obscured other unpalatable realities. Many of the outlines of apartheid thinking had been in place almost from the start of European settlement nearly 300 years before. Ever since, exploitation had been extended and expanded. Consequently, during the first half of the twentieth century the creed of racial separation was actively encouraged, ruthlessly rationalised and legally codified, first by the mining magnates and then by the Milner administration: agents, official and unofficial, of the British Empire.

Frank had proudly declared himself 'the complete Empire citizen'. In this he followed Jan Smuts, the Boer general who, having fought the British during the Boer War, became their greatest ally. In the First World War, Smuts served in the British War Cabinet. In 1941, after joining the Imperial War Cabinet, a contingency plan endorsed by George VI proposed that if Churchill became incapacitated, Smuts should lead the Allied war effort.

Frank knew Smuts reasonably well. Early in the war he had been in Smuts' office for the Prime Minister to sign a letter requesting military authorities 'to render every help' to the war correspondent. Smuts left his office briefly and Frank, who had learned to read upside down while setting type in his father's printing works, read the communiqué on Smuts' desk. It contained classified battle orders. So Frank knew where to head with his new letter of authorisation, ahead of any newspaper rivals.

Smuts had written a book, *Holism and Evolution*, to expound his belief that it is 'the tendency in nature to form wholes that are greater than the sum of their parts'. In an interview with Frank, Smuts explained, 'That is why I continue to say Britain and the Commonwealth have evolved the most successful experiment in history, which is the best influence for good in the world and offers civilisation's best leadership.'

A small man who once bestrode international affairs, Smuts failed to get to grips with his country's major predicament. Following his election defeat, Frank began to see the flaws of his hero. 'In the Empire most of us had been brought up to accept an artificial scheme of society whereby all whites were established securely above the black for no other virtue than being white,' he wrote. But he was under no illusions about the future under apartheid. 'The Nationalists are expunging the faint glimmerings of liberalism nurtured by the English and during the sort of benevolent despotism of General Smuts.'

At that moment, Frank received a telegram from the *Daily Express* offering him the plumb job of chief cricket correspondent. More urgently, it pleaded with him to cover the Olympic Games, due to begin in London within a few weeks: the first Olympics since the 1936 fiasco with Leibbrandt. So directly after the birth of his only child, Frank flew to London. As he was due to return shortly with the English cricket team for their 1948–1949 tour of South Africa, my mother and I stayed with my Granny Trixie in Johannesburg. This set the tone for most of their married life. While not on the scale of Captain Wallis' epic circumnavigation, my parents continued that pattern of incessant and restless travel.

Boy in limbo

Most of my peripatetic childhood is a blur: a cheerful haze of what I remember, and what I imagine I remember but was told by adults or have subsequently read. Perhaps I should look once more to Marie-Henri Beyle (Stendhal). In the 1830s, he embarked on his audacious memoir, and although the manuscript lay neglected for nearly 50 years, incomplete and unrevised, it retains an exhilarating freshness. At one point he confesses, 'so far as my childhood is concerned I only have very clear impressions without *dates* or *likenesses*. I write them down more or less as they occur to me.'

My mother told me that I didn't celebrate a birthday on land till I was seven. We were constantly travelling with the English cricket team to South Africa or Australia by mail ship. So like the two generations before me, though at an early age, I was split between the 'mother country' and its distant outposts. I still have a pile of yellowing certificates issued in the name of 'King Neptune' to attest that as a boy I crossed the Equator by sea more times than Vasco da Gama. The first was awarded on the day before my first birthday on the *TSS Umtali* as we sailed to England, and commands that 'all whales, sharks, crustaceans, etc., must refrain from molesting or otherwise taking liberties with his person'. A year later, as we headed for Australia on the *SS Stratheden*, another fading and torn scroll prohibited 'all kippers, haddocks and other denizens of the deep from molesting him'.

It occurs to me now that only former 'white' colonies, Australia and South Africa, were deemed wholesome enough for a late imperial lad, since I was never taken to the other cricket playing Commonwealth nations like the West Indies, Pakistan or India.

Instead, on those occasions, my mother and I would return to Johannesburg for the summer to stay with Granny Trixie.

With the blithe assurance of a man entirely engrossed in his job, my father remarked in an article how pleasant it was for his wife and infant son to travel with him, apparently unaware how difficult it would be for a new mother to uproot twice a year, sail to the southern hemisphere, find accommodation and a new school, then repeat the whole operation six months later in London. At one point I was pictured in the *Daily Express*, about to enter a taxi for another journey, clutching by its tattered furry foot the 'most travelled teddy bear in the world'.

Sometimes during British winters, while Frank toured abroad, my mother and I stayed with Granny Trixie for several months at a time. It was a childhood of perpetual summer, and Granny Trixie's bungalow seemed to me, despite the scorched lawn, like the Garden of Eden.

My globe-trotting teddy bear

The map of memory

Set against that luminous sunshine there was always a shadow: darkening, lengthening and sinister. So, my map of childhood is almost entirely illusory. The official map had been redrawn, aiming to show that South Africa was a white nation and that black

Africans should be restricted to designated areas. The advent of apartheid prompted a frenzy of map-making. Ethnographers and cartographers attempted to demarcate hitherto fluid patchworks of tribal entities, some of which had never existed.

On my own miniature map of 15 Cradock Avenue in Rosebank, there's the stoep where Granny Trixie sits all day. Tucked away at the side is the 'maid's room'. The stoep, though shaded, is filled with light, while the maid's cramped room is perplexingly dark, even at noon. The two remain entirely separate. Even so, I am vaguely aware that the maid's largely hidden world is linked to the local police station, from where my mother always returns cursing softly about permits.

Barbara also spends some afternoons in the township of Orlando. It is, she explains, a scheme to teach African women skills, from cooking to dressmaking. Sometimes she took me with her. I remember a cavernous community centre with women seated on uncomfortable chairs listening to the white lady. Most vivid is the day that she parks outside a tin shack. My mother stands outside talking to adults while I wander inside. It's alarmingly dark. Flies buzz round my head. As my eyes focus, I can make out that the cramped room is almost filled by an enormous bed. Several children squat on the floor.

They stare in astonishment at the skinny white boy. Finally their eyes swivel back to the huge bed. I follow their gaze. Under layers of blankets, in the oppressive heat of a Highveld summer afternoon, lies an elderly black women. Her eyes meet mine vacantly. Even though several flies hover round her eyes, she doesn't blink. But I'm sure she doesn't see me. It's like staring at a ghost, and I know instantly that she's dying.

Looking back, that's what I see.

Or have I overlaid this with images from the township shacks that I have visited since? No matter. The redrawn map of apartheid didn't simply outline boundaries for implausible ethnic statelets. It was also designed to isolate people by weaving invisible and consequently frightening mental barriers. And my mother, however tentatively, crossed that imaginary frontier; and, memorably, took me with her.

Onward Christian soldiers

But leisurely sea voyages between hemispheres, and the lark of a different school every six months, couldn't last. The solution was that old colonial tradition for officials posted to distant stations of the empire: send the boy to a boarding school in England.

It was housed in a red-brick Victorian building in a dowdy town outside London. We wore green blazers and lawn-green caps. Africa seemed unimaginably far away. In geography lessons though, we did learn about African countries that were still 'ours'. On Saturday evenings we were treated to black and white documentaries on West African colonies: beaming men shinned up trees to collect cocoa pods, then paddled dugouts through pounding surf to ships waiting to take the cargo to England, where it would be turned into chocolate for us lucky lads.

At the close of every unchanging day, the 50 or so boarders gathered for prayer in the oak-panelled dining room. To accompany hymns, the headmaster's stout and kindly wife thumped her piano with the fervour of a Salvation Army crusader. As dusk crept over the playing fields, it was inexpressibly sad to hear reedy male voices once again trill, 'The day thou gavest Lord is ended, the darkness falls at thy behest.'

We also sang with gusto 'Onward Christian Soldiers', though we had no idea that at the same time in faraway Ghana the followers of Kwame Nkrumah, clamouring for independence, opened their political meetings with 'Onward Christian Soldiers, marching as to war'. The words were undoubtedly more meaningful for Ghanaians, whose country had previously been named the Gold Coast by its colonial masters, than for little white boys in Surrey mostly concerned with that week's soccer results.

'At the sign of triumph Satan's host doth flee; / On then, Christian soldiers, on to victory!' If only we'd known, this hymn was delightfully subversive (so had been banned in 1903 at the coronation durbar in Delhi to celebrate, in his absence, the succession of Edward VII as the Emperor of India) because it expressed a sentiment not encouraged among schoolboys in the Home Counties: 'Crowns and thrones may perish / Kingdoms rise and wane'.

Mesmerised, as we gazed out at the school's manicured lawns bathed in a gentle sunset glow, I wondered about that other, seemingly tantalising life in the southern hemisphere. Were my memories real, or perhaps based on overheard adult conversations? Looking back, Stendhal found that 'things imagined and things seen become confused'. So unlikely did those recollections appear amid the metronomic routine of a Surrey prep school that it became increasingly hard to pin them down. Gradually South Africa loomed like a fanciful, make-believe realm of limpid sunshine and adventure, a thrilling antipode to England's pleasant, well-tended pastures green.

A boy's own quest

At school assembly I recited my own secret invocation to summon up that more enticing universe: Tyger Hoek, Zebedelia, Nylstroom, Umzimkulu. Some of those names aren't on the map any longer, but like a sorcerer's spell they transformed grey shorts and shirt into khaki as we track our quarry through the veld. We step warily in case the crackling of a dry twig gives away our presence to the prey we're stalking, whether wild beast or human foe. We sleep under the stars. The night is filled with shrill cries and throaty roars. We don't know what is out there in the inky-dark and in that long vigil before dawn, we fear the worst. We sleep with our guns perpetually beside us.

In effect, I didn't just have some imaginary friend, I occupied an entire imaginary country: a realm of wonder where anything, even the impossible, was possible. After several years the headmaster grumbled in my term report: 'When I consider Bryan's future I am filled with despair.'

This verdict followed a uniquely embarrassing episode. Instead of studying during the evening homework period, that errant lad had been scribbling a satire of school life in the style of the Old Testament. Later, in the dormitory, he'd read this out aloud like a serial. But one night our young author left the new verses in his locker downstairs, and by popular demand had to sneak back to fetch them. Unluckily he was intercepted by the headmaster, who demanded to know why he was creeping around in pyjamas. After closer questioning, the mortified boy sheepishly handed over his scribbled biblical parody. Alas, that evening's episode involved the Latin master and school matron, with copious begettings and begattings. The headmaster

OUTRIDERS OF EMPIRE

read this in silence and muttered 'Follow me.' The blue and purple welts on my buttocks took days to subside.

If only our presumed pornographer had been able to cite the illustrious literary tradition of mixing satire with sex. Or how the term 'Monomotapa' was used in the eighteenth century as a device to obscure the place of publication. In 1748, the French encyclopaedist Denis Diderot wrote a lascivious parody of Louis XV, with the monarch portrayed as the bored Sultan of the Congo. He possesses a magic ring that can provoke women's labia to careless gossip. *Les Bijoux Indiscrets* (The Indiscreet Jewels) registered that it was published '*Au Monomotapa*'. But that callow schoolboy knew nothing of Diderot, Monomotapa, or anything at all to do with begetting and begatting.

Instead, what the lad did know about were the stirring tales of astonishing adventures that white men could have in Africa.

An empire of fiction

One Saturday the cricket first XI were on their way to a match with a rival school when they noticed that their mid-order batsman and star fielder was not on the bus. Turning back, they discovered the miscreant hadn't heard the team call as he'd been absorbed in H. Rider Haggard's *King Solomon's Mines*. For these old thrillers weren't just rollicking adventures. They were daring quests. Brave men set out for a distant land in search of something astounding, almost beyond belief: a lost city, say.

There didn't seem to be any quests left in England; not since King Arthur and the Knights of the Round Table. But in Africa!

185

Gallant Englishmen could abandon the comfort of home, travel among martial tribes and undergo far-fetched dangers. Having endured privations and overcome perils, they triumph and return home, wiser and considerably richer. In *King Solomon's Mines*, Allan Quatermain divulges that many years previously he'd met an old prospector who told him, 'how he had found in the far interior a ruined city, which he believed to be the Ophir of the Bible'.

Rider Haggard had been on the staff of Sir Theophilus Shepstone when he annexed the Transvaal in 1877, and it was the future author who ran up the British flag in Pretoria. That was undoubtedly where he heard about Carl Mauch's 'discovery' of what the German claimed to be 'the supposed realm of the Queen of Sheba'.

In *King Solomon's Mines*, billed as 'The most amazing book ever written', the map had been drawn 300 years before on a rag by a Portuguese trader 'with his blood for ink'.

In *Allan Quatermain*, the sequel, the hero makes a remark bound to ensnare the bored schoolboy. No man who has led an exciting life, he avers, 'can with impunity go coop himself in this prim English country, with its trim hedgerows and cultivated fields, its stiff formal manners and its well-dressed crowds. He begins to long – ah, how he longs! – for the keen breath of the desert air; he dreams of the sigh of Zulu impis breaking on their foes like surf upon the rocks, and his heart rises up in rebellion against the strict limits of the civilised life.'

On each quest they are accompanied by loyal servants who have a regal presence. In *King Solomon's Mines*, Sir Henry Curtis booms 'I like your looks, Mr Umbopa, and I will take you as my servant.' At the crucial moment, Mr Umbopa exposes his serpent tattoo to reveal himself as 'Ignosi, rightful king of the Kukuanas!'

In *Allan Quatermain*, the imposing tall and fierce Umslopogaas declares: 'I was high-born, ay, of the blood of Chaka, the great king …', to which the white man responds 'And now, behold, Umslopogaas, I know thee for a great warrior and a brave man, faithful to the death.'

Yet it is Mr Umbopa, finally installed as king, who expresses the ethos that permeates these imperial escapades. 'It is strange,' he answered, 'and yet had ye not been Englishmen I would not have believed it; but English 'gentlemen' tell no lies.'

Expanding youthful horizons

Another favoured author described his thrillers as 'shilling shockers'. John Buchan had been among the 'kindergarten' of Oxford grad-uates imported after the Boer War to administer the South African colonies. In his *Prester John*, Davie Crawfurd leaves school, 'where my progress was less notable in my studies than my sports', and emigrates to work in the remote Zoutpansberg mountains. *Prester John* is haunted by fears accumulated over centuries, for Davie's antagonist is a 'nigger priest', the Rev. Laputa, who expounds the perfidious gospel of 'Africa for the Africans'.

There are secret maps, hair-raising chases. But the sly undercur-rent is a lust for wealth. At the end of *Prester John*, after Davie has wrestled the Rev. Laputa to death, he gropes in the dark cave and finds 'British sovereigns, Kruger sovereigns, Napoleons, Spanish and Portuguese gold pieces, and many old coins ranging back to the Middle Ages and even to the ancients.' Having helped to suppress the uprising ('and white Africa breathed again'), Davie is rewarded with a share of the treasure and returns home a rich man.

For the Surrey schoolboy, however, as for generations before him, the preferred 'boy's own' author was G.A. Henty. Though Henty died in 1902, by 1960 when our colonial lad was devouring his works, it is estimated that Henty's 122 historical novels had sold 25 million copies. His rip-roaring adventures ranged across the empire. It's often the same plot in a different imperial setting: a British youth signs up for a thrilling outdoor life free of parental control. In *The Young Colonists: A Story of the Zulu and Boer Wars*, the Colonel tells the teenage hero 'Your life is indeed an adventurous one. It needs endurance, pluck, coolness, and a steady finger on the trigger.'

Henty boasted that if young fellows read his historical novels attentively, they would easily pass an exam on imperial history. If I could have been tested on Henty or Rider Haggard novels, no master would have had to despair of my future, nor my mother been obliged to hide my school reports as long as possible from my father.

It didn't occur to an avid consumer of these yarns that some of Henty's teenage heroes – Chris King (*With Buller in Natal*), say, or Gregory Hartley (*With Kitchener in the Soudan*) – would have been army officers in their mid-30s by the time of the First World War. Fired with notions of honour and empire, those officers would have led their men out of the trenches on the first day of the Battle of the Somme. Out of the 120,000 British troops who charged into battle that July morning in 1916, there were 57,470 casualties, 19,240 of them killed. Sixty per cent of all officers fighting that day also died.

Every year at school we dutifully remembered the dead on

Remembrance Day. We were not told that the fatality ratio among black African porters conscripted by the British during the First World War was considerably higher than the toll among the empire's white soldiers, though in the case of forced African labour the cause of death was mostly disease and exhaustion. Among British Imperial forces in East Africa, 11,189 white soldiers died compared to 95,000 black porters and labourers, 90 per cent of all British and allied fatalities in that campaign: a contribution which remains almost entirely disregarded.

About two million black Africans took part in the First World War, of which one million died. Most lie in unmarked graves. A British document from the 1920s, only discovered in 2019, states, 'most of the natives who have died are of a semi-savage nature and do not attach any sentiment to marking the graves of the dead'. Erecting headstones, the memo concluded, 'would constitute a waste of public money'. This was signed off by the chairman of the Imperial War Graves Commission, Winston Churchill.

Echoes of empire

The British Empire, emerging victorious from that war, carried on much as before. After the Second World War, one senior colonial officer wrote, 'What we require out here are young public school men who have failed conspicuously at all book work and examinations in proportion as they have excelled at sports.' That was a good description of my schoolboy self. Even in 1960 we were still being educated to be officers or administrators for an empire which was crumbling.

The onus was to prepare us for a 'good' public school. In his essay,

Such, Such Were the Joys about his own prep school, George Orwell wrote, 'It was universally taken for granted at St Cyprians that unless you went to a good public school (and only about 15 schools came under this heading) you were ruined for life.' The empire was run largely by officers from that limited pool. Orwell himself, on leaving Eton, joined the Indian Imperial Police in Burma, and in another famous essay wrote about shooting a rampaging elephant because he felt that in front of local villagers he had to keep up the prestige of the white man: 'A sahib has got to behave like a sahib …'.

In 1943 Sir Ralph Furse, Director of Recruitment at the Colonial Office, wrote a memorandum on the training for post-war colonial officials: 'as the more educated native moved to the centre of the stage', he argued, more sensitivity would be required. So what was needed for Britain to retain its influence, he concluded, was more of the cultivated ancient Greek spirit rather than a muscular Roman preoccupation with *Pax Britannica*.

Sir Ralph (Eton and Oxford) presided over an administrative caste system. Character and breeding were paramount. Intellectuals were regarded with suspicion. The Colonial Office's *Appointments Handbook* counselled that 'Weakness of various kinds may lurk in a flabby lip or in averted eyes, just as single-mindedness and purpose are commonly reflected in a steady gaze and a firm set of the mouth and jaw.'

This was the kind of imperial guff that I was devouring at school in novels like Rider Haggard's *Allan Quatermain*. 'What a splendid looking man he is!' ponders the narrator Quatermain as Sir Henry's face is illuminated by the evening fire. 'Calm, powerful face, clear-cut features, large grey eyes, yellow beard and hair – altogether a magnificent specimen of the higher type of humanity.'

Although South Africa appeared to remain static, aided by draconian police powers, north of the Limpopo there were confused British attempts to both placate and contain demands for African advancement. The Central African Federation clumsily bolted together what today are Zimbabwe, Zambia and Malawi. The stated aim was to create a 'partnership' between black and white. But as the Federation's second Prime Minister stipulated, blacks were to remain the 'junior partner'.

Sir Roy Welensky, a former engine driver and trade unionist, had been the heavyweight boxing champion of Southern Rhodesia. My father's interview with him was the first item of political reportage I remember reading, but that's only because I thought the introduction so belly-achingly funny. It began something like this: 'The last time I saw Sir Roy, the burly Prime Minister was spread-eagled on the canvas below me, blood spurting from his nose after I had knocked him down in the second round.'

That was probably in 1960 during Harold Macmillan's six-week tour of British colonies in Africa, culminating with his famous 'Winds of Change' speech in Cape Town. Privately, Macmillan referred to African nationalists as 'barbarians'. Nevertheless, the patrician British Prime Minister (Eton and Oxford) was acutely aware of the chilly post-war gusts blowing changes for his own country.

Like Sir Ralph, Macmillan was partial to the Greek/Roman analogy, and he fondly imagined that Britain could play the role of seasoned classical Greece to the assertive new Roman Empire, the United States ('big, vulgar, bustling', he called it): an affectation which still deludes many well-bred Englishmen into believing that the influence of their former empire lingers on.

Baffled by the facts of life

Though failing to graduate to any of Orwell's significant 15 public schools, I did squeak into a minor public school that, in the classic Furse requirement, was dedicated to building 'character'. Sir Ralph had specified that his ideal candidate as a colonial officer was a chap who'd been a school prefect and captain of the school XI. I certainly fitted the bill. But by the time I was poised to leave, there was no longer an empire available for my meagre talents.

At home there were anxious parental conferences: what on earth are we to do with 'the boy'? The solution, not surprisingly, was the traditional colonial option: dispatch the errant lad to a distant out-post of empire. Or, by 1967, its ghostly residue. I was astonished, then exhilarated, to be informed that it had been decided the best prospect for me was to go to university back in South Africa.

The evening before I was due to sail for Cape Town, I overheard my mother exhorting my father that it was time for him to divulge to his son the facts of life. An embarrassed Frank shuffled into my room and after hemming and hawing muttered, 'Look, about women, I've got only one piece of advice – never tell a woman that you love her.' A month later in Cape Town, on the eve of my departure by train for Grahamstown, Uncle René took me to his gentlemen's club in Queen Victoria Street.

Uncle René assumed the air of a man on a delicate mission, and I guessed that he had been instructed by Auntie Betty to disclose to me the arcane lowdown on the fancier facts of life. Unlike my father who, I discovered from a limerick written by former press colleagues, had been reputed a noteworthy ladies' man in his youth, Uncle René was undoubtedly a man of slender romantic experience. However, he clearly relished his educational role of the roughish man-about-town.

'You go to university to learn two things,' pronounced Uncle René, as he surveyed the menu. 'To learn about wine … and about women.' Glancing up, he bestowed upon me his aspirant Monte Carlo *roué*'s wink. 'And about women,' he purred, 'I will give you only one piece of advice, Bryan – always tell a woman that you love her.'

9

✝

ON A FRAGILE FRONTIER

A chronicle insanity

IN THE SOUTH AFRICA, to which I'd naively stepped back as an
18-year-old, whiteness wasn't simply a colour. It was a belief system,
almost a theology. Ironically, this was particularly true for those
whites who maintained that they were no longer of Europe but had
become an indigenous tribe: the Afrikaners.

Seven years previously, in April 1960, three weeks after the infa-
mous massacre of black protesters at Sharpeville, a wealthy white
farmer, David Pratt, fired twice from point-blank range at the
Prime Minister Dr Hendrik Verwoerd with a .22 pistol. So much
blood gushed from the felled ideologue that his bodyguard fainted.
This was at the opening of the annual Rand Easter Show, that year
celebrating the fiftieth anniversary of the Union of South Africa.
Verwoerd recovered remarkably quickly.

Pratt's failed assassination attempt had taken place a week before
my twelfth birthday and my mother, who had known his family,
told me that Pratt was really strange and had imagined that he was a
fried egg. I was spellbound by this idea; but why fried, I wondered,
rather than scrambled or poached?

Pratt, I learned later, suffered from epilepsy and depression.
Nevertheless, he had a lifelong commitment to non-racialism and
at his trial declared his implacable hatred of 'the stinking monster
of apartheid'. From the dock, he proposed the exceedingly sane

dictum: 'If you live under guilt, you are never free.' But at his trial his doctors claimed that he harboured 'grandiose delusions of the political saviour type'. Yet that, surely, was precisely the malady from which Dr Verwoerd suffered, with his grandiose master plan to isolate each of the country's assorted pigments and keep them rigidly apart.

Six years after Pratt's bungled shooting, Verwoerd was stabbed to death in Parliament by another man who was also quickly declared insane. Both David Pratt and Dimitri Tsafendas were politically committed, but so far as the ruling party and a great many white South Africans were concerned, anyone who wished to assassinate Dr Verwoerd had to be off their rocker. Both men, one a liberal and the other communist, were declared unfit to stand trial by reason of insanity. So this is unavoidably a chronicle of madness: a folly which a minority of the population, but a majority of whites, took to be normality.

The portents were all there to see; except for those habituated to the asylum. Barely two months after Pratt fired two .22 bullets into Verwoerd at point-blank range, producing a geyser of blood, the zealous Prime Minister had recovered sufficiently to deliver yet another Union anniversary speech, this time in Bloemfontein. 'I have in my hands here a dove,' Dr Verwoerd proclaimed sonorously, 'which I now send out into space as a symbol of peace and prosperity, which we wish all people on earth. It will be our messenger of goodwill.' Once Verwoerd had tossed the snow-white dove into the air, however, this symbolic wingéd messenger of racial separation did not soar into a pure blue yonder of peace and prosperity for all.

Instead, it crashed straight back to earth unconscious.

An outpost of empire

As the train snaked round the last gradient in an ashy dawn Grahamstown looked dour. Once past grimy stockyards, and under luminous sunlight, prospects brightened. Attractive colonial buildings were fronted by wooden balconies and shaded arcades, its vaunted status as a city established by the Cathedral of St Michael and St George in the handsome High Street.

The winsome 'white' town seemed like a tranquil English market town of the 1950s. It was surreal, as though I'd accidentally journeyed back in time – except that the ramshackle 'native location' across the valley, directly facing Gunfire Hill and Fort Selwyn, sprawled over a ridge named after the prophet who had led Xhosa warriors in a doomed fight against British settlers.

The modern aspiration was to mimic an English university town. Teenage white boys and girls still wore the kinds of school blazer and straw boater which were rapidly being jettisoned from the imitated originals. Some academics liked to imagine that their compact university was a sedate replica of Oxford colleges in Africa. There was also a surfeit of churches, which led to a fanciful boast that, like Oxford, this was a city of dreaming spires.

The towering landmark spire of the cathedral had been designed by Sir Gilbert Scott, the leading architect of the Gothic revival in Victorian England. Scott had earlier won the competition to design a new building in Whitehall to replace the waterlogged old Foreign Office – where a previous Foreign Secretary had narrowly escaped death when a ceiling collapsed onto his desk. By then, the empire spanned 9.5 million square miles of the globe, and it was felt that Britain needed an administrative palace worthy of such grandeur.

Sir Gilbert designed an ornate Gothic edifice, but at that moment the gruff Lord Palmerston returned as Prime Minister and squashed the plan. Palmerston felt that only a classical Greek or Roman style would convey the majesty of the Foreign Office's prodigious mission.

To the surprise of his admirers Sir Gilbert, the leading advocate of the Gothic revival, caved in and designed the current imposing but self-important Italianate building – which in 1968, the year after I arrived in Grahamstown, changed its name to the Foreign and Commonwealth Office. This titular dilution reflected the reality that since the end of the Second World War, Britain had lost suzerainty of over 30 distant countries, including all its African colonies, save – in name only – Rhodesia, which had made a Unilateral Declaration of Independence in a doomed attempt to preserve white minority ascendancy.

Fading into mimicry

Dizzying changes in the rest of the world were seldom apparent in Grahamstown.

Founded as a garrison town, eight years later English settlers were sent out to act as a buffer against the Xhosa nation, on what was then the furthest frontier of the Cape Colony. Half of the settlers in 1820, however, were from cities, so unsuited to farming. Many soon retreated to town, where the clammy grip of the British class system reasserted itself. Driven by a powerful local squirearchy, a strain of Eastern Cape separatism flourished; in 1864, even prodding the Cape Parliament to convene a sitting in distant Grahamstown in order to placate the fractious provincials. Ever since, the town has been in steady decline.

In 1887, *The Eastern Star* newspaper transferred from Grahamstown to Johannesburg, changing its name to *The Star*. Nevertheless, a strong sense of separatism persisted, with an emphasis on the English heritage derived from the 1820 settlers, about whom a hallowed status had grown. My history tutor, and thereafter lifelong friend, was an irreverently witty young Australian who taught at Rhodes University while researching his thesis on Anthony Trollope's travel book, *South Africa* (1878). Jim, later to become Dr Jim Davidson and a highly acclaimed writer, helped to put this cultish 1820 pretension into perspective by referring to it as 'ancestor worship'.

Trollope had visited the city during his lengthy tour of South Africa in 1877, and remarked, 'The people of Grahamstown are very full of their own excellencies.' Ninety years later, most whites still were.

It soon became apparent that within the city's constricted white population it was ludicrously easy to identify the local Special Branch political police. The majority of white students, however, seemed neither to notice or care about the degradation on which their privilege was based. In the dining halls, 19-year-old white youths would click their fingers at elderly black retainers and shout 'Hey, Chief!' Many from what was then Rhodesia casually referred to 'munts' or 'Afs', even if a black attendant was present, as though when not being given commands they became invisible.

The hypocrisy was startling. A couple of times a year, after the government had passed yet another authoritarian law, professors and lecturers in academic gowns and some students would march silently round the cathedral in protest. Then everyone went home while the university authorities continued to conform to the repressive prescriptions of the regime. I still have a notice filched from the gate of the university rugby field: 'This entrance, and the area to which it gives access, may be used by EUROPEANS ONLY (members of the 'White' group).'

Worse, as has since been discovered, some of the most senior administrators actively colluded with the Special Branch in providing information about dissident students. It was a grievous shock to witness the meek implosion of benign nineteenth-century British liberalism in the face of intransigent twentieth-century intolerance.

An outpost of progress

As Queen Victoria celebrated her Diamond Jubilee in July 1897 with an extravagant display of imperial might in London, Joseph Conrad published a startling short story called *An Outpost of Progress*. It's an acidic tale of colonial venality and hypocrisy: 'pushed a little (and only a little) beyond the actual facts of the case,' he said. The story drew on Conrad's experience of working in the Congo and presages his masterpiece, *Heart of Darkness*, two years later.

During my final year at university, I resolved to hitchhike up to the former German colony of South West Africa, now Namibia, but then still controlled by South Africa. There – illegally, because it was a restricted security zone – I reached the river marking the border with Angola: a bizarre journey that I recently discovered has an eerie resonance with Conrad's parable of two white men abandoned at a remote trading station far upriver.

An Outpost of Progress begins, 'There were two white men in charge of the trading station. Kayerts, the chief, was short and fat; Carlier, the assistant, was tall, with a large head and a very broad trunk perched upon a long pair of thin legs.' It was close to the Angolan border that I met a demented replica of Carlier, the tall one.

It had taken days to get there. Somewhere beyond Windhoek, a farmer dropped me on a lonely road at dusk. Through the trees I spotted the glow of a fire. In a clearing, an elderly African sat on a log boiling water in a rusty can. He motioned me to sit, and from an animal-hide pouch he pinched some grains of instant coffee into a mug.

We struggled to communicate. The Americans had just landed the first astronauts on the moon, so pointing up at the sky, I enunciated, 'There-are-men-on-the-moon.' My companion gazed at me warily. When I repeated this, louder and slower, the old man burst into laughter. He woke me at daybreak with the sound of a truck approaching, and as I scrambled back towards the road I could still hear him chuckling.

In the small town of Tsumeb, I wandered into a bar to see if anyone might give me a lift further northward. An engineer, who had studied at Rhodes, suggested instead that he could give me a ride right up to the northernmost border. He was working on a government construction project a couple of kilometres from the river that marked the frontier with Angola.

'You said it was a restricted zone,' I objected.

'Yeah, but the security guys know me,' he insisted. 'They'll never check. You're in the back with my kids. You duck down and they'll wave us through.'

It didn't occur to me to wonder how I'd get out again.

On the way up, past the security post, we sped through a flat expanse dotted with dry waterholes, lofty palms and gnarled baobabs. As we neared the Angolan border, the engineer remarked that we were taking a detour deeper into the bush, as I'd be staying the night with their soil analyst. He lived ahead of the main construction team in a prefab cabin where there were two bedrooms.

'And one,' murmured the engineer, 'is now free.'

He explained that this soil analyst (I'll call him Carlier) and his former boss (I'll call him Kayerts) had been stuck out in the bush for two years. The previous week, he said, Kayerts had finally gone 'bush happy'.

'Mad Hatter's tea party,' chortled his wife.

'By the end they hardly spoke to each other,' admitted the engineer. 'Their only socialising was on Sundays. They'd cross the river to some beer hut in Angola. First they'd drink ten or so beers, then fill the empties with gin and drink that neat. Last Sunday when they came back the senior guy went apeshit. Got his rifle, walked all the way to our construction site. Shot out windows, peppered the manager's *bakkie*, blasted a generator and calmly kept reloading. I counted 18 holes in our water tank.'

'Anyone hurt?' I asked.

'No, but he killed six chickens.'

It was dusk when we reached a boxy cabin in a clearing. A tall, gaunt man, Carlier, came out. He didn't say a word as the engineer explained that I'd be staying the night and they would collect me at noon the following day. Inside, Carlier pointed to a door and muttered, 'That's you,' then disappeared into his own room.

The next morning I woke early, starving. There was no sign of Carlier, so I tiptoed into the kitchen and opened the fridge. It was stocked with huge cartons of orange juice and as I was pouring myself a glass Carlier appeared, dressed only in torn khaki shorts. Violently he grabbed the carton out of my hand. Carlier stared at me without blinking for so long that I thought he might strangle me.

'Never touch a fucking thing here,' he hissed.

Hearts of darkness

In Conrad's story, Kayerts and Carlier begin energetically after the company steamer drops them at their isolated post. But trade in ivory proves sluggish. As months pass, indolence and heat overcome them, though they are delighted to find an old magazine which discussed *Our Colonial Expansion*. 'It spoke much of the rights and duties of civilisation, of the sacredness of the civilising work, and extolled the merits of those who went about bringing light and faith and commerce to the dark places …'.

Bored and seemingly forgotten, it cheers them up to imagine that they may one day be remembered as 'the first civilised men to live in this very spot!'

After five months, a band of armed black strangers arrive. They palaver with the station's sole other employee, Makola. Their presence is frightening. But Makola informs the Europeans that these 'bad fellows' can procure a large haul of ivory. Carlier and Kayerts shut themselves away from the nightlong drumming. The next day, the local villagers have vanished; they've been sold into slavery. In return, there are six magnificent tusks.

Torn between greed and revulsion, the two Europeans begin to unravel. They curse 'the Company, all Africa, and the day they were born'. Carlier 'talked about the necessity of exterminating all the niggers before the country could be made habitable'. They bicker, and come to blows over whether they may have sugar in their coffee. Kayerts chases Carlier with a revolver. Shots go off.

Kayerts hides away, unsure what has happened until Makola appears to inform him of Carlier's fate. 'Come along, Mr Kayerts,' urges Makola. 'He is dead.' This is a trial run for the brusquer phrase from *Heart of Darkness*: 'Mistah Kurtz – he dead.'

At that moment there's a hoot from the company steamer. The Managing Director has arrived at last. He rushes ashore to find two corpses. Carlier, the tall one, has been shot, and his boss Kayerts has hung himself from the cross they had erected over the grave of their European predecessor. In a grotesque parody, Kayerts appears to be standing to attention: 'And, irreverently, he was putting out a swollen tongue at his Managing Director.'

Startled by the soil analyst's aggression, I collected my rucksack and hurried back along the track we'd driven the previous evening. After a while, I came across a village of about 20 thatched huts. Women stared. Children giggled.

'Hey,' greeted a young man. He'd worked in Windhoek and spoke halting English. I asked if he knew about the rampage of Carlier's boss the previous Sunday. 'Sure,' he said. 'That crazy white guy! Walked right past here with his gun. Bam-bam! Shot my brother in the leg.'

I was waiting on the track when the engineer and his family arrived. I didn't mention Carlier's odd behaviour. Instead, they announced we were going to a Sunday picnic by the river organised for the construction team. Carlier was not invited.

'He'll be off to that Cuca hut for his beer and gin today,' shrugged the engineer.

Half a dozen beefy men, their beefy wives and beefy children, all white, were already encamped by the river. Beers were open and meat grilling over fires. After lunch they invited me on the river in a powerful launch, the wash slapping noisily against swampy banks. Drunkenly, a couple of men fired at ducks and missed. On the way back they aimed at a fish eagle perched on a riverbank tree. It fell soundlessly into the reeds, and they didn't bother to stop.

In the car returning to the construction site, I asked about Kayerts shooting a villager in the leg. 'Oh?' said the engineer, surprised. 'No, don't think so.'

We drove on in silence. It had been arranged that I could spend the night in the caravan that served as a clinic, before leaving early the next morning with a truck that would take me part of the way out of the security zone.

'No, definitely not,' added the engineer as the lights of the construction site came into view. 'I would've heard.'

A clammy embrace

Back in Grahamstown, the tepid liberalism of most English-speakers seemed much like the reformist grand dame – 'Sophie Chattel-Monkheim was a socialist by conviction and a Chattel-Monkheim by marriage' – in the short story by the Edwardian satirist Saki: 'Sophie had very advanced and decided views as to the distribution of money: it was a pleasing and fortunate circumstance that she also had the money. When she inveighed eloquently against the evils of capitalism at drawing room meetings and Fabian conferences, she was conscious of a comfortable feeling that the system, with all its inequalities and iniquities, would probably last her time.'

In reaction, though equally ineffective, my best friend – a rebellious art student – and I began issuing provocative leaflets, which

*Author as an angry young man
(drawing by Jeff Chandler)*

we printed on a decrepit university mimeograph machine and distributed round the campus after dark. Jeff, despite his English name, was from an Afrikaans family which later disowned him over his revolt. Emboldened, we also painted slogans on campus roads late at night. Local papers took an interest. 'Rhodes rash of mystery slogans', warned one. A longer article appeared in the Johannesburg *Sunday Express*, cautioning 'No-one knows who are the movers behind the group, which has been issuing pamphlets calling for change.' Readers were reassured that if caught the culprits would probably be expelled.

It was my final year at university and I was living in a converted stable. Late one night Jeff and I were interrupted mid-graffito by security guards as we painted a colossal slogan right across the road. We fled, racing in opposite directions. After this close escape one of the local Special Branch cops (I remember him as Sergeant Gouws) took to visiting the stable yard in the afternoon. The burly sergeant would lean on the bottom half of my stable door and ask with ponderous irony, 'How are we doing today, my young friend?' Not bothering to wait for a reply, the supposedly secret policeman would nod and amble off.

Surely the Special Branch had more dangerous and dedicated subversives to track? Then it occurred to me: maybe Gouws is filing fantastical reports to distant police headquarters, making our trivial youthful pranks sound like a serious conspiracy or real revolutionary threat in order to justify his cushy posting in this sleepy town.

Historians differ as to the major incubator of South African society: was it the shifting, violently disputed frontier? Or the discovery of diamonds and gold, with the introduction of migrant labour and jail-like compounds for industrial production? The late Robert Shell, brilliant chronicler of Cape slavery, maintained that slavery reflects the true gestation of South African culture – with its pitiless efficiency, duration and, above all, its morbid intimacy. Slaves were considered as being incorporated into the family unit, similar to the ancient Roman custom: a cloying system of control, physical and psychological, thus a form of domestic totalitarianism.

Such lasting and perverse intimacy may help account for the repetitively macabre personal violence in South Africa. The twisted familiarity, which also allowed local Special Branch policemen to be effortlessly identified, later turned particularly malicious in the Eastern Cape where they developed a reputation for sadistic murders.

There was a harsh, burning intensity to that time. But even the most dedicated dissidents, black or white, were forced to make daily petty accommodations confronted with the ubiquitous 'Whites only' or 'Non-Whites' signs. Finally I began to agonise more seriously: youthful anger aside, are you really prepared to risk prison, even torture, to change this cushy life of privilege? I also had to admit to myself that I longed to travel, have adventures, see the world. A decision couldn't be put off much longer. Soon I was bound to receive call-up papers for military service.

All at sea

As I write, it's a soft spring evening. Fishing boats chug out of our bay, receding into an amber dusk. Watching them as they beat into the swell of the Atlantic, I am vividly reminded that nearly fifty years ago I set out on a similar craft. Not into a hazy sunset, but against the full ferocity of a Cape winter. Sometimes small private incidents, rather than great public dramas, can be the most illuminating on an intensely personal level. Convinced that a spell of seafaring was a crucial apprenticeship for an aspirant writer, during my last university winter vacation I convinced a friend to arrange for me to work on a trawler. A curt message instructed me to report to Cape Town docks the following Sunday at 11 p.m., prepared to sail for ten days to the stormy Agulhas Bank.

It was a dark, vaporous mid-winter night in Cape Town harbour. Eerie floodlights lit the otherwise deserted quay. The trawler had an entirely coloured crew and a coloured captain. Out of the gloom, from behind some dockside machinery, stepped an elderly black man.

'Pssst,' he hissed.

He gestured for me to slink into the shadows where we couldn't be seen. In the dark, he glanced round warily to make sure that there was no one to overhear. 'Don't go, white boy, not on that boat,' he whispered urgently. 'It won't be safe, believe me. Look at those guys!' Most of the crew had piratical scars, many had fingers missing from chopping fish on the pitching seas. 'It's dangerous out there, people get hurt, fall overboard,' warned the old man, the fierce gleam of an ancient mariner in his eye.

'Listen to me, I know these guys,' he implored. 'They won't be happy. Not with a white passenger, like he's on some fancy big liner. Maybe whitey fall overboard ...'.

It was irresistible. I went. Immediately we left the harbour, the small boat tossed mercilessly. The cramped steering cabin was fogged with cheap cigarette smoke and stank of fish. The captain tersely forbade me to work.

He wasn't going to risk some unknown white youth, out on a lark, suffering an unfortunate accident for which he would get the blame. Colossal waves, which would easily have washed an unwary crewman overboard, crashed across the deck. I wanted to be sick. After a while, a loud cheer rose from the men on deck.

'What's that?' I managed to ask.

'We've just left South African territorial waters,' replied the unsmiling captain. 'For the moment, we're free.'

Right next to the kitchen galley was a tier of bunks where we had to take it in turns to sleep. An oily reek from the galley, along with the violent bucking of the ship, made me feel perpetually sick, though I didn't dare show it and so admit to being merely a useless white passenger.

The atmosphere on the tiny bridge remained tense.

On day two, the disapproving skipper started chatting to the helmsman about soccer. Timidly I mentioned that as a teenager in London I had watched Chelsea play all the big teams at Stamford Bridge. Spontaneously I reeled off the line-up of that Chelsea squad: Peter 'the Cat' Bonetti, 'Chopper' Harris, Bobby Tambling, Terry Venables … until the entire team had been reverently identified. The ice was broken. My now lapsed adolescent obsession with sport had finally, kindly, paid out an unexpected and undeserved, but extremely generous dividend.

Even so, this vividly brought home to me that however much I might fancy myself a 'grievous radical' (in Charles Dickens' pithy self-definition), as a white person in South Africa, I remained a spoilt and exploitative passenger. A refrain began to beat in my head: to go or stay, go or stay?

The bitter pill

That December, I moved to Cape Town and worked briefly as a cub reporter on a local paper. But the nagging question became ever

more insistent. During hot summer evenings I paced the streets of
Cape Town, rehearsing the arguments over whether to abscond or
remain.

I was repeatedly drawn to the boisterous, cobbled streets of
District Six, a ramshackle neighbourhood at the foot of Devil's
Peak, overlooking the harbour and Table Bay. It was a multi-racial,
working-class district of peeling, double-storeyed Victorian buildings, tenements with wrought-iron balconies, tailors' shops, spice
bazaars, old cinemas, churches, mosques and nine synagogues.

Over half a century before, when my grandfather Lewis Rose
had published a newspaper series by the nation's hangman, the circulation had surged: 'particularly in District Six,' he boasted, 'the
poor quarter of Cape Town largely populated by Malay 'Cape boys'
and poor whites'. For obdurate apartheid ideologues, such flagrant
racial intermingling proved intolerable. By 1970, when I was rest-
lessly walking those cobbled streets, the government had already
declared District Six a 'white area'. But the forced removals had not
yet begun in earnest and so, unlike the staid white suburbs, it still
pulsed with an effervescent, raucous vigour.

Many of the overcrowded houses were crumbling. Much of the
area was a slum. There were gangs: the Jesters, Killers, the Globe
Gang. Once I was held at knifepoint by a youthful hoodlum who
was probably experimenting to see how pale a white man could
turn.

Another time, an older man held a pistol to my head. It was a
Luger. He was angry and stoned. He said that he had served in the
Second World War, but being 'non-white' he hadn't been allowed
to carry arms. He seemed to blame me. He had brought the Luger

back as a souvenir. After 20 minutes or so he calmed down and called over some friends from next door, insisting that we drink several bottles of cheap wine together. Finally, my tormentor slapped me heartily on the back, and as I disappeared down the cobbled street he yelled: 'Walk tall, whitey!'

Near the edge of the district there was a derelict, padlocked shop. Perhaps its owner had already been forcibly evicted. This shop was called, I think, Professor Colombi's Dispensary. A notice was taped inside the cracked and dusty window. The sign was soiled, but it was typed in capital letters so that it was just possible to decipher: WE HAVE PILLS FOR ALL YOUR TROUBLES – STOMACH TROUBLES, ULCER TROUBLES, EAR TROUBLES, EYE TROUBLES, WIFE TROUBLES.

To go or to stay? It was an insistent, troubling refrain.

To go or stay? Go or stay ...

10
✠
NEW WORLDS, OLD IDEAS

A parting gift

STANDING ALONE at the stern of a merchant ship as it sailed out of Cape Town felt, at first, as though the burden of centuries was being sloughed off in our wake. Back on shore a controversy raged. The Western tradition portrays Jesus Christ as blue-eyed and rosy-cheeked, while his apostles, though gnarled, are also depicted as white. So some local white pastors were insisting that their coloured flock refer, respectfully, to 'Baas Matthew', 'Baas Mark', 'Baas Luke' and 'Baas John'.

Out in the bay, the cargo boat rolled with heavy grey swells. It was a darkening, late winter's afternoon in 1970. Gulls wheeled and shrieked. The hump of Robben Island slipped by. Evening lights glimmered faintly from the receding city. Finally the monolith of Table Mountain slithered over the murky horizon and nothing of Africa remained visible. Suddenly, unexpectedly, and with pang of dismay, I thought: I'll never see South Africa again.

Down in my cabin, stowed in my scruffy suitcase, were parting gifts from Auntie Betty. For some time she had taken it upon herself to reform what she regarded as my immature view of humanity: a *naïveté*, Uncle René had growled, that was positively reckless in South Africa. Auntie Betty's educational campaign involved birthday and Christmas presents of books on animal behaviour, with the implication that I should learn a sobering lesson about the racial limitations of human nature. The supreme coup, conducted the day before I sailed away to the old world, was the presentation of two books by their philosophical guru Robert Ardrey.

Largely forgotten today, Ardrey was then hugely fashionable. After a successful career as a playwright and Hollywood scriptwriter, Ardrey married a South African actress and began to go on safari. From watching lions and reading about laboratory experiments with dormice, he formulated sweeping theories about civilisation and race. Works such as *African Genesis* (1961) and *The Territorial Imperative* (1966) gave him an international reputation. His theme was stark: men are basically weapon-wielding apes. Stanley Kubrick credited Ardrey as an inspiration for his cult film, *2001: A Space Odyssey.*

In the midst of this lugubrious philosophising, Ardrey gained an Oscar nomination for his screenplay for the 1966 movie *Khartoum*, an epic about the famous siege starring Charlton Heston as General Gordon and Laurence Olivier in blackface as the Mahdi.

Auntie Betty revered Ardrey and urged me to study the great man's ideas. It quickly became apparent why his reductive behavioural verdicts appealed to so many white South Africans. The message in Ardrey's first book was simple: man is territorial, man is brutish, and black ones are the worst. After observing wild animals in the bush, Ardrey retreated to his home in Rome and composed apocalyptic sermons. He argued that over many centuries northerners, or white people, had erected a flimsy barrier against barbarism. At the end of *African Genesis* he states that although all humanity is scary, 'most of all I am afraid of the African street. There are smiles, broad and white. But what lies behind the smile? I do not know.' Is it, he asks, the tribe in the hills or witch-doctor's magic?

The other gift was Ardrey's second book, *The Territorial Imperative*, which piled on the gloom. 'The territorial nature of man is genetic and ineradicable,' he decreed. This was the credo which under-pinned apartheid: that different races couldn't coexist so had to be corralled into separate enclaves. Robert Ardrey went further. Every African nation was sinking into chaos and bloodshed, he wrote: 'Whereas the pariah state South Africa is attaining peaks of afflu-ence, order and internal solidarity.'

This is what white South Africans like Auntie Betty yearned to hear. There was even weightier reassurance in his *magnum opus*; but that arrived too late in South Africa for her to hand over before I boarded ship for Europe.

Ardrey's ambition in *The Social Contract* was no less than to over-turn the humanism of eighteenth-century European philosophers. Citing more studies, mostly on animals, he concluded that 'the black race' did not fully qualify as part of *Homo sapiens*. For devotees like Betty and René, validation for their prejudices was now vouchsafed by laboratory experiments with muskrats and stickleback fish. *The Social Contract* was mailed to London as my Christmas present that year.

A relative empire

An aura of ill-defined perils has been our birthright.

In 1923, aged 11, my mother had informed her little English friends solemnly, 'I am about to leave for a very dangerous country!' At that moment the British Empire appeared to be at its zenith. It comprised 400 million people in 58 countries, seven times larger than the Roman Empire during its furthest reach. To mark this ascendancy, a great jamboree was staged at Wembley and King George V opened the British Empire Exhibition on St George's Day of 1924. The showgrounds covered 220 acres with stands from every imperial domain. It was a celebration of global power, and attracted 27 million visitors. *The Times* described the exhibition as 'a true shrine of Empire'.

In his short story *The Rummy Affair of Old Biffy*, P.G. Wodehouse has his fearsome psychiatrist Sir Roderick Glossop, the 'loony doctor', exclaim that this presented the greatest 'educational collection of objects, both animate and inanimate, gathered from the four corners of the Empire …'. In contrast, Wodehouse had his cheery hero Bertie Wooster slope off to the Planters' Bar in the West Indian Pavilion. For once, the clueless Bertie was on the mark. For despite Britain expanding its vast sway after the First World War, the cost of that war tipped the empire into its long decline.

Even so, in 1924 my father was 17 and already a keen empire enthusiast. In the aftermath of the Second World War, having been a roving sports journalist and war correspondent, Frank wrote, 'I feel that in my way I am now the complete Empire citizen. In the last few years my job has taken me to Canada, Australia, New Zealand, India and Palestine, Ceylon, Malaya, Newfoundland, Gibraltar, Malta, the Sudan, the Rhodesias, Bechuanaland, Zululand, Swaziland, Kenya, Uganda, British Somaliland and East Africa, so I can say there are few places daubed with red on the map that I have not visited.'

He was, my father admitted, equally split between South Africa and England, both of which he called 'home'. Uncle René, who used to raise the flag of Monaco in the woods near Cape Town, was also split. Originally from Holland, his dream world centred on Monaco and the principality's music hall monarchy. When he retired from his office job in Cape Town, René and Betty bought a tiny flat in an anonymous high-rise in Monte Carlo. After my aunt died, I used to call Uncle Rene occasionally, and once he asked me to send him an omnibus edition of the comic novels by P.G. Wodehouse.

'They're so like real life, aren't they?' he enthused.

In the fantasy universe of Uncle René, the clueless escapades of Bertie Wooster, his resourceful butler Jeeves or the Old Etonian Psmith appeared to be much as René had pictured the Principality of Monaco from afar: a stylish contrast to boorish South Africa, where one might exclaim 'Gadzooks!' before setting out for a weekend house party with an 'aged ancestor' in 'darkest Worcestershire'. For Uncle René, this represented a *Belle Époque* chic, where all that is inconceivable in your own routine world might spring to life, and where urbane gentlemen changed for dinner and in a tight spot, like Psmith, shrug insouciantly, 'I am as broke as the Ten Commandments.'

On my one visit to Monte Carlo, I had a row with René about apartheid, and when I got home my mother left a letter on the dining room table for me to read. It was in her sister's outsized handwriting. 'René is dismayed by Bryan's opinions,' Betty wrote. 'He can make neither head nor tail of them. But I think I can fathom your son's strange and wilful ideas a little as I read a lot of books.'

If only I could have answered the phone like Bertie Wooster when his fox-hunting aunt rings in Wodehouse's *Jeeves in the Offing*. 'A healthy pip-pip to you, old ancestor,' offers Bertie breezily on hearing Aunt Dahlia's booming voice (sounding 'as if shouting across a ploughed field in a high wind'). To which his aunt replies, 'And a rousing toodle-oo to you, you young blot on the landscape. I'm surprised to find you up as early as this. Or have you just got in from a night on the tiles?'

Instead, Auntie Betty, trapped in her Monte Carlo eerie, concluded regretfully that I was a renegade and delinquent. Perhaps she was right. But putting aside any personal defects of my often angry young self, it seems odd that my aunt, who was essentially a kindly person, should hold such abhorrent views. In that, she was little different from the majority of white South Africans who voted in ever greater numbers in support of apartheid.

Consequently, recalling Auntie Betty, I'm still left wondering: where did it all go wrong?

X marks the spot

My father would have been shocked and Auntie Betty scandalized by my contention that a lust for riches was present from the outset of European occupation, long before the discovery of diamonds and gold. In 1652, a small Dutch contingent established a rudimentary settlement at the southern tip of Africa in order to supply fresh produce to passing Dutch East India Company ships. Yet within three years we can see the spark of a more ambitious aspiration. In December 1655 the first commander of the tiny Cape garrison, Jan van Riebeeck, recorded his desire to locate the glorious kingdom of

Monomotapa and its fabled wealth.

The Empire of Monomotapa loomed large on many European maps of Africa. Gerard de Jode's *The True Shape and Situation of Africa*, printed posthumously in 1593, shows Monomotapa stretching almost as far as the Cape of Good Hope. Willem Janszoon Blaeu, as the official cartographer for the Dutch East India Company, had access to all company charts under a vow of secrecy. But his maps of Africa were based chiefly on accounts of previous Portuguese exploration, as well as port gossip and rumour. Blaeu's exquisite 1635 map shows Monomotapa sprawling across nearly all of southern Africa. Blaeu also identified two imaginary cities: Davul and Monomotapa.

By February 1659, Van Riebeeck was ready: 'After protracted exhortation seven adventurers volunteered to undertake an expedition inland right up to Monomotapa.' They were assured that 'It is not more than 120 or 130 miles N.E. of here', and they were directed that they should continue to 'the city of Monomotapa, the seat of their Emperor in a land rich in gold ...'. A month later the dejected troupe returned, 'and reported that they had found the country everywhere so barren, parched and ill-supplied with pasturage and water that they were forced to turn back'.

Undeterred, Van Riebeeck launched more expeditions. After all, the commander possessed a spectacular map. Jan Huygens van Linschoten, a Dutch merchant, had worked as bookkeeper for the Archbishop of Goa, the Portuguese enclave in India. Portugal, as well as Spain and the Netherlands, had made revealing maps to foreigners a crime punishable by death. But Van Linschoten used his position to gain access to secret maps about Portuguese trade routes. In 1596 he published his account, including a detailed map of southern Africa that not only identified the colossal empire of Monomotapa, but provided exact coordinates for the cities of Davagul and Monomotapa.

Although most of the detail was phantasmagorical, the commander of the struggling garrison had no doubts about its reliability. He instructed the leader of the next foray, Jan Danckaert, to take a copy of that precious map as it showed where 'the Emperor of Monomotapa mostly has his residence and most of his gold'. Van Riebeeck promised bountiful compensation to Danckaert's raggedy troupe for 'gold, precious stones, pearls or anything else', obtained 'however cheaply'. The expedition was not a success, foiled by illness and dissent.

Undeterred, Van Riebeeck planned another sortie to be commanded by Corporal Pieter Cruijthoff: 'he has the courage to see that things are carried out more satisfactorily and is able to maintain the necessary authority over the men.' Cruijthoff and his men were also assured they would be 'liberally paid' for returning with 'gold, precious stones, pearls or the like'. Nevertheless, Corporal Cruijthoff failed to locate the empire … thrice.

Van Riebeeck's successor remained undaunted. The scarcer the facts, the more fevered became the speculation. In 1663 a French soldier and hunter, Jonas de la Guerre, led yet another mission in the hope of opening up trade with Monomotapa. After three months he returned with his men in a 'deplorable state', and all on foot, having been forced to eat their own oxen. Like A.A. Milne's children's conundrum, the more they looked for this fabled El Dorado, the more it wasn't there.

Empire of dreams

It was there: just not in the way Europeans had engraved on their maps, or even remotely as they had fantasised. The Portuguese historian João de Barros described in *Décadas da Ásia* (1552) 'a huge region ruled by a gentle prince called Benomotapa'. This potentate ('being the lord of all') had many wives, and 500 musicians sang wherever he went. Above all, De Barros asserted, 'The land is full of gold …'. Other reports testified that the Emperor lived in a great stone palace much like Amsterdam Town Hall. But Monomotapa remained stubbornly elusive.

In fact, a large territory was occupied from the mid-fifteenth century by a confederation of tribes covering much of what is today Zimbabwe and Mozambique. There are conflicting interpretations, but the notion of Monomotapa was inferred by the Portuguese from terms such as *Mwene* (roughly, prince) and *Mutapa* (territory). Europeans tended to project onto African societies their own assumptions, and so froze more flexible social structures into prescribed hierarchies, as well as imposing the idea of set boundaries to delineate a nation or empire.

From this dominant realm, there had long been trade in ivory and copper with Arabs at eastern ports, as well as gold obtained by panning in streams or digging shallow deposits on the high plateau. But rumours inflated sketchy reports into a legend. So in 1569, Francisco Barreto was appointed to lead a Portuguese invasion. The goal was to gain for Portugal the kind of astounding wealth that Spain was importing from the Americas. The king began by convening a commission of lawyers and theologians to adjudicate on the morality of attacking Monomotapa.

The *Mesa da Consciência e Ordens* duly declared that due to the murder of a Jesuit priest there, a war against Monomotapa would be righteous, and 'in the name of the Gospel'.

Though said to be the most illustrious band that had set sail from Lisbon, the expedition was a disaster. Barreto made the fatal decision to proceed inland along the malaria-infected Zambezi River. Men died every day. Not understanding the causes of malaria, his accompanying Jesuits claimed they were being poisoned by Muslims, so the Portuguese soldiers impaled villagers alive, used some for target practice, and fired others from cannons. Barreto also succumbed to disease, and the rump of his expedition retreated empty-handed. Of 1,000 soldiers, 180 returned.

Nearly 30 years later, Van Linschoten described how 'the black people' went naked, had 'insatiable desires' and cut off their foes' 'privie members'. These were dispensed by the king to reward his warriors, so that 'the bride or wives of those knights doe weare mens members about their neckes, which among them is as great an honour, as it is with us to wear the Golden Fleece, or the Garter of England ...'.

Ignorance continued to breed myths and prejudice. It was said that the impressive stone ruins, later called Great Zimbabwe, could not have been built by black Africans. Some speculated it had been created by Prester John. Well into the twentieth century, European scholars variously ascribed it to the Phoenicians, the Chinese, Persians, Arabs, or as the ruins of biblical Ophir, the supposed source of King Solomon's riches.

Between 1869 and 1872, the English artist and explorer Thomas Baines led two gold seeking expeditions into what he described as the 'Monomotapa of Medieval Geographers' and the 'supposed realm of the Queen of Sheba'. Neither produced the hoped-for riches, and left Baines ill and destitute. Baines had travelled armed with a formal letter from the colonial administrator Sir Theophilus Shepstone, addressed to 'all chiefs of native tribes and their peoples'. This letter contains the following caveat: 'If gold exists where it is said to exist, no power can stop the stream of those who seek for it, however much they may wish to do so; and it is the way of a wise man to guide what he cannot prevent.'

So it came to pass: the story of modern South Africa.

Oh strange new world

It is ironic that as the Portuguese gradually penetrated inland, fuelling the extravagant legend, the kingdom itself began to disintegrate. Monomotapa finally petered out as an identifiable entity during the First World War. From conjuring a seductive mirage in the European imagination, that 'empire' is now commemorated in the name of a multi-storey hotel in Harare, the city which is also home to the professional Monomotapa United Football Club.

In contrast to European responses to Africa, the pioneer explorers of the Americas were inclined to conjecture that they had arrived at, or near, paradise; possibly the Garden of Eden. Christopher Columbus recorded on his third voyage that he had found 'the Terrestrial Paradise'. Subsequent voyagers made similar associations. Amerigo Vespucci, after whom the continent is named, asserted, 'I thought I was near the earthly paradise.'

As the English began to develop ambitions in the Americas,

Dr John Dee, as advisor to Queen Elizabeth I, projected a mystical vision of British expansion into a new Arcadia. This eccentric magus is thought by some scholars to be the model for Shakespeare's sorcerer Prospero in *The Tempest*. And Prospero's daughter, hitherto a shipwrecked castaway, famously gasps on seeing men for the first time: 'O brave new world, / That has such people in't!'

Such optimism is not to be found in the European exploration of Africa. Since antiquity, the southern hemisphere had chiefly been regarded with trepidation. Misconceptions about Africa reflected a cauldron of the European subconscious, with every suppressed terror and desire bubbling to the surface.

The English pilgrims who sailed on the Mayflower, 32 years before the founding of a Dutch settlement at the Cape, left with an aspiration of starting afresh, leaving behind the disappointments of the old world in the hope of establishing a more moral society. But if the Americas evoked expectations of a New World, Africa appeared to threaten a steamy abyss, an anti-Eden, where Europeans might be sucked into a monstrous pit of depravity.

European prejudices intensified with, and ideologically justified, the increasingly profitable Atlantic slave trade. So while the English pilgrims in Virginia intended to settle there permanently, the European presence in Africa was initially restricted to precarious enclaves for trade, purely in order to exploit its resources, mineral and human.

Consequently, along the entire west coast of Africa, as European sailors and merchants pushed ever further south, there was no New England, no New Amsterdam, nor a New York: no new anything at all. Only the Gold Coast, Ivory Coast and Slave Coast. This was not a realm of novelty or wonder, but one to be raided and used.

Here be wild beasts

In 1767, the year Samuel Wallis made landfall in Tahiti, a fuller attempt to classify humans into racial groups was made by the Swedish botanist, Carl Linnaeus. In *Systema Naturae,* he'd already published an innovative classification system for all living organisms, including '*homo sapiens*'. By the twelfth edition in 1767, Linnaeus added attributes for the 'varieties' of humans: *Americanus* (red, regulated by custom); *Asiaticus* (yellow, governed by opinion); *Africanus* (black, ruled by caprice); and *Europeanus* (white, guided by laws). In addition, he added the *Monstrosus* (the Patagonian giant) and the *monochid* (one-testicled) Hottentot (Khoikhoi).

Bushmen (San) did not merit a mention. Invariably regarded by Europeans as less than human, late into the nineteenth century the 'wild Bosjesmen' of southern Africa were even hunted and killed like wild animals. Even in the latter half of the twentieth century, when still called Bushmen, they remained widely reviled.

During one autumn break at university, I was invited to the farm of an Afrikaans family on the Karoo plains. There had been a protracted drought. Sheep were dying. Vultures circled. The farmer, his face seared the colour of teak, invited me on his daily tour of the vast property, and among the scattered koppies showed me rock paintings, hundreds of years old.

'What happened to the Bushmen?' I asked.

'They were still here in my grandfather's time,' he said and led me to a rocky outcrop and along a rubble-strewn defile. 'Bushies constantly raided everyone's livestock,' he explained. 'Eventually a commando was called and all the farmers came with horse and gun. They were hunting a big group so it was easy to follow their dust trail. The commando herded them – men, women and children – right here. But those crafty little Bushies had retreated deep into the ravine. Guns were useless while their arrows were deadly. It was decided to starve them out. After only a few days, though, most men said they wanted to get back to their farms.

'The Bushies were sheltering under a rocky overhang. Some of our younger guys were sent to fetch barrels of vinegar, while others collected brushwood, anything that would burn. Then the vinegar was poured over the rock of the overhang, and on top of it they built a huge bonfire, which was set alight. Finally, that rock got so damn hot that the entire overhang cracked, split and smashed down onto the Bushmen below, killing the lot.'

Charles Dickens conveys this exterminating credo. Despite his empathy for the downtrodden in England, he did not extend compassion to aboriginals in the colonies. 'Think of the Bushmen,' urged the novelist in 1853 in his own weekly magazine, *Household Words*. 'Think of the two men and two women who have been exhibited about England for some years. Are the majority of persons – who remember the horrid little leader of that party in his festering bundle of hides, with his filth and his antipathy to water, and his straddled legs, and his odious eyes shaded by his brutal hand, and his cry of 'Qu-u-u-u-aaa!' (Bosjesman for something desperately insulting I have no doubt) – conscious of an affectionate yearning towards that noble savage, or is it idiosyncratic of me to abhor, detest, abominate, and abjure him?'

Dickens went further: 'To come to the point at once, I beg to say that I have not the least belief in the Noble Savage. I consider him a prodigious nuisance, and an enormous superstition. His calling rum fire-water, and me a pale face, wholly fail to reconcile me to him. I don't care what he calls me. I call him a savage, and I call a savage something highly desirable to be civilised off the face of the earth.'

A litany of insults

Such opinions lingered long after Dickens. In 1910 the *Encyclopaedia Britannica* labelled Bushmen as 'of generally unattractive countenance ... the eyes are deeply set and of crafty expression'. Bosjesmen were often indiscriminately lumped together with what were termed Hottentots. Lenin used the term 'Hottentot' as shorthand for people who had not reached what he considered to be a reasonable level of culture. In 1922, an outraged review of James Joyce's *Ulysses* on the front page of the British newspaper *Sporting Life*, normally devoted to horse racing, concluded that his novel would 'make a Hottentot sick'. My *Chambers Encyclopaedia* (1955) specifies that 'Bushmen have proved resistant to civilisation', while my dog-eared copy of *Roget's Thesaurus* (1972) draws these parallels: 'A Goth, Vandal, Hottentot, savage, barbarian, yahoo ...'.

Those prejudices have a lengthy pedigree. Sir Thomas Herbert, who later accompanied King Charles I on his last walk to the scaffold, described 'Afrique' as being full of 'black skinn'd wretches' who 'are of no profession, except rapine and villainy'. In his book *Some Yeares Travels Into Africa and Asia the Great* (1631), he depicted mythical kingdoms where men's shadows took on sinister shapes and wanton women showed off 'their bummies' to the new moon.

Yet when Sir Thomas reached the southernmost tip of Africa, he was enthralled by the sight of Table Mountain. He called the Cape 'this Elysium', but he was incensed that semi-naked 'monsters' could live in a demi-paradise. So Sir Thomas resorted to the ancient calumny about Ham. 'The country is rich and fruitful in her womb,' he wrote, 'but owned by an accursed progeny of Cham, who differ in nothing from bruit beasts save forme.'

They are godless, thieving and ugly, he thundered, and live in caves, 'coupling without distinction, the name of wife or brother unknown among these incestuous Troglodytes'. He denounced them as '*Anthropophagi*, a degree more barbarous than the Lyons', claiming that 'these savages eat men alive or dead, even their own old folk'. Finally, Sir Thomas found himself so repulsed that he had to seek refuge in Latin for a summation of their unregenerate beastliness: '*inhumani … impuri … falsissimi, fraudulentissimi, cupidissimi, perfidissimi*'.

Twenty one years later, with the arrival of Dutch Calvinists, for whom bustle and toil exemplified a path to salvation, their sloth was reviled. But Hottentots also represented potential use as trading partners, however reluctant, for their sheep and cattle. In contrast, neither Aboriginals in Australia nor Bushmen in South Africa proved of economic value to the settlers. Thus both were subjected to the annihilating fury of invading Europeans. The English civil servant John Barrow, in his 1801 account of his two years' service at the Cape, remarked, 'I myself have heard one of the humane colonists boast of having destroyed with his own hands near three hundred of these unfortunate wretches.' Some colonists mounted their victim's skulls on the wall as trophies. Others made tobacco pouches from women's breasts.

A succession of Englishmen delighted in drawing droll comparisons between South Africa's supposed savages and the colonised Irish. King Charles I's comforter, Sir Thomas, remarked of the Hottentots, 'Their language is apishly founded', adding that it is 'voyced like the Irish'. Dickens likened listening to a troupe of 'Zulu Kaffirs' performing at Hyde Park Corner to 'an orator in an Irish House of Commons'. And commenting on a proposal to extend self-government to the Irish, the Tory Prime Minister Lord Salisbury quipped, 'I would no more give an Irishman the vote than I would to the Hottentot.'

When Charles Darwin visited the Cape on *HMS Beagle* in 1836 he made a brief trip into the countryside, hiring as his guide a 'Hodmadod', of whom he spoke favourably. But Darwin later reflected, 'Wherever the European has trod, death seems to pursue the aboriginal. We may look to the wide extent of the Americas, Polynesia, the Cape of Good Hope and Australia, and we find the same result.'

Denis Diderot – though not as enamoured as he had been with the good-natured and good-looking Tahitians – had been right to urge, 'Flee, Hottentots, Flee!'

Imperial social experiments

The response of the first European visitors to Tahiti was the opposite: the island was a garden of earthly delights and the people uniquely good-looking.

'The women are all handsome,' recorded Samuel Wallis, 'and some of them extremely beautiful.' Nine months after he left, the Comte de Bougainville arrived, not knowing Wallis had preceded him, and rhapsodised, 'I thought I had been transported to paradise. Everywhere we went we found hospitality, peace, innocence and joy and every appearance of happiness.'

Diderot seized on Bougainville's portrayal of Tahiti in his *Voyage autour du Monde* as a cudgel with which to thump French society. His satire, *Supplement au Voyage de Bougainville,* based on Bougainville's fortnight in Tahiti, helped to promote the idea of '*le bon sauvage*'. Diderot foresaw only harm being brought by Europeans, and warns Tahitians 'one day you will be almost as unhappy as they are'.

The inspiration for Diderot's ridicule of French society was a young Tahitian whom Bougainville had brought back to Paris, wishing to test whether an artless 'child of nature' could be transformed into a refined Frenchman.

Aotourou proved a sensation, though after 12 months interest waned and he died of smallpox on his way home.

Captain Cook arrived a year after Bougainville, and though less inclined to romanticise, was also impressed by the attractiveness of the Tahitians. Sir Joseph Banks, the botanist aboard Cook's *Endeavour,* liked to portray himself as a dashing rake, and before he married, he remarked that for a wife, 'had he been inclined' he would take a Cape Town Dutch woman, but Tahiti was the nirvana for erotic enchantments.

Five years after Aotourou had been transported to Paris, another Tahitian was taken aboard *HMS Adventure* by Commander Tobias Furneaux, who had served with Captain Wallis on the *Dolphin.* Mai, or Omai as he was commonly known, was introduced to London society by Sir Joseph and became a celebrity, feted by the leading dignitaries, including King George III.

He remained in England for two years, by which time Banks had tired of his novelty value. Eventually Captain Cook, on his third voyage, was instructed to return Omai to Tahiti, where the dire predictions of Diderot proved prescient. Landing with many gifts, Omai soon offended important Tahitians, and Cook realised that his charge needed to be removed to another island. On Huahine, Cook's carpenters built Omai a house called Beritani (Britain). But Omai's goods were soon pillaged, and in less than three years he was dead.

Earlier the British had conducted another experiment, though more commercial. The British East India Company had been considering establishing a provisioning station on the coast of South Africa, when in 1613 two Khoi men were kidnapped from Table Bay by a returning East Indiaman. The idea, according to a contemporary, the Rev. Edward Terry, was that once they learned enough, the English trading company 'might discover something of this country which we could not know before'. One captive died on the voyage. But as soon as the *Hector* docked in London, the survivor, Xhoré, was taken to the home of the governor of the East India Company.

Sir Thomas Smythe, the most powerful merchant in Britain, instructed that his captive guest be clothed fashionably, and Sir Thomas personally supervised his tuition in English ways, particularly the language. This was not a success. Xhoré, unlike Omai, had no desire to humour his captors or perform a pantomime of European imitation. According to the Rev. Terry, Xhoré 'was very well used'; everyone was therefore flummoxed by Xhoré's apparent total lack of gratitude. Every time Sir Thomas tried to probe him about Saldania (as Table Bay was then known), Xhoré fell to the floor, beating the carpet fiercely and wailing, 'Xhoré home go – Saldania go!'

Less than six months after his arrival, the experiment having been a complete failure, Xhoré was put back on the *Hector* and returned to Table Bay. The experiment was more than a fiasco; it was a humiliation. The unlettered Khoi chief had outwitted Sir Thomas. As the Rev. Terry ruefully recorded, 'It would have been well if he had not seen England. For as he discovered nothing to us, so certainly when he came home he told his countrymen (having doubtless observed much here) that brass was but a base and cheap commodity in England …'.

In the Cape the result was that 'we never after had such a free exchange of our brass and iron for their cattle'.

Intimate investigations

The reports of passing travellers reveal a fascination with Khoi genitalia: the testicles and penis of men, 'steatopygia' or the ample backsides of women. Above all, visiting Europeans were riveted by the female Khoi pudenda. Successive writers tried to answer the question as to whether there was a female 'Hottentot *tablier*' (apron); i.e. if they possessed extended labia. Even Monsieur Diderot took an interest in this recondite topic. After questioning the soldier Robert Gordon, he wrote that the Colonel had examined two women and saw '*un clitoris exorbitant*'.

Captain Cook also felt obliged to investigate 'the great question' when the *Endeavour* called at Cape Town on the return from his first circumnavigation. Cook interviewed a local doctor, who claimed that in treating Hottentot women he found 'skinny appendages proceeding from the upper part of the labia ... and were in different subjects of different lengths, in some not more than an inch, in others three or four inches'. One of the foremost disciples of Carl Linnaeus, the Swedish naturalist Anders Sparrman who accompanied Cook on the *Resolution*, apologised to his 'more delicate readers' in his *A Voyage to the Cape of Good Hope* (1786) for not wrapping up the subject in Latin or delicate phrases. But he felt obliged 'to make enquiries'.

Another contemporary report noted that this esoteric topic 'usually excites the curiosity of European sailors', and that there were Hottentot ladies who 'will offer to satisfy his curiosity for a halfpenny'. It is quite probable that when the *Resolution* anchored in Table Bay, the ship's carpenter – my great-great-great-great-grandfather James Wallis – conducted his own amateur investigations.

Over a decade later, after entreaties from the French explorer François Le Vaillant, a Khoi woman eventually ('confused, abashed and trembling') permitted him to study her genitalia at his leisure. Some more years later, in 1810, another Khoi woman Sara ('Saartjie') Baartman was first exhibited in London, then after four years she was sold off to a Frenchman and displayed in Paris. There Sara was studied by the naturalist Georges Cuvier, who remarked, 'there is nothing more celebrated in nature than the Hottentot apron, and at the same time there is nothing which has been the object of such great argumentation'.

Regularly cited as a self-glorifying comparison between 'civilised' Europeans and bestial 'lower beings', the 'apron' continued to be a focus of voyeuristic fascination well into the twentieth century, with speculation as to whether this was natural or artificially induced. In fact, much earlier, Le Vaillant had deduced, correctly, that the 'apron' was fashioned or contrived: a cultural practise.

In another context, Le Vaillant wrote, 'I will soon report some facts that will prove, more surely than idle speculation, which is the barbarian: the savage or the white man.' As if to prove his point, after the death of Sara Baartman in 1816, Curvier dissected her body and pickled her brains and genitalia, which remained on display in jars in the Museum of Man in Paris until 1974.

A major influence on nineteenth century views on race was Dr Robert Knox, regarded as an expert on aboriginal people, having served as an army surgeon on the Cape frontier. His lectures were attended by the young Charles Darwin. Knox developed a theory of racial categorisation, asking, 'Who cares particularly for the Negro, or Hottentot or the Kaffir?' Knox promptly answered his own question: 'Destined by the nature of their race to run, like other animals, a certain limited course of existence, it matters little how their extinction is brought about.'

Dr Knox is better known today for the purchase in Edinburgh, for dissection, of 17 vagrants killed by William Burke and William Hare, hence the popular ballad: 'Burke's the butcher, Hare's the thief / Knox the boy who buys the beef.'

As late as 1997, shortly before I returned to South Africa, I wrote to the Natural History Museum in London asking if it was true that they had on display five heads of Xhosa warriors obtained during the frontier wars. The reply was that the museum had seven heads, 'although they have never been on display and have always been part of our worldwide anthropological research collections'. The letter declared that there was no evidence that the heads were obtained during the frontier wars, as 'the material was donated to us' by the Royal College of Surgeons.

Hearts of whiteness

Having traced imperial and familial records up till the present, I agree with the narrator of Joseph Conrad's *Heart of Darkness*, 'The conquest of the earth, which mostly means the taking it away from those who have a different complexion or slightly flatter noses than ourselves, is not a pretty thing when you look into it too much.'

The 'scramble for Africa' was a violent scrimmage. In 1870, ten per cent of the continent was under European control. Just over 30 years later, 90 per cent of Africa had been occupied. This conquest was made possible by the availability of commercially produced quinine and the repeating rifle. A brand-new machine gun, named after its inventor Hiram Maxim, was used for the first time in battle by Cecil Rhodes' British South Africa Company. His mercenaries invaded Lobengula's Ndebele kingdom with five Maxim guns. In one engagement they killed 1,500 warriors with the loss of four men, and a week later slaughtered an estimated 2,500 Matabele.

Such weapons enabled competing European powers to annex approximately 100 million extra subjects. Even the uncompromising explorer, Henry Morton Stanley, who opened up the Congo for King Leopold II of Belgium, confided to his diary: 'We went into the heart of Africa self-invited – therein lies our fault.' Leopold had declared that he coveted a slice of 'that magnificent African cake', and under the guise of a philanthropic mission, he seized the Congo Free State as his personal fiefdom. The depravity was unparalleled.

About half the population was killed. Yet every time there is conflict in Africa, articles appear in the West repeating the same lazy headline: the Heart of Darkness. It took Conrad several years to digest the pitiless colonial behaviour he had witnessed while working as a temporary captain of the streamer *Roi des Belges* on the Congo River in 1890. Yet even as Conrad began describing the fictional quest upriver in search of the 'prodigy' Kurtz, with horrifying stories of his atrocities multiplying, a French expedition set out from Senegal with the aim of unifying all French territories in West Africa. Though the novelist couldn't have known about it, this official mission bears a macabre resemblance to the gruesome novella that he was composing about the Congo.

The leaders, Captain Paul Voulet and Lieutenant Julien Chanoine, were rising stars of the French army. Their secret orders were to carve out a vast chunk of empire.

Instead, the French Central African Expedition became a homicidal odyssey of rape, torture and massacre. When two of his soldiers were killed, Captain Voulet ordered 150 women and children executed in retaliation. In one village, 400 were slaughtered; in another, 1,000. Local guides who displeased Voulet were strung up alive so their feet could be gnawed by hyenas. Girls were hung from trees; heads were impaled on sticks.

As word filtered back to Paris, the Governor of Timbuktu, Lieutenant-Colonel Arsène Klobb, was sent after them. Like

Marlow tracking Kurtz, Klobb followed an 'infernal trail' of devastation and charred bodies.

Lt-Colonel Klobb caught up with his quarry on 14 July, shortly after Captain Voulet had given his officers a bottle of champagne to celebrate Bastille Day. Ordering his men to fire at Klobb, Voulet raved, 'I am now an outlaw. I disavow my family, my country, I'm not French anymore, I am a black leader', and decreed, 'We will create an empire.' Chanoine and Voulet were shot by their own soldiers.

In 1902, following an enquiry, the French government ruled that the two officers 'had been driven mad by the dreadful heat'. Once again, blame was placed on Africa.

But this atrocious saga, like Conrad's novel, is not about Africans. It's a chronicle about Europeans in Africa. *Heart of Darkness* was serialised in early 1899, exactly as Arsène Klobb was chasing his fellow officers through the desert.

'All Europe contributed to the making of Kurtz,' reflects Conrad's narrator. The seafarer Marlow, aboard the Thames pleasure yacht *Nellie*, tells his companions the grim tale of his quest for the crazed Kurtz in the Congo jungle. Marlow is scathing about European motives for carving out colonies in Africa. 'To tear treasure out of the bowels of the land was their desire,' he relates, 'with no more moral purpose at the back of it than there is in burglars breaking into a safe.' Marlow had read the eloquent report by Kurtz for the International Society for the Suppression of Savage Customs. But an added note on the last page ('scrawled evidently much later, in an unsteady hand'), exhorted: 'Exterminate all the brutes!'

Unlike my grandfather, Lewis Rose, or my father Frank, Conrad harboured no illusions about the ambitions of empire. At the time of the Boer War, Conrad wrote to a friend, 'There is an appalling fatuity in this business. If I am to believe Kipling this is a war undertaken for the cause of democracy.' Then the novelist reverted to French, perhaps because in English he always preserved such exquisite civility, '*C'est à crever de rire!*' ('It's enough to make you die laughing!')

✠

ORPHANS OF THE HEART

Following ghostly footsteps

WHEN MY FOUR grandparents emigrated to South Africa, though the British Empire was still to reach its farthest span, nearly all the great Imperial advocates were glancing uneasily over their shoulders, fretting that time was running out. The criterion against which they measured themselves was the Roman Empire.

Almost as though it was a set work, the select and favoured dutifully read – as, deferentially, did I – Edward Gibbon's *Decline and Fall of the Roman Empire*. Winston Churchill first studied it as a 22-year-old army officer in India. In South Africa, Cecil Rhodes re-read the book obsessively, and even paid for fresh translations to be made from the original Latin sources that Gibbon had consulted.

Rudyard Kipling rather overdid the Roman analogy in praising Rhodes' buccaneering ally Dr Jameson, whom Lewis Rose was later contracted to support by launching a newspaper. Crudely, but revealingly, after the massacre of the Matabele with the new Maxim guns, Dr Jim, as Administrator of the conquered territory, declared the opening of the town of Bulawayo from the entrance of a new hotel, The Maxim. Kipling nevertheless eulogised Dr Jameson as 'the noblest Roman of them all'. Perhaps it is lightly ironic that, not long after sailing out of Table Bay (failing to foresee any decay or fall of apartheid in my lifetime), I should head for Italy.

Kipling was not only a forceful poet of empire. He was haunted by decline; the anxiety that the sands of time eventually run out for all empires.

'On dune and headland sinks the fire,' he lamented in *Recessional*. 'Lo, all our pomp of yesterday / Is one with Nineveh and Tyre.' Four times Kipling repeated the melancholy refrain, 'Lest we forget – lest we forget!'

But we do, all the time.

Absconding to Europe

My motive for going to Italy was the precise opposite of my parents. They had gone on honeymoon – Venice, Florence, Rome – in the freezing winter of 1947, prior to their plan of returning to South Africa and making a new life there. Mine was to get away from South Africa. For several years after I had sailed from Cape Town, believing that it was forever, the South African Defence Force posted letters to me, care of my mother in England, instructing National Serviceman 70547542 to report for military service in Pretoria. My mother never bothered me with this annual summons, and many years later confessed that she had always requested, in reply, that if the army ever did succeed in locating her elusive son, would they kindly inform her of his whereabouts?

Towards the end of his memoir, Stendhal describes his rapture on arriving in Italy as a lieutenant in Napoleon's army. Looking back, the novelist admits that he would be forced to romanticise if he attempted to recall his emotions as a young man, and urges 'O unfeeling reader, forgive my memory, or rather skip fifty pages.' As this exhortation appears on the last sheet of Stendhal's unfinished manuscript, there were no more pages left to skip. Instead, O reader, I will now do the skipping for you by travelling discreetly from fair Verona, my first delightful Italian home, to unruly Naples.

Having endured centuries of invasion and conquest, that resilient, ancient city had learned to survive by guile and subterfuge. When the troops of Charles VIII of France occupied Naples in 1495, they soon discovered nasty lesions on their genitals. Anticipating the later spat between Captain Samuel Wallis and Bougainville over who had introduced venereal disease to Tahiti, the French christened this infection 'the Neapolitan disease', while Neapolitans retaliated by calling it the 'French disease'.

The likelihood is that the gruesome itch had been brought back by Columbus' men from the New World – and some of them took part as mercenaries in the defence of Naples. Thus, when French troops occupied the city, Naples repaid this violation from the festering embrace of its legion of prostitutes. After which the 'great pox' spread swiftly throughout Europe – and eventually to Tahiti.

In the eighteenth-century, Naples had been a major European city, a centre of scholarship and culture. 'The most beautiful city in the universe,' judged Stendhal. But after that began the slow decline, as if history were leaving Naples stranded in its own colourful myths and ancient preoccupations. In my sweltering room – a converted storage space below a brothel – my novel set in Cape Town swelled manically. It echoed an unsolved mystery from the abortive Russian Revolution of 1905.

A mass march in St Petersburg to present a petition to the Tsar was led by Father Georgi Gapon, whose organisation, the Assembly of Russian Factory and Mill Workers, was funded by the Tsarist secret police. As the crowd snaked towards the Winter Palace, soldiers fired, killing about 200 protestors. Was Father Gapon an *agent provocateur*, or did he get carried away by the passion of the moment? Gapon fled abroad, but returned in 1906 only to be murdered: whether by vengeful revolutionaries or the Tsarist secret police remains unclear.

The plot for my fervid novel was partly based on a charismatic friend who, it seemed likely in retrospect, had been either a police spy or *agent provocateur*. Yet given the feverish conditions in which it was being written – in a poky, sweaty storeroom, as murky at noon as at midnight – my manuscript was also rapidly losing the plot.

One summery dawn, I wandered past the Royal Palace to the small park and belvedere, from where there was a panoramic view over the Gulf of Naples. Across the bay, Vesuvius seemed to loom close enough to touch. Abruptly, after nearly a year, I realised why Naples seemed so improbably familiar. The sinuous bay and that prodigious, mountainous landmark? Of course, Table Bay!

Above all, I realised, the cobbled backstreets reminded me of District Six. Like the *Quartieri Spagnoli* of Naples, District Six had been a defiant universe of its own, a rowdy challenge to respectability. It had also been such an affront to South Africa's ruling zealots that by now they had stepped up the pace of evicting the hybrid residents and bulldozing their homes to make way for 'whites only'.

Into the underworld

The genial Roman poet Horace enjoyed holidaying at the empire's most fashionable resort near Naples, where his friend Virgil had lived for many years. But Horace dryly lamented that the Bay of Naples was so full of rubbish that even the fish complained.

This was still true. Within a month of my arrival there was an outbreak of cholera, blamed on toxic mussels. Soon there were deaths. Panic spread. Then I fell ill: diarrhoea, vomiting, dehydration, exhaustion. All the symptoms. I joined jostling queues to see an army doctor. A young officer, groggy with fatigue, sighed 'You'll live,' adding, 'drink beer.' So in the shabby grandeur of the Galleria Umberto, the cavernous glass-domed nineteenth century arcade, I dutifully sipped beer during hot evenings. By the time the plague passed, it had claimed 24 lives.

Virgil, in the *Aeneid*, located the entrance to the underworld at Lake Avernus, a volcanic crater lake just west of the city ('Perdition's dank door remains open day and night'.) Nearly 2,000 years later, Naples seemed like a spectral netherworld. Opposite the Galleria, the jumble of narrow streets (known as the Spanish Quarter from the time when Spanish invaders quartered their troops there) persisted as a stronghold for the two professions forever drawn by the military: prostitutes and criminals.

On the floor above me in the rundown *palazzo* was a small and homely bordello with several resident ladies. As the US Sixth Fleet had its main base in Naples, I always knew when its warships had returned to port, as in the early hours, from the lightless stairwell, I'd be woken by drunken cries of 'Hey, *Senorita*! You there, *Senorita*?'

The most courteous of the middle-aged courtesans upstairs was

242

Carla, a matronly figure with a pretty oval face and sad eyes. When the US Fleet was in, Carla always had a single beau for the duration of the furlough. They were invariably raw youths, probably homesick rural hicks grateful for the motherly attentions of an older woman. One morning, Carla came to my door and held out a scrappy handwritten letter in English. She couldn't read it. The author was called Freddie aboard a US aircraft carrier. 'Do you miss me?' he asked. 'I miss you so much, Carla.'

Her proposition was simple. She would pay me to translate these letters into Italian and her replies into English. I declined the offer of cash in return for the use of their outsized zinc bathtub. I still have more than a dozen of those letters.

Carla's first letter to Freddie produced a swift response. 'I know you have another man in Naples – but when I come back you'd better give him up as Freddie will be in town,' he wrote.

Soon a letter arrived from Ronald, saying that he'd been made a fool of twice by women; but, 'In the few days we were together, I never knew a woman so tender and honest.' Ronald asks Carla to send him a photo. So did Danny, followed by Price.

In May came a letter from Sugar Bear, his address, 'At Sea'. Sugar Bear seemed worldlier than Carla's other suitors. 'That last night we spent together is still on my mind,' wrote Sugar Bear. 'You were good. (We both were good). I really did like you, that's no lie. I know you said the same to me, it could have been because your job is to make the customer feel good. Just maybe you do have some feeling for me. I can't really say.' Towards the end, Sugar Bear remarked 'Why didn't you say that you had gotten $10 out of my coat? At first I was pissed, but I got over it.' Finally, Sugar Bear also asked Carla for a photo, and added: 'I'll always remember you.'

Paths of forgetfulness

Compulsively exploring the back streets, I realised I had become infatuated with the city, exactly as had happened not long ago in my wanderings in Cape Town. With no one to answer to, I experienced a sense of weightless freedom followed by acute pangs of aimlessness. It was at that point I met Valentina. She lived in an empty sentry box outside the long-vacant Royal Palace.

Valentina Fedina must have been in her late 60s. With grey eyes, a weather-beaten face, frizzy ginger hair and scarlet lipstick slashed across her mouth, she dressed like a rag doll: all frills, tatters and faded glory.

She had been a young girl when her family fled from Russia in 1917 to escape the Bolshevik Revolution. That was why her unruly mongrel was called Mosca, Italian for Moscow. How she ended up in Naples was never clear, although sometimes she mentioned a late, unlamented husband. Once, she remarked indifferently, 'We were awfully rich.' Valentina seemed to enjoy living in the sentry box. 'It protects me from sun and rain,' she explained. 'It also has a seat, so I can sleep sitting upright, most comfortably.' The added appeal of this address, I suspected, was that during the day it allowed her to face the busy *Piazza del Plebiscito* and survey the passing strangers, many of whom stopped to pay court to her like some raggedy queen on her throne.

Now, in addition to being disturbed late at night by drunken American sailors, I was regularly woken before dawn by a cheery,

'Cooee, Mr Rostron!' Usually the excuse was some stray thought that Valentia pretended she wished to discuss.

'I wonder,' she once asked, 'what you consider might have happened if Mr Trotsky had prevailed over Mr Stalin?' It being too early to ponder such historical riddles, I'd suggest that we adjourn for a cappuccino and brioche, while thinking: damn, there goes today's budget for lunch.

One day she let slip that she had a sister. 'But one no longer has contact with family,' explained Valentina airily.

Yet as winter gathered, even she confessed that the sentry box was not entirely satisfactory. I wheedled out of her the sister's address in New York, and wrote to explain Valentina's situation. A terse response (c/o Carla) said that funds would be sent directly to a *pensione* – to ensure the money was not spent on anything else, but sufficient to assure Valentina of a bed till the following spring. The condition for this help was that Valentina never attempt to make contact again.

A postcard with a cartoon of Vesuvius belching smoke arrived from Valentina with an invitation 'to dine' at her new *pensione*. Cramped and filthy, the building looked as though it was about to collapse. With Mosca frolicking behind, Valentina led the way up two flights of stairs to show me her room. There was barely enough space for the iron bedstead and her collection of plastic bags. '*Violà*,' she trilled, 'a room of my own!' We progressed to the dining room, stinking of rancid fat. It was packed.

There must have been at least 40 men at three long tables. Even in the gloom it was clear that they were all tough Asian sailors, or Lascars: an old term for crews from the Indian Ocean serving on

European ships. 'In honour of this unique occasion, the hotel management has made special arrangements,' Valentina informed me, pointing proudly to what seemed to be a card table with collapsible chairs on each side. Slowly we wended our way across the darkened dining room, and every so often Valentina would halt to address a cluster of baffled Asian sailors.

'I should like to present – if I may – my dear and most distinguished friend, Mr Rostron,' Valentina proclaimed each time in a resounding quaver, as though introducing the Grand Duke Sergei to a huddle of titled foreign diplomats.

Time, I thought, to emerge from this crepuscular underworld.

Lone mother of dead empires

The winter of 1947, when my parents went on honeymoon to Italy, was exceptionally bitter. In the disordered aftershock of war, trains ran irregularly. There was little fuel. *Pensiones* had no heating. A snap of the newlyweds in Venice catches them in a gondola, huddled in overcoats, swathed in scarves, hats pulled low. Behind, the *palazzi* of the Grand Canal are almost blanched out by swirling fog.

There's another photo of them wrapped up on the belvedere overlooking Florence, this time with my Auntie Alix's older sister Esmé, my mother's other great-aunt. There are several more grainy honeymoon snaps: on Esmé's rambling Tuscan farm *Monteverdi*, and in Rome, again looking extremely cold. By then the widow Almagià, Esmé had been married to two wealthy Italians, and her elegant Roman villa was packed with Chinese artefacts from when she, Alix and their brother Bertram had been brought up in Tientsin.

I moved from Naples to Rome 27 years after my parents' honeymoon and regularly walked to the foreign Press Club through 2,000 years of architecture. Rome was a bombastic pageant of empire, and one of the monuments I passed almost every day was the *Ara Pacis*, a massive marble altar commemorating the Emperor Augustus and dedicated to *Pax*, Roman goddess of Peace.

To mark the 2,000th anniversary of the birth of Augustus, but chiefly to boost Benito Mussolini's pretensions that his fascist regime was the twentieth century incarnation of imperial Rome, the colossal monument was tortuously exhumed in 1937 from under a nearby *palazzo*. What I didn't know then was that this stately Renaissance palace, once the residence of cardinals, princes and dukes, had been owned by Esmé's in-laws. The Almagiàs, including Esmé's second husband Saul, helped to pay for the difficult feat of excavating the *Ara Pacis* in the hope that *Il Duce* would leave the Almagià family, one-quarter Jewish, alone.

For a while I rented a room near the Villa Borghese from an obese former New York wrestler, who had staked all his savings on moving to Rome in the hope of carving out a new career playing gangsters in Italian movies. Eddie spent every morning in the expensive pavement cafés of the Via Veneto expecting to be spotted by a film director. But he'd return disconsolate at midday, complaining, 'Dammit, that's where the movie stars hung out in Fellini's *La Dolce Vita*. Where'd the hell they all go, Brain? Now it's fulla friggin' American tourists.'

In the Villa Borghese Gardens nearby was a statue of Lord Byron, grandson of Captain 'Foul-Weather Jack'. In his epic poem *Childe Harold*, Byron salutes Rome as 'Lone mother of dead empires!' The preceding lines are engraved on the statue's plinth, and hauntingly evoke the city with high-flown Byronic clairvoyance:

> 'Oh Rome! City of the soul!
> The orphans of the heart must turn to thee …'

It was the tail-end of the *Dolce Vita* era. Every summer, along with the swallows, the Eternal City attracted a rich cosmopolitan flotsam, trailing an enervated whiff of decadence. Rome was an indulgent refuge for charmers, chancers and dreamers.

For foreign newspapers, I investigated stolen artworks and smuggled statues. One paper dispatched me to interview a Tuscan peasant who had placed an ad in South Africa: 'Genuine racist, seeks work'. After a while, I moved to a tiny flat in a cobbled street behind Santa Maria in Trastevere, and suddenly, bizarrely, had a brief career as a movie actor. Whether a naïve Swedish boyfriend or CIA agent disguised as a priest, a scruffy but pitiless German terrorist or impeccably groomed officer of the Austro-Hungarian Empire, my unique talent was, effortlessly, that I didn't look Italian.

Recalling a time of great happiness in Italy as a young man, Stendhal admits: 'What can one say of such a moment without lying, without lapsing into fiction?'

Theory runs amok

Stendhal's memoir, however, starts with a fib. The very first sentence of *The Life of Henry Brulard* informs us seductively that 'I was standing this morning, 16 October 1832, by San Pietro in Montorio on the Janiculum Hill in Rome, in magnificent sunshine.'

This was a brazen act of creative reorganisation, for the novelist was travelling that month in the mountainous region of Abruzzi, west of Rome. For several years, in contrast, I did linger at that very spot, either in the early morning or evening, and can confirm the essence of what Stendhal claimed to see and feel that day: 'A few small white clouds, borne on a barely perceptible sirocco wind, were floating above Monte Albano, a delicious warmth filled the air and I was happy to be alive.'

My small flat overlooked a square with steps leading to the Janiculum, the hill above Trastevere which offers stupendous views over Rome. Walking up almost every day past San Pietro in Montorio, I didn't know that when crossing the Via Garibaldi, I was passing right in front of the home of the American author whose books Auntie Betty had thrust upon me with such proselytising zeal.

The mystery is not that my auntie revered Robert Ardrey, but that leading newspapers and magazines in America and Europe dispatched their top reporters to interview the writer in his apartment. Never modest, Ardrey's ballooning conceit can be judged by his third book which borrows its title, *The Social Contract*, from Jean-Jacques Rousseau. Mr Ardrey's aspiration was not only to compare himself with one of Europe's foremost thinkers – but to do so favourably, by tipping poor old Jean-Jacques on his morose head.

Rousseau maintained that humans come into this world innocent, but are sullied by civilization; that 'natural man' is corrupted by the artificial citizen ('Man is born free, but everywhere is in chains.') Ardrey, over two hundred years later, argued the exact opposite: that men are intrinsically brutal, and only develop a thin patina of civility through (Western) civilization.

Ardrey had no truck with fancies of 'noble savages' and scorned any idea of equality. In his *Social Contract* (1970), our modern philosopher resolutely declared that science had confirmed that 'the black race', while athletically more endowed than whites, was intellectually inferior; and consequently, 'must be regarded as a distinct subdivision of *Homo sapiens*'.

This was the credo of many white South Africans. Luckily I never bumped into the world-fêted writer as I strolled past his apartment every day. For by then I had been told of the legendary night of terror at a fashionable restaurant, caused by a wild animal that the intrepid thinker had brought back to Italy as an eye-catching gift.

A decade earlier in *African Genesis*, Ardrey had illustrated his doctrine of innate and ineradicable instincts by describing a well-known experiment with a young otter in South Africa. This showed that even on being removed from the wild as an infant, the otter retained all its primal instincts after three years in captivity.

Nevertheless, Ardrey presented an imported South African otter, waggishly called Cheetah, to an American artist living in Trastevere, a baroquely camp character called Zev. One night Zev took his new pet to a chic restaurant (perhaps *Dell'Orso*, a favourite of Ardrey's) and Cheetah panicked. Unused to the volume of noise in a crowded Roman restaurant, the otter went berserk. Women scrambled onto chairs; crisp white tablecloths and male diners in stylish suits were spattered with otter shit.

I knew of this saga because Cheetah had been exiled in disgrace to *Monteverdi*, the Tuscan farm of cousin Gigi, son of Esmé. I resisted the temptation to relay this discrepancy between lofty theory and low farce to Auntie Betty. Of course, at the time I had no idea that her hero was my neighbour in Trastevere. In his last years Robert Ardrey went to live near Cape Town, in Kalk Bay, a 15-minute drive from Betty's former cottage on the chicken farm. By then, however, my aunt was marooned in a soulless Monte Carlo high-rise, trapped in René's Bertie Wooster fantasy of European refinement, far away from their fears of African savagery. But, like the famous Mr Ardrey, not so very remote from feverish European nightmares of Africans as: *'inhumani … impuri … cupidissimi, perfidissimi.'*

Out of Africa

British Empire loyalists, seeing Rome as an imperial template, relished citing *Pax Britannica* as a justification. Though a direct echo of *Pax Romana*, there was little *pax* in either empire. This was acknowledged by the Roman historian Tacitus, if not by most British historians. Recording the career of his father-in-law, the general who governed Britain and conquered Scotland, Tacitus attributes a bitter denunciation of Roman ruthlessness to a Caledonian chieftain: 'They make a desert and call it peace.'

Along the same lines, in 1851, the British socialist Ernest Jones remarked of the British Empire, 'On its colonies the sun never sets, but the blood never dries.'

Pax Britannica is regarded as lasting from 1815 to 1914, even though it has been estimated that by the time Queen Victoria celebrated her Diamond Jubilee in 1897, there had been at least 60 wars, great and small, throughout the empire: roughly one for every year of her reign. In parish churches all over England, bearing witness to the ferocity of that 'peace', there are ragged regimental flags commemorating local lads who fell in campaigns across the globe fighting what the Romans called '*barbari*'.

Yet the Romans displayed far more fluid attitudes to citizenship and identity, tending to make cultural rather than racial distinctions. This allowed 'barbarians' – Britons, Gauls, Germans, plus others of a different colour – to be assimilated, valued, and often promoted. The British, on the other hand, clung to a caste-like devotion of racial hierarchies, hence the marked distinctions between the 'White Dominions', such as Australia or South Africa, and the subject peoples of India, the West Indies or Africa.

Pride in 'the white man' was central to the British notion of imperial mission. Nowhere was that sense of national identity more tested than in Africa. Most chronicles of explorers and 'shilling shocker' novelists share archetypal motifs: city-bred gents undergo a perilous quest. Risky ventures into the 'Dark Continent' are a journey into the European subconscious. Amidst jungles, deserts, wild beasts and warlike tribes, they are tested to the uttermost before emerging triumphant. Modern thrillers set in Africa often mimic those themes.

Before leaving Italy, I starred in a ropey adventure B movie which – so far as anyone could follow the plot – repeated this formula.

Author starring in 'Skin 'em Alive'

A ne'er-do-well young German called Rudy (me) gets beaten up because he can't pay his gambling debts. He flees to Africa in search of his unscrupulous older brother, Franz, a vicious mercenary. After silly, scary, exotic and erotic adventures in the wilds (tons of sand ferried onto a backlot of Cinecittà Studios in Rome), I vanquish my nasty brother in a fist fight, win the bag of diamonds and return to Europe: a wiser, much richer man.

In search of fame

The further away I drifted, the more self-righteous seemed western attitudes towards Africa: habitually supercilious, often absurd. On moving from Italy to New York, I was, like Psmith, 'as broke as the Ten Commandments'.

At that moment my mother (who had been in the habit of posting me articles about writers who, having seen the light, churn out a blockbuster) sent a clipping about a publisher who was on the lookout for hungry new writers. It quoted Mr Bernard Geis as saying, 'We give our writers lots of money and tell them to go away and write.'

Later this publisher was portrayed in a film, *Isn't She Great*, starring Bette Midler, about his discovery of the author who virtually invented the mass-selling potboiler. Jacqueline Susann's first book, *Valley of the Dolls*, had been rebuffed by dozens of publishers until she met that same showman, played in the film by a manic John Cleese. He makes a spectacular entrance by sliding down a fireman's pole. I recognised that pole immediately.

The article explained that Mr Geis packaged deals, concocted storylines and even linked writers to team-constructed plots in search of an author. 'If the cash runs out,' Geis added, 'we give them more.'

Quickly I typed a 40-page outline for a thriller set in Italy. Geis responded that though tempted, 'the narrative art is an elusive one and, in this case, we are not quite prepared to gamble that the moonbeams would be caught in your net.' Despite doubts about Bernard Geis' prose, I weaved a bigger, better net: a 50-page synopsis for a political thriller set in South Africa. This time, to my astonishment, he phoned. Invited me to 'take' a meeting.

The first clue that I might not be cut out for this genre came when the publisher told me, 'We like your writing.' In *Isn't She Great*, Susann's editor sighs, 'Your manuscript is nigh unto incoherent' (to which Bette Midler replies, 'Is that bad?') In fact, for years *Valley of the Dolls*, published in 1966, was only outsold by the Bible. Previously Susann had bombed as an actress, whereas before moving to New York I'd stared in a B movie and had written two youthful novels set in South Africa. The first was short and brutal. The other, sweated over in my garret in Naples, was long, fevered and probably 'nigh unto incoherent'. I had shelved both, as in a Brooklyn motel I struggled with a new novel, hungry and insolvent.

Mr Geis looked tanned and rich. He came straight to the point: 'Like the writing, Bryan. Don't like the politics. We're off politics.'

'You lack a sustained love interest,' chipped in a lady editor.

'What we need is something incredible,' decreed Geis. 'Something so totally astonishing it could affect the life of the reader.' He paused. 'Like, if the Titanic had sunk off Cape Town, you could've raised it there, brought in the CIA, the KGB …'.

Then BG came up with his humdinger: 'South Africa, what d'ya think when ya think South Africa?' he mused. 'You think hot, right?' Abruptly he was struck by a bolt of inspiration. 'How about if … yeah, if some desperadoes kidnapped South Africa and towed it to Antarctica!'

The lady editor said that she'd read my new novel.

'It's not exactly a thriller,' I mumbled.

She shrugged. 'Our last prospective author wanted to know where to put the dialogue.'

Geis led me back to his large office with the fireman's pole.

'Bryan,' he boomed. 'I like my authors to slide down the pole. Test of nerve, wanna try?' Hell yeah, if that's what it took to earn, as Jacqueline Susann gloated, 'a shit load of money.' But as I vanished through the hole in the floor I heard a cackle from above: 'Of course, you've gotta write the goddam thing yourself, y'know.'

Ah. Actually write such *schlock*? Oh no. Before hitting the ground three stories below I knew I wasn't sliding down to bestsellerdom, chat shows, celebrity or riches.

The formula had long ago been spelled out to Olive Schreiner by Rider Haggard. After reading *The Story of An African Farm*, the best-selling author of *King Solomon's Mines* visited Olive at her London lodging (causing a scandal over unannounced visits by male callers). Haggard advised Olive to make her books more cheerful: rather rich, she remarked, from someone responsible for 'a murder or a suicide on every other page'. She also recorded that a critic, a friend of Haggard's, had grumbled that he would have preferred her 'little book': 'if it had been a history of wild adventure … of encounters with ravening lions, and hair-breath escapes.' But as Olive remarked, 'This could not be. Such works are best written in Piccadilly or in the Strand: there the gifts of the creative imagination, untrammelled by any fact, may spread their wings.'

The land of childhood

After a year in New York – *Pax Americana* – I returned to London, where my father suddenly seemed very frail. His once stocky boxer's build appeared shrunken, and his cheeks blushed like a child. Frank's conversation was increasingly about the past.

The philosopher Hegel, claiming that sub-Saharan Africa was insulated and static, declared: 'it is the Gold-land, compressed within itself – the land of childhood, which lying beyond the day of self-conscious history, is enveloped in the dark mantle of night'.

Though by an unspoken truce my father and I never discussed such matters, I suspect that Frank might have nodded in agreement with Hegel's generalisation. The Western perception of Africa as slumbering outside of history till awakened by the arrival of white men is still prevalent. Over the next few years, however, Frank seemed to be irreversibly retreating in his own memories, back to the land of childhood: an oddly serene preparation for being enveloped in the dark mantle of eternal night.

My mother believed that his loss of immediate and short-term memory was due to blows to his head as a boxer when a young man. His stories ebbed steadily in time, becoming more and more distant, reaching back to his youth and childhood. When repeating anecdotes, by then I knew better than to interrupt Frank's reminiscences.

As his memory drifted ever further back, his carapace of toughness slowly fell away. He told me of the time as a small boy, when they lived in Boksburg, that he'd been given the Christmas present he had always longed for. A neighbouring teenager swore to him that if he threw it deep into the nearby lake he would be rewarded with a much better, definitely more wonderful gift. I never heard Frank laugh so uninhibitedly as when he described how he had hurled his present as far as he could into the lake.

The map of memory

The only time I saw my father cry was when he was nearly 80. As an ex-South African amateur middleweight champion and former war correspondent, Frank was not a demonstrative man. Even more startling, this uncharacteristic display of emotion was precipitated by an event which had occurred over half a century before.

There was no warning. One moment he was talking about something quite commonplace when, seemingly unnoticed by the old man himself, he began to weep. Waxy tears, oddly from only one eye, slithered slowly and pitilessly down Frank's rosy, crinkled cheek.

My father seldom permitted a crack in his defences. As a young man he had fought exhibition bouts against several of the greatest boxing champions, including British world welterweight champion 'Kid' Lewis, the former world heavyweight champion Primo Carnera and Young Stribling, the chivalrous American, who – starting with his mother, Ma Stribling, as trainer – fought a record 286 professional contests. Although rated by many as one of the best heavyweight boxers of all time, Stribling abhorred violence and died young in a motorcycle accident.

In old age, Frank stubbornly fought to the end never to drop his gruff self-protective guard. Yet he'd begun to be less combative, no longer so insistent on always being right. Instead, he was increasingly inclined to remember episodes from the past. On that winter evening at my parents' home, there was little change at first in his voice as he suddenly switched subject and started to recall an incident that had occurred when he was a young reporter on *The Star*.

My father was a natural reporter; energetic, gregarious, wily and curious. At the time he was 23, covering the gamut of news from crime to tedious municipal meetings. But thanks to his athletic prowess, Frank also wrote about sporting events. On this particular occasion he was reporting on his first cricket Test match: a major opportunity for a still-junior member of staff.

Frank stared straight ahead as though my mother and I weren't there. The Test match against Percy Chapman's English touring side took place over the Christmas period of 1930, at the Old Wanderers Ground in Johannesburg. Long since moved and rebuilt, the Old Wanderers' cricket stadium was then situated where Johannesburg's main railway station stands today, a convenient ten-minute brisk walk away from *The Star*. It was the first of five Test matches, a highly anticipated contest, as three years before at the same ground South Africa had lost against the previous English visiting team by a resounding ten wickets. By December 1930, sports-obsessed white South Africa was keyed up to avenge that humiliating defeat.

It was a nerve-wracking trial for the ambitious young journalist.

Working for an afternoon paper, his task was to type fast and dispatch his report without delay to *The Star* in Sauer Street. There was, he said, a system of 'runners' to relay 'copy' back to the newspaper for changing afternoon editions. In South Africa, this job was done by black Africans. The pace was frenetic. The reporter had to type at top speed, then the 'runner' cycled back to the office as fast as possible. There were no bylines, and as the Test match reports for successive afternoon editions covered four long broadsheet columns, it is likely they were compiled by more than one reporter.

Frank stylishly looked the part. There are black and white photos of him in wide-shouldered suits, snap-brimmed hat tilted jauntily as he stares back with the poise of a Hollywood-style newshound who perpetually wisecracks out of the side of his mouth.

In December 1930, with huge public interest, there was considerable tension to meet deadlines. The see-saw drama is caught in the headlines. On the first day the sports page initially lamented, 'South African wickets fall cheaply', followed by the 'City Late' edition's, 'South Africa's disaster'. But the next afternoon saw a complete reversal, 'England's collapse', and a few hours later, 'Thrilling Springbok third wicket stand'. On the final day, *The Star* heralded, 'Test fluctuation and thrills', while the evening edition was able to crow, 'Springbok's brilliant win'.

There was, recounted Frank, one particular 'messenger boy': an older man, a sports fan who had followed my father's boxing career closely. This 'old man' often discussed boxing with him, or asked Frank who he tipped to win a title fight.

It was disconcerting sitting at the dinner table, listening to my father as he wept openly. There was no self-pity. He made no attempt to wipe away the tears. He spoke calmly, evidently feeling compelled to relate this memory accurately and factually. He clearly recalled the occasion as vividly as though it had happened the previous day.

It was, he said, the worst thing he ever did.

On that day the black messenger made some mistake, what I don't recall. Perhaps in his haste he had dropped and lost the typed article. The result was that the older man had to confess that Frank's deadline had been missed. My father, who had a quick temper, lost control.

In a fury, he lashed out. That young white man, the ex-South African junior middleweight boxing champion, punched a black messenger whom he himself described as old. He hit him in the face.

The old black man, said Frank, simply stood there. For a while he was silent. Then he began to cry. Not from pain, continued Frank. From shock and disappointment. Tears streamed down the old man's face, and he shook his head disbelievingly.

'Oh baas,' he whispered. 'Oh baas, ooh my baas ...'.

There was nothing that any black man could have done. Even if he had been young and fit, it would have been unthinkable to strike back at a white man. So he stood there, weeping gently. It was at this point that Frank turned to me for the first time, and I remember it precisely as this is the most personal thing my father ever said to me. He had stopped crying, but one side of his face was still wet. Looking me directly in the eye, he repeated, quite firmly, 'The worst thing I ever did.'

Stalked by a phantom

Memory, of course, can be fickle. Was the 'old messenger' really old? As meeting deadlines depended entirely on speed and stamina, it seems unlikely. Perhaps he just seemed so to an athletic young man.

But 'old' was definitely the description, and in my father's account he takes on an almost allegorical role. What is striking about Frank's story now is that this African man has no name, no other identification. He is like a figure out of a Greek chorus, faceless and mythic. Simply 'the old messenger'.

Nevertheless, that seemingly arbitrary recollection, safely interred for nearly 60 years, distressed my father profoundly, overwhelming him with the injustice of that one fleeting act, committed against someone whose name he could not even recall.

Previously Frank had seldom spoken of his past. Yet as Alzheimer's exerted its pitiless hold, stripping away some of his tough, even bullying, veneer, this seemed to release a gentler side. It was as though my father's erratic memory was peeling back calcified accretions of habit to reveal something which had long lain dormant: the potential, always present, that our choices could have been different.

My father died in January 1989, having been rushed to hospital after a heavy fall. He lay in his National Health Service bed, confused and defenceless, most of the time unable to talk. But when he was lucid, he was childishly sweet. Although there were other patients in the ward and a wall-mounted TV blared all day, as Frank steadily faded before our eyes, he thought he was billeted at the Grand Hotel in Eastbourne to report on a tennis tournament.

Afterwards my mother asked me to go through his old suitcases in their grimy cellar to see what was stored there. Battered, ripped in several places and secured with rope, they were plastered with tags recording over half a century of travel round the world. Inside were folders of forgotten articles, editor's memos, ancient expense claims, and at least three outraged letters of resignation that were never sent. As well as randomly scattered sheaves from the manu-script of Frank's uncompleted memoir, there were expired passports and dozens of photographs.

One photo in particular startled me.

It appeared to be a snap of myself as a scrawny, fair-haired teen-ager in the classic boxer's pose: fists up at the ready, *en garde*. I studied this snapshot repeatedly, utterly mystified, as I had given up boxing well before the apparent age of that gangly youth posing so self-consciously for the camera. Finally, I understood.

I had known Frank only as burly and broad-shouldered, with chestnut hair and a craggy face. As a boxer his nose had been broken twice. He had also sustained innumerable scars on his mouth and around the eyes. My father was frequently absent as he reported on

The mystery boxer

sports events across the globe, and when at home he was an intimidating, even overbearing presence; almost, I felt, a stran-ger. In his memoir, though, I read to my astonishment that as a child he had been sickly, nearly dying from diphtheria. All sport had been forbidden until, after being bullied at school by an older boy called Denby, his father Bill over-ruled Annie and took Frank to a boxing gym to learn to defend himself.

I also discovered something else from his memoir that he never told me in person, 'After half a lifetime spent on the inside of boxing,' he had confessed, 'I hope my small son will keep well out of it.'

So despite the likeness, that skinny lad in the photo wasn't me. It was my father.

A shrinking world

It's strange to gaze back at what has occurred during the lives of my grandparents, parents and myself. Much of it seems unlikely or fantastical.

Equally startling, peering back even further, is what has been recalled and what forgotten. On my return to England in 1980, one of my first newspaper assignments was early on a chilly Saturday morning at a distant corner of Heathrow Airport, where the Prime Minister was due to greet the return of Britain's last governor of Rhodesia. It was an historic moment: Britain had divested herself of her final colony in Africa.

Margaret Thatcher was enormously grateful to the portly Lord Soames, Winston Churchill's son-in-law, that the transition to an independent Zimbabwe had gone peacefully after years of armed conflict under white minority rule. A declassified memo reveals that the Prime Minister's press secretary advised her confidently, 'There will be very considerable press/radio/TV interest in this.' How wrong he was.

There were no more than half a dozen journalists huddled on the tarmac to witness Mrs Thatcher congratulating Lord Soames, whom the memo calls 'the conquering hero'. The curtain was coming down on the empire. It had been a long story, forever hailed with pomp and ceremony. This was the penultimate act, yet apart from an occasional burst of chauvinistic bravado, the British had largely lost interest.

Since the end of the Second World War, the number of subjects under British control had shrunk by roughly 700 million. Like those fast-dwindling imperial domains, attitudes had also narrowed. Only a few months after I was born, the British were still confident enough to pass the 1948 Nationality Act, guaranteeing all empire citizens the right of entry into Britain, with the right to work there. Thereafter, access was steadily eroded as the island withdrew into itself and attempted to winch up the national drawbridge in order to shut out the aftershock of having subjugated a quarter of the globe.

Map on the wall

In London, I used to gaze at an exquisite little map of the '*Cabo de Bona Esperanca*' that hung above my desk at home. It was a present from a friend in Italy. On the back, a Verona art dealer's sticker dates this as 1665, and attributes the work to the famous Amsterdam mapmaker Joannes Jansson. The sienna-tinted map shows the *Fort de Goede Hoop* and about 50 farms, including those of Simon de Groot, Gerrit Kloeten and Swarte Pieter. Beyond a thin black line indicating the Berg River are several red dotted rings: the *Kraalen of Hutten der Hottentotten* (kraals or huts of Hottentots).

Fascinated, I contemplated this tiny map as though it was a sort of talisman. Outside, in my memory, it is a grey-green, greasy

Limpopo of a crepuscular London evening. The few people out on Talbot Road scurry by, umbrellas flapping against the slanting drizzle. The tall building opposite is dark and silent. On grey, mulchy days my map of the '*Cabo de Bona Esperanca*' represented a different horizon.

It is, I believe, the first map to mark the position of the original European homesteads in South Africa and to name their owners. But the date can't possibly be 1665, a mere 13 years after the founding of a European outpost on the southern extremity of Africa. For a start, Joannes Jansson died in 1664. Some authorities catalogue this as the work of the Dutch publisher Frederick de Wit, giving its date as 1675. However, the only town shown in the interior is *Stellenbos*, founded four years later. And if you look closer, the *Frans Quartier of Draakesteyn* is also indicated, with a symbol for a church marked *Franse Predikant*, French priest, yet the Huguenot refugees fleeing religious persecution in France arrived only in 1688.

In fact, my map is a diminutive insert which has been removed from the bottom right-hand corner of a much larger map published in Amsterdam in 1710, by the widow of the great Dutch cartographer Nicolaes Visscher. On the main map, I discovered, Africa is called '*Cafrerie ou Pays des Cafres*', while South Africa is identified as the 'Place of Hottentots' and 'Wandering Kaffirs', with one tribe designated as cannibals.

As is common with maps of that era, there is much that is inaccurate or entirely fictitious. In comparison, my insert – which some opportunist dealer must have cut out from the bigger '*Carte de l'Afrique*' and framed – is positively chaste. Some names, with a slight alteration, are still in use: like *Ronde Bosje* (Rondebosch).

The more I studied this map, the more familiar it seemed. Maps are not neutral. They tell a story. They make the world known to us by including some things and downplaying or excluding others. And all maps overlay a previous story. In my framed insert there are only Dutch names: *Hout Bay, Zee Koe Valey, Blauwenberg*. There are no clues that there are any indigenous people within the confines of white settlement. There are plentiful rivers, sweet valleys, fruitful pastures. It's as if a modest European utopia has been established in a beguilingly vacant arcadia at the opposite end of the earth. It is the enduring myth of white South Africa: a dream of Eden before the fall.

To the east, though, beyond a winding line that traces the Berg River – and which also denotes an uncertain frontier – are those slightly ominous red rings representing the mysterious *Kraalen der Hottentotten*; while westward, out in Table Bay, is *Robben Eyland*, identified in italics as *'where the slaves walk in chains'*.

I'd assumed that apartheid would last my lifetime. Yet like the glories of Nineveh and Tyre, as Rudyard Kipling cautioned, nothing lasts. Nearly three decades after being summarily stripped of my South African citizenship for evading military service, there was a dramatic change, with negotiations between the dying white regime and the liberation movement. And so early on the morning of 27 April 1994, the day of South Africa's first democratic election, I collected a brand-new passport at the back door of the South African High Commission in London, and strode round the block to vote.

12

✟

JOURNEY'S END: ALMOST AFRICA

The view from here

THIS WEEK the fish factory has been stinking again. It's only two or three times a year that the odour of processed fishmeal permeates the entire valley. Luckily a mild ocean breeze has rinsed the air, leaving just a lingering whiff.

The sky is a flawless blue and out in the bay a lone fishing boat, returning after a night's trawl, turns in a wide arc to enter the harbour. Sand from the beach, though, has banked into treacherous mounds across Harbour Road, and a couple of the rusted 'cockroach' taxis that race along the seafront have been trapped in fine-grained quicksands. Gusts of sandy granules swirl along adjacent streets until they splatter across our windows.

Out of my study window I can see in the distance sunlight shimmer from tin *hokkies* (shacks) perched on Sentinel Hill at Hangberg – quaintly known as the fishing village, although it's a straggling slum. Most residents are 'coloured', the term which stubbornly persists for those of mixed race, many forcibly moved there from the farmland down in the valley during apartheid.

In the hollow of the valley are the middle-class, mostly white homes, and numerous 'security estates' have sprung up in the 22 years since we've lived here. Fastest growing of all, however, is the black shantytown clinging to the steep flank of Skoorsteenkop Mountain. Drifting across the valley, if the wind blows in the right direction, you can hear an unruly mix of sounds: donkeys braying, jiving weekend revelry, even an occasional gunshot and on Sundays, raucous revivalist meetings. High up on the rockiest incline, the newest arrivals pitch their hovels. The area is known as *Dontse Yakhe*; 'pull your own shack'.

At first glance, viewing this sun-drenched and apparently somnolent scene, not much appears to have changed. Under the surface though, the entire axis has shifted. Now that our rigid racial straight-jacket has been stripped off, for some this strange new world can be extremely unsettling. We have to make things up as we go along. There's no telling where it may all end.

Down by the beach, the old police station has almost disappeared. A few years ago, this station was completely operational. But once the cops moved into a smart new station the old building began to fall apart, blasted by wind and sand and swiftly stripped by opportunist shack builders. Today you have to scramble over spongy sand dunes to discover that now only a couple of pillars peep out amid the rubble and sand, their former significance as forgotten as any ancient Greek ruin.

Is this, I wonder, how our lives will appear to future generations: a mystery, with shards of ruin vanishing or suddenly reappearing, matching the whims of the wind?

Cracks in our map

Many white South Africans seem not to wish to peer too closely into the past. For those of us who grew up under apartheid, what once seemed normal is now revealed as a mass delusion. Seen through that fissure in memory, we would all have to admit we were in some way complicit.

Yet attempting to find your way on an uncharted map can also be disorienting – like someone suffering from Alzheimer's, where the world suddenly appears unfathomable – and makes some people very uneasy.

On a visit to Johannesburg a while ago, I wandered round a neighbourhood where for months at a time my mother and I would stay with Granny Trixie while my father toured some distant sports nirvana: India, Pakistan, Ceylon or the West Indies. Almost everything in Rosebank had changed, with just enough surviving to be confusing.

Cradock Avenue had been a dusty, jacaranda-lined street. The red dust was still there, but that's because much of the street was a building site, adding more and brasher 'retail opportunities' to an already busy mall precinct. Covering the entire block, once home to my primary school, is a ten-storey corporate headquarters. Nearby, a smart Chinese restaurant has replaced the dingy 'Greek store', where the alcoholic couple who rented a room from Granny used to bribe me to buy their grog.

It took an age to guess where Granny's small, white stucco bungalow had once been, with that sun-scorched front lawn and red tin roof. After a great deal of vacillation, I decided that the ghost of Number 15 must lurk at the spot then occupied by the raggedy African craft market. A lonely jacaranda still stood outside.

Once, the only black people permitted by day were maids, nannies and 'garden boys'. Come the evening, they became invisible: vanishing into a servant's room at the back of the boss' property, or melting away into distant townships. To a seven-year-old, it all seemed perfectly ordinary. But one day my father, during a stop-over from some distant land, came home in a towering rage. He had been to the local post office after repeated delays in sending cables. On that occasion I recall Frank telling my mother that the post office manager had been contrite, but apologised that there was nothing he could do.

The government's policy required that all sorting staff be 'European'. Meanwhile, the lower-paid postmen who delivered the letters had to be, by decree, black. The snag arose from the fact that a number of white sorters were semi-literate; consequently, the black deliverymen had to waste time reorganising the letters for their postbags. Now that, I thought for the first time, was odd.

Today, the once dozy suburb throbs with cafés and restaurants. Many of their patrons are black professionals. Meanwhile, traders in the African craft market sit at the entrance of their stalls full of tourist knick-knacks and carved animals, playing cards or speak-ing loudly on cell phones, perhaps in Lingala to their family in the Congo.

'Anomie' describes a mental or emotional state where accepted values have broken down and not yet been replaced. People marooned in such a vacuum, even entire societies, feel that they lack a clear goal or shared purpose. A significant number of white people in South Africa have responded to the changes around them by retreating, baffled, from any real engagement with this new soci-ety; many sound perpetually anxious or resentful, a plaintive note of exasperation echoing in their conversations.

A strident minority remain permanently enraged. In contrast, there are other white folk who are delighted, even excited, to have broken out of the confines of skin colour. It's reckless to generalise, but given our history, South Africa persists as a Republic of Generalisations. So, really, it's fair to ask: how did we migrants from Europe find ourselves in this strange no man's land of anomie?

A last colonial outpost

In the distance I can see the shadowy back of Table Mountain which blocks us off from Cape Town. This valley is an idiosyncratic *cul-de-sac*; a microcosm of South Africa. Three communities – white, black and coloured – live within sight of each other, but in separate areas: social and racial boundaries which stretch back centuries.

Within months of European settlement at the Cape, the Dutch commander visited Hout Bay, admiring its dense forests, while noting that the Khoi leader Harry (Autshumao) and nomadic herders frequently pastured their cattle here. The amphitheatre-like nature of our valley, cut off by mountains and sea, gave Van Riebeeck the idea of establishing an early apartheid-style reservation in the valley by blocking off all passes: 'By these means Harry and the Kaapmans, having been enticed hither, could be confined within the said bounds where they would have sufficient pasturage for all their cattle, and then, out of the increase, the needs of the company could also be supplied ...'. What Van Riebeeck had not allowed for was that the Khoi knew every hidden path out of Hout Bay. But unlike the later zealous social engineers of apartheid, he recognised that his internment scheme 'would be quite impossible'.

Instead, Van Riebeeck planted a bitter almond hedge, so that the fledgling European outpost 'will be beautifully enclosed as in a half-moon, and everything will be well protected against raids by the Hottentots'. He also considered cutting a canal across the peninsula, effectively creating an island. Ever since, separatist fantasies have persisted. Cut off by mountains and appended to the tip of Africa like an afterthought, Cape Town feels semi-detached, mentally and socially, from the rest of Africa.

Hout Bay, tucked even further behind the bulk of Table Mountain, endures as a diminutive, largely racially segregated enclave. This might have been reassuring to my late Auntie Betty and her husband René, with their genteel European pretentions and fear of African independence. Most of the newer residential complexes here reflect Mediterranean aspirations, with names like 'St Tropez' or 'La Mer'.

In fact, I suspect Auntie Betty would have been far happier in this faux colonial realm rather than spending her declining years in a hideous Monte Carlo high-rise. Uncle René could have continued as Honorary Consul for Monaco. It's a perfect fit. A stone's throw from our home, is another small complex, called, yes: Monaco Close.

All that glisters

The Spanish conquistador Hernán Cortés is said to have informed an emissary of the Aztec Emperor Montezuma that 'I and my companions suffer from a disease of the heart which can be cured only by gold.' That affliction led to a city springing up on the Highveld: *eGoli* to the legions of African migrants who flocked to sweat in the bowels of the earth in order to assuage the white man's malady.

I have also descended underground in Johannesburg, though at the Public Library, the only institution to retain copies of the newspaper that my grandfather, Lewis Rose, founded and edited from 1911 to 1915. No one at the library appeared to know anything about the *Sunday Post*. Eventually I was allowed down to the basement, the descent becoming ever gloomier due to lack of lighting.

In the vast storeroom, much of the overhead lighting wasn't working. I searched in this half-light until a grey-bearded stacker finally appeared, and without hesitation led me to the correct section, in total darkness, which contained the dusty copies of the *Sunday Post*.

It was eerie to be almost certainly the first person in a century to read my grandfather's words. I recognised his muscular style immediately. On the inaugural front page was the editor's response to offerings from would-be contributors. To 'GDD', he growled: 'No trace of merit.' To SAM: 'Hopeless drivel.'

Editorials reveal the concerns of Lewis Rose and his readers: 'The White Man's Burden', 'The Future of the White Man'. Another, 'The House Boy', reflects unease over the intimacy entailed by the presence of household servants, wondering: 'How far the 'Black Peril' is directly traceable to the elevation of the raw kaffir to the post of domestic servant …'. Later, the paper attempted a lighter note with a feature by the future novelist Sarah Gertrude Millin, entitled 'Servants I have sacked'.

Naturally Lewis Rose's newspaper, bidding to be the voice of a gold-rush city, was spellbound by the yellow ore that could apparently cure the heart condition which afflicted Hernán Cortés. For the Christmas edition of 1912, the *Sunday Post* carried the longest article of its four-year existence. This detailed the continuing search for those legendary ancient gold mines around which Rider Haggard and John Buchan spun their 'shilling shocker' yarns. 'El Dorados Of Long Ago: History's Riddle', teased the headline. This was the phantom of Monomotapa, resurfacing in my grandfather's ailing Sunday paper just as the ancient kingdom itself was fading into oblivion.

The Sunday Post correspondent, identified as 'F.J.P.', described unearthing 'skilfully constructed shafts … now thickly overgrown with bush'. He posed the question: 'Who then were the workers, and whence did they come?'

It was a mystery.

'Certainly our beloved Bantu brother knew nothing of the arts of extraction', he declared. Were those ancient miners, he wondered, Arabs or Phoenicians? Leaving that riddle unanswered, 'F.J.P.' concluded: 'Surely we are not going to sit idly by and allow this vast, almost illimitable storehouse to remain untouched and neglected!'

An empty map

Terra nullius (nobody's land) was a stock colonial justification. If 'untouched and neglected', it was up for grabs. During the eighteenth century, most maps of Africa were adorned with exotic designs or fearsome beasts to disguise the fact that so little was known of the continent, especially the interior. Vast spaces were left blank.

From the outset there were ingenious interpretations. The Elizabethan magus and polymath Dr John Dee, who coined the term 'Brytish Impire', urged his queen to challenge Spanish dominion

in the New World by claiming that North America had been discovered in 1170 by the Welsh prince Madoc, and long before that
by King Arthur. Dee may have been persuaded to swap his pretty
wife on the instructions of the unseen angel Madimi, but he was
also a scholar renowned throughout Europe. Dee's treatise submit-
ted to Queen Elizabeth I asserted that 'The Lord Madoc, sonne to
Owen Gwynedd, led a Colonie and inhabited in Terra Florida or
thereabowts.'

A century later, the Enlightenment philosopher John Locke provided intellectual justification for the appropriation of *terra nullius*
by proposing that ownership derived from labour. Locke, regarded
as a founder of classic liberalism, contended that 'land left wholly to
nature, that hath no improvement of pasturage, tillage, or planting,
is called, as it is indeed, 'waste' …'. Thus possession, he wrote, must
devolve to he who 'mixed his labour, and joined it to something
that is his own'.

My father, when frail, became violently agitated during our dispute over whether most of South Africa had been empty before
Europeans penetrated into the interior. Frank insisted, as he had
been taught at school, that white settlers moving north and African
tribes migrating south converged at roughly the same time. He
had become dangerously puce in the face, so I didn't mention the
archaeological proof of African occupation for over ten centuries.
Or that a former government propagandist from Pretoria, who
had decamped to London in disgust with disseminating apartheid
lies, used to turn up at my newspaper office in the late 1980s to
hand over evidence of the disinformation being pumped out by the
South African government. Thus the South African ambassador in

London was merely recycling fraudulent government propaganda when he asserted in a diplomatic magazine that, prior to white settlement, South Africa consisted of 'totally uninhabited territories'.

Mapping our insecurities

Among my father's possessions that I found after his death is a colourful chart presented to him at the 1932 Olympic Games. Frayed at the edges, it was rolled inside a certificate recording that Frank had served on the Olympic boxing jury. The gift has illustrations of several 'Atlantic and Ethiopic Ocean' islands. The Olympic Committee probably thought this would be a fitting gift because at the bottom is an inset with a diagram of Table Bay and 'Robin Island', plus a plan of the stone-walled Dutch castle.

In fact, this chart had been removed from Emanuel Bowen's 'Complete Atlas' of 1752. Bowen, Geographer Royal to George III, helped purge the customary encrustation of decoration and mythical creatures that had previously filled the empty spaces on maps of Africa. He replaced them with cautionary observations such as 'man eaters', 'savage people', or 'This nation is said to make use of lions in fighting'.

Now framed, it is next to the largest map on my wall, published 30 years later. Entitled 'Africa, agreeable to the most approved maps and charts, by Mr Kitchen', this depicts the entire continent. Thomas Kitchen further uncluttered the map of Africa, leaving vast blanks in the interior, though southern Africa is divided between first 'Monomotapa', then 'Caffreria', followed by 'Hottentots'. At the farthest extremity, marked *Dutch Ft*, is the tiny European settlement, looking insignificant and isolated.

Scrutinising the sequence of maps on my wall, covering just over a century, I can see a steadily darkening progression. As the frontier pushes forward, a sense of apprehension deepens. These maps not only delineate known outlines, but also chart an interior world: a projection of what colonisers longed for but feared as well.

On Kitchen's 'most approved' map, much of North Africa is merely identified as 'Desert of Barbary' or 'Negroland'; Central Africa is shown as a white expanse, with names like 'Mujak' and 'Zendero' in what appears to be an empty vastness. This vacuum is what was habitually identified on other contemporary maps as *terra incognita*: a short mental step to *terra nullius*, or nobody's land.

A third map, titled 'South Africa', hangs alongside that of Mr Kitchen, but was printed 33 years later, in 1815. The work of J. Thompson and Co., successful Edinburgh publishers, this shows how far the frontier had advanced. Rivers and mountains are named, as are the growing number of villages and towns. There appear to be almost no indigenous people within the colony's borders, and the countryside carries little trace of their memory. Instead, there's a different litany: *Riebeecks Casteel, Tyger Hoek, Jackals Fontein, Zwartkops River, Theopolis.*

There are also helpful tips: 'Wild Hilly Country uninhabitable for Want of Fresh Water'. Curiously, despite the amount of detail, several garrison posts already established on the disputed east-ern frontier are missing, including Graham's Town where I later attended university. Colonel John Graham, after whom the town was named, ruthlessly obeyed his orders to 'take the most effectual measures to clear from His Majesty's territories the Caffre nation'.

Graham destroyed huts and crops, killed women and children, and drove the Xhosa people back across the Great Fish River – which on my 1815 map demarcates the furthermost eastern boundary. The colony soon expanded, but in the depiction of the unknown on the other side of the troubled frontier you can sense the beleaguered *iKoloni* mentality which eventually led to apartheid, and more subtly persists among some whites today. The frontier, from the Atlantic to the Indian Ocean, is underlined in red, green and yellow. Beyond the eastern boundary is designated KAFFERLAND.

To the north is a great white space. There's no habitation in that unnervingly vacant tract: not a village, kraal or hut. Further north is a dotted trail recording the journey of the Rev. John Campbell. His tracks run parallel with the Orange River, then vanish off the top of the map.

There appears to be nothing in that mysterious hinterland. As a guide to our colonial mental map, it is labelled simply, ominously: *Wild Boskesman's Country.*

A dark and stormy night

The night my mother died, there was driving winter rain and a howling wind; the turbulence that gives the Cape of Good Hope its less cheery title: the Cape of Storms.

Barbara was 92, and had driven her car the day before. On her desk afterwards I found, in her slightly wobbly handwriting, a list of things to chat about when I called, as I did every evening. Barbara had never thought she would return to South Africa. But at the age of 85 she agreed to this move because she knew that, as an only son, I wouldn't leave my widowed mother alone in London. She made only one condition: she wished to remain independent, and so would not live with my wife and myself, but on the other side of Table Mountain in a retirement village closer to town.

There I would call her every evening at roughly the same time. Her reminders of topics for our evening talk, written on the day that she died, included the benefits of solar heating and the name of a South African writer she wished to discuss. It was a conversation we never had.

Given her age and colonial upbringing, it is astonishing how open-minded she remained. Born in 1912, the same year in which the African National Congress was founded, the changes that my mother witnessed in her lifetime were astounding. She took it all in her stride. The nostalgia and prejudice of many of the other white residents of the retirement village, as well as a recurrent ignorance about the past, constantly astonished Barbara, alternately amusing or infuriating her.

My mother hated racial chauvinism and evidently always had, despite the fact that her father had been a firm defender of white dominance. As Lewis Rose had been a staunch supporter of General Smuts, Barbara once told me how shocked she had been when, aged 17, she accompanied her mother to take tea with Smuts' wife Isie, known as 'Ouma', who insisted on referring to 'kaffirs'.

After my mother died, reading her wartime diaries which described the arduous travels through the Middle East with the South African entertainment unit, I came across this entry: 'The Corporals gave a party for us and I spent most of the evening talking to Smuts' son, Captain Smuts, whom I took an instant dislike to, finding him rather stupid and extremely pompous. We nearly came to blows over the coloured people. He said he thought they were a degenerate, drunken lot and that they were being overpaid at five shillings a day. It's impossible to argue with stupidity like that.'

Barbara seldom talked about herself. It was only after she died that I unearthed files of old theatre reviews, from Johannesburg and the West End, revealing how talented she had been. But it was in reading her wartime diaries that I discovered a different person to the doting, slightly overanxious mother I thought I knew. Instead, here was an adventurous young woman, spirited and inquiring.

My ever-surprising mother; though born into an establishment white *milieu*, she never believed that she belonged to a superior caste. Even at over 90, Barbara had no wish to live in the past or cling to the wreckage of unearned privilege.

On her desk, alongside the list of items for our evening talk, I found a poem in her shaky handwriting that she must have copied out on the day before she died. Called *Margaritae Sorori*, it ends:

'My task accomplish'd and the long day done
My wages taken, and in my heart
Some late lark singing,
Let me be gather'd to the quiet west,
The sundown splendid and serene,
Death.'

Revelations in the DNA

Frontiers shift constantly. South Africa has only been a unified country since 1910, so our mental map can be as arbitrary as geographical boundaries, which adapt to changed circumstances. Until recently I knew little of my family lineage, and have discovered that much of what I'd been told and accepted as fact was mistaken.

Some years ago my goddaughter Vuyelwa and I were invited to take part in the first phase of the Africa Genome Project, which aimed to create a genetic map of migration patterns for the various groups that have settled in South Africa. Vuyelwa, at the time an 18-year-old high school student, is a second generation Capetonian, whose family had previously lived in the Eastern Cape; on the other hand, I am only a third generation South African. She is black; I am white. Our DNA tests were taken from cheek swabs, and produced unexpected, even shocking results.

Vuyelwa's lineage, and that of her sister Nomsa, is thought to have originated about 80,000 years ago in East Africa. It is associated with the 'Out of Africa' move, so while some of that group migrated north to populate the world, other branches dispersed throughout Africa. According to her DNA report, Vuyelwa's sub-group possibly arose in Central Africa near Sudan around 35,000 years ago. It's been an epic migration all the way to Cape Town.

From their own DNA sample, women can trace only their female lineage, and need a male member of their immediate family to track their paternal roots. This was not available for Vuyelwa or Nomsa. Men (once again) have an unfair advantage: both sides of the family can be traced through a male DNA sample. This is where I came in for an astounding revelation.

Before my various grandparents immigrated to South Africa at the turn of the twentieth century, either they or their parents had set out from Scotland, Lancashire or Ireland. Beyond that, our family trees seemed to evaporate into indifference, apart from the cherished but apocryphal tale of being related to Tahitian royalty. The DNA results turned the accepted but scant stories of family genealogy, believed firmly by my mother and father, upside down.

Family myths unmasked

The DNA evidence traced my mother's lineage to about 30,000 years ago, mainly in north-west Europe, probably part of the population following the retreat of the ice sheets from Europe. This group is especially prevalent in Scandinavia – exactly where Frank had imagined that his origins lay; perhaps from early Viking raids on England.

What would have shocked my father is that the DNA sample revealed that his side of the family originated many thousands of years ago in South and Central Asia, Iran and the Caucasus. It also appeared that there may be ties with the Romani people, who have their ancient roots in the north-west regions of India. The Romani are an itinerant ethnic group, better known (usually pejoratively) as gypsies. I can't imagine Frank being gratified to be told that he was descended from gypsies, although all his life my father was an obsessively itinerant newsman.

Most dramatic of all is that my DNA revealed that I have a verified, if inexplicable, genetic bond with Africa. A search of the worldwide database turned up only a single living match: from

Cabinda, an enclave of Angola. My father would have huffed indignantly, or scoffed cynically. Auntie Betty would have been utterly scandalised.

There must be a mistake, I thought. But the chief scientist at the Johannesburg laboratory where the testing was done confirmed this astonishing match. His reply was eminently sensible, if sobering: it was entirely feasible that someone in Cabinda should now carry a Y chromosome passed down by one of my forefathers, 'given the history of the slave trade routes and the European settlements along the coasts of Africa'.

Oil-rich Cabinda was one of the first points on the Central African coast where Europeans began trading. Could it be that one of my forebearers — of whom we have absolutely no record — was a sailor on a ship trading down that part of the coast in the seventeenth or eighteenth centuries? Or that I have an ancestor who was a slave trader, and left, as it were, his indelible mark? I'll never know.

Whatever the reason for my startling link to Angola, all that can be said with a degree of certainty is that it is another consequence of the spread of empire. And that despite my family's role in global conquests, ironically, we all started out from Africa.

Effectively my ancestors departed from Africa on foot and had to wait, like all whites in South Africa, for the invention of technologies — ocean-going ships, gunpowder and guns — in order to return to Africa as settlers with a perceptibly lightened pigment.

Ever since, we have been telling a very dubious story.

Lurid travellers' tales

Europeans writing about Africa, from the ancients to modern news-papers, have routinely taken flight from reality to weave tales of danger and the exotic. In the eighteenth century, books by explorers were often best-sellers. Some felt free to invent anything that they wanted for a sensation-hungry and sometimes gullible public, as no one back home was in a position to contradict them.

One ruse to establish the veracity of your story was to attack a pre-vious adventurer. The Frenchman François Le Vaillant – perhaps the greatest, certainly the most humane of early European explorers – bolstered his credibility by scorning a book of 50 years before as 'fables'. Le Vaillant unfairly accused Peter Kolbe, the German explorer, of never venturing beyond Cape Town and of merely repeating tavern talk. Le Vaillant was in turn equally unjustly belit-tled. The British administrator Sir John Barrow, in his successful *An Account of Travels into the Interior of Southern Africa* (1801), called Le Vaillant 'an unblushing liar' and ridiculed his claim to have explored beyond the western frontier.

Another writer, George Thompson, contended that Le Vaillant had fibbed about venturing beyond the eastern frontier. But while Le Vaillant may have embellished a good story, he was not merely an observant and open-minded explorer. As an ornithologist and naturalist, he was a trailblazer. The Frenchman harshly criticised white settler cruelty ('In this place all the horrors invented in hell are committed'), and acknowledged his Khoi guide, Klaas, as 'my equal, my brother'.

Le Vaillant remarks on one white couple's putrid hovel and adds that one of their slovenly daughters had made eyes at him.

Nevertheless the Rev. John Campbell later came across the widow Van der Westhuizen, and reported that this harridan was delighted to learn that she featured in a celebrated book, but asked whether the eminent author had mentioned the thrashing she claimed to have administered because of his 'improper behaviour' towards her daughter.

The ploy of denouncing rivals was taken to an audacious conclusion by Christian Frederick Damberger in his popular *Journey Into The Interior of Africa* (1801). Before each account of venturing where no white man had ever trod before, Herr Damberger rips apart Le Vaillant's descriptions, thus making his own story sound authentic. He also provided a map of his hazardous journey, which climaxed with his enslavement by pirates. In fact, his account was entirely made up. Damberger, a Leipzig cabinetmaker, never left home, let alone visited Africa.

Reading those old leather-bound volumes, it became apparent that even some of the most scrupulous of European writer-explorers had journeyed a long way in order to have their preconceptions confirmed. I should have paid attention.

Late one afternoon in the British Library, after hours of reading an apparently unreliable 1796 English translation of François Le Vaillant's *Travels*, I copied into my notebook what seemed to be evidence of the Frenchman's gullibility. Alas, it wasn't Le Vaillant, great-uncle of the poet Baudelaire, who was the dupe. What I had copied, and later committed to print, was a version by his English translator of Le Vaillant being woken one morning by a strange bird. I was enthralled by his deduction: 'By its flight, however, I could tell that it was a goat-fucker.'

In my weariness I'd forgotten that old English s's look perilously like f's. One incensed academic pointed out, quite rightly, that it was not the intrepid Le Vaillant who 'doesn't know his arse from his arfe' – for the translation had actually referred to a 'goat-sucker'. The Frenchman was, in fact, giving the first report of a Fiery-necked Nightjar, whose long fluting call I sometimes hear on a hot summer's night. Like other nocturnal birds, nightjars were once associated with witchcraft, so were named *Caprimulgidae,* goat-suckers, as they were believed to drink goat's milk under the cover of dark.

All the same, my goodness: a 'goat-fucker'! Who could resist that? Not me, obviously. Like so many before, I too had seen what I wanted to see and proved a sucker for a tall tale, believing of Africa the absolutely unbelievable.

The dominion of myth

For the Greeks and Romans, everything south of the Sahara represented an inhospitable mystery. There dwelt the *Blemmyae*, with faces on their chests, the one-legged *Scopapods*, blind *Troglodytes*, sexually profligate *Garamantes*, and the terrible *Anthropophagi*, devourers of human flesh: later regularly depicted on European maps.

Similar inferences were drawn in return. Many Africans imagined that business-like Europeans transformed the bodies of their black victims in clinical, cost-effective processes: grinding African bones into gunpowder and fermenting black victims' brains into the cheeses that they ate or transmuting blood into the red wine they drank.

Modern urban legends continue to be almost as tenacious as the myths of antiquity. The difference is that today apocryphal tales spread a great deal faster globally.

We thrive on myths. As Britain withdraws in on itself, we hear nostalgic boasts of how, 'we stood alone against the Nazis'. But Britain did not fight alone. Britain fought with the entire empire at its side. Millions, black and white, rallied from all over the world: more than two million from India, about one million from Africa. Of the eleven million men that served under the British flag, five million were from the colonies. White South Africans were armed, but 80,000 black Africans were enrolled for strictly non-combatant duties, along with 23,000 coloureds – including that aggrieved Cape Corps veteran who once held a Luger to my head in District Six.

So the question lingers: have today's heirs of empire come to an honest reckoning with their acquisitive past?

The sharpest riposte to claims that empire was 'A Good Thing' is the contrast made by the historian Mark Mazower in his book *Dark Continent*, referring not to Africa, but to twentieth century Europe. While Hitler admired the British Empire, especially the way Britain ruled India, his territorial ambitions lay in Europe, to the east, with the stated aim of reducing the despised Slavs to a servile worker class; a colonised people. Unlike the older imperialisms, which had seen their expansions and 'civilizing burdens' as being outside Europe, Mazower points out, 'National Socialism did not: and just here, no doubt – by turning Europeans back into barbarians and slaves – lay the Nazis' greatest offense against the sensibility of the continent.'

It's a mirror most Europeans decline to gaze on, fearful of the reflection.

A personal reckoning

Nevertheless, after a long journey, this is the shore upon which I have landed. And while I've tried to understand what drove my itinerant relatives, I cannot answer for the departed. I can, however, attempt a personal accounting of my intricately layered inheritance.

There is a discernible pattern: loyalties, mutual assumptions, shared beliefs and myths handed from one generation to the next, trickling all the way down to myself. Viewed from the dizzy heights of today, however, the most persistent motif over 250 years is that of frontiers.

Not simply physical ones, either. The most persistent frontier is the one that runs right through our head.

For most of those 250 years, boundaries for the British were almost limitless. We mostly went where we pleased. Many of the frontiers that first appeared on maps of distant lands were allocated by bureaucrats in London to demarcate new possessions. This cavalier approach was summed up crisply by the last Prime Minister to run Britain from the House of Lords. In an after-dinner speech, Lord Salisbury remarked cheerfully of the fierce European colonial rivalry in Africa: 'We have been engaged in drawing lines upon maps where no white man's foot has ever trod; we have been giving away mountains and rivers and lakes to each other, only hindered by the small impediment that we never knew exactly where the mountains and rivers and lakes were.'

As a result, debates and quarrels about colonialism, particularly among white South Africans, tend to be broadly inward-looking: concentrating almost entirely on what 'we' feel, as heirs of the Imperium, rather than trying to listen to what the formerly colonised may have to say.

The problem from which the mother country has never quite recovered was identified by that timid but famous novelist who accidently locked himself in the lavatory of my grandfather's home in Johannesburg. The English, observed E.M. Forster, 'go forth into a world that is not entirely composed of public school men or even Anglo-Saxons, but of men who are as various as the sands of the sea; into a world whose riches and subtlety they can have no conception.'

As that mother country, the small island which oversaw boundless boundaries, retreats behind a diminishing frontier, its former colony South Africa, despite being trapped for so long in blueprints of ethnic isolation, is tentatively loosening those mental frontiers. It's a strange, unpredictable society: one so endlessly fascinating that I wouldn't want to live anywhere else. Yet 50 years after seeing Uncle René raise the flag of Monaco in homage to Prince Rainier, 6,000 miles away in Europe, I still wonder: *have we whites truly come to terms with living in Africa?*

Not exactly. Not yet.

The map of now

The last map on my wall is an austere chart of the '*Cabo de Boa Esperanca*'. The jagged coast, tinged with yellow, is etched with sawtoothed barbs to indicate mountain ranges. A mesh of lines crisscross the empty interior. Dated 1726, this folio has been removed from a copy of the history of the Dutch East India Company by the Calvinist minister François Valentijn. His shoreline sketch shows on one side Table Bay with *Robben Eylandt* and on the other, separated by the presence of Table Mountain, is the misnamed *Sout Bay*, Salt Bay; or, more correctly, Hout Bay where I now live.

With a gap of 250 years, our zigzagging family saga has completed a ghostly rendezvous. Captain Samuel Wallis stayed for a month in Cape Town on his return voyage to England, having been compelled to relinquish his quest for the mythical *Terra Australis Incognita*. As there was an outbreak of smallpox in Cape Town, Wallis requested permission to erect a tent, 'upon a spacious plain, at about two miles distant from the town, called Green Point'. From our home, Green Point is a half-hour drive along the twisting Atlantic coastline.

Shortly afterwards, a temptation for Europeans writing about Africa was identified by the naturalist who sailed with Captain Cook (along with my ancestor James Wallis, the ship's carpenter). 'Men with one leg, Cyclops, Syrens, Troglodytes and the like imaginary beings, have almost entirely disappeared in this enlightened age,' wrote Anders Sparrman. 'At the same time, however, many have been hitherto induced to give credit to tales almost as marvellous, with which authors … have seasoned their relations in order to go down better with the public.'

Sparrman himself went in search of unicorns.

And the rest of us, what were we seeking?

The shifting sands

My family, I have discovered with some astonishment, went forth and colonised, trailing so many contradictions. My grandfather

Lewis Rose hankered to be British, though he didn't travel to England until he was 41, and only returned to Johannesburg because Granny Trixie insisted. It appears that despite his renown and influence Lewis Rose never came to terms with living in Africa.

My other grandfather, William Rostron, the crabby socialist printer, did not live to see a more equitable world for the working man, or even achieve financial security for himself. Aged 68, he was described in a lawyer's letter as being 'on his beam ends', and at 77 'Bill' Rostron was taken to court after he had agreed to buy, but failed to pay for, Benny and Phil's fish and chips shop.

Auntie Betty and Uncle René felt themselves to be displaced in Africa, but their ideas and values were hopelessly anachronistic. My mother Barbara once told me that before Betty met René she had been jilted by an older suitor in Johannesburg who had refused to do the honourable thing. 'You must inform Daddy,' demanded a hysterical Betty. 'Tell Daddy he must find a gun and force Johnny to marry me!'

René waited years to inherit enough money for them to escape from Cape Town and spend their last days acting out his fantasy of European sophistication in the '*royaume d'opérette*' of Monte Carlo. There, isolated in their cramped high-rise flat, they bickered. Sadly, my pompous Uncle René turned out to be less of an amiably daffy Bertie Wooster and more like one of the self-important middle-class snobs from the droll short stories by my grandfather. Indeed, one of Lewis Rose's laboriously crafted epigrams might have been coined for Uncle René: 'A nest-egg? My dear fellow, a nest-egg would be no earthly use to Algy. What he wants is an incubator.'

My father Frank proved to be at home anywhere, so long as he was chasing a story and had a deadline to beat. When too frail to do so any more, he found himself stranded in a confusing *terra nullius*. Or rather, Frank lost himself in an uncharted no man's land of memory, stranded physically in my parents' bedroom in London as emotionally he retreated to the South Africa of his youth.

In the end it was my mother Barbara who managed to adapt from the colonial world in which she grew up, accepting with grace what it might mean to be a white person in Africa without a habitual sneer of cold command.

Denis Diderot was right: empire corrupted the imperialists. Even we orphaned great-grandchildren of empire were brought up to believe ourselves superior.

'*Hélas! Madame*,' exclaimed one of Diderot's witty friends, history is but, '*une fable convenue*': fables that men have agreed upon. Well, history will have to answer for itself. But I have discovered that Voltaire's epigram does broadly fit the many tales, or convenient fables, faithfully passed down by my own family.

Undertaking this personal odyssey has traced for me a different, very subjective circumnavigation. Having finally populated my once skimpy register of ancestors, I now have a fuller appreciation of what this unfinished story might mean. My own private map has not only massively expanded, but has even changed complexion.

Our goddaughters, Nomsa and Vuyelwa, are now grown-up, and we have another 'grandson', Ntshuxeko ('Freedom' in Tsonga), 13, who insists, 'I'm not black, I'm chocolate brown, and you're not white at all, but peach.' It's a spontaneous and refreshing perception in a country where, not long ago, every aspect of life was rigidly legislated as either black or white. From such small benedictions things can change, releasing us from the grip of a cruel past and reshape what was once a doctrinaire map of exclusion into a fresh horizon of human inclusion.

Unexpectedly last night, from the mountain behind us, for the first time since last summer, I heard the elegiac four-note quaver of a secretive Fiery-necked Nightjar. And this afternoon I walked with my dog, Kwesi, in the early summer sunshine over those unstable dunes by the beach, flattened after ferocious spring winds. There was no sign of the ruins of the old police station; not a spar or brick to be seen in the snowlike sand. All evidence: gone, gone, gone, lingering only in our fickle memory.

ACKNOWLEDGEMENTS

My first debt of honour is to Jim Davidson. As a young history tutor at Rhodes University long ago, he pushed me as a student to try to think for myself. (Jim also coined the saucy pun on p28).

I am extremely grateful to the historians Paul Maylam and Christopher Saunders in South Africa, Deryck Schreuder in Australia and, in the US, the scholar Greg Clingham for their advice. From France, Christopher Hope offered comment and encouragement from the start, as did Dalbert Hallenstein in Italy.

Investigating what at first appeared to be the staggering collection of Old Master paintings owned by my great-great-grandfather in Sydney, Richard Beresford at the Art Gallery of New South Wales provided invaluable expertise, guiding me in the quest to sift what were once believed to be genuine masterpieces from what later proved, alas, not to be originals after all. Also in Australia, Bill Wallis and Noel Wilkinson generously shared their research into our distant relatives who emigrated from Britain in the nineteenth century.

For the history of the early Communist Party of South Africa, Allison Drew's sympathetic biography, *Between Empire and Revolution: a life of Sidney Bunting, 1873-1936*, proved particularly helpful in clarifying the background to the work of my grandfather, the irascible printer Bill Rostron.

Finally, my deep appreciation to Edward Davies whose friendship, enthusiasm and support has been unstinting over many years.

ABOUT THE AUTHOR

Born in Johannesburg, Bryan Rostron has worked as a journalist in Italy, New York, London and South Africa, writing for the *New York Times*, *The Guardian*, *The Spectator*, and *Private Eye*. He was the South African correspondent for the *New Statesman* and contributes to South African papers. He is the author of six books.